Picture Book Activities

Fun and Games for Preschoolers
Based on 50 Favorite Children's Books

Trish Kuffner

Meadowbrook Press
Distributed by Simon & Schuster
New York

Library of Congress Cataloging-in-Publication Data
Kuffner, Trish.
    Picture book activities / Trish Kuffner.
        p. cm.
    Includes bibliographical references and indexes.
    ISBN 0-88166-392-1 (Meadowbrook) ISBN 0-743-21617-2 (Simon & Schuster)
        1. Reading (Preschool)—Activity programs. 2. Picture books for children. 3.
    Children—Books and reading. I. Title.

    LB1140.5.R4 K84 2001
    372.41'2—dc21   2001030800

Editorial Director: Christine Zuchora-Walske
Proofreader: Megan McGinnis
Production Manager: Paul Woods
Desktop Publishing: Danielle White
Cover Art: Dorothy Stott

Published by Meadowbrook Press, 5451 Smetana Drive, Minnetonka, Minnesota
55343

www.meadowbrookpress.com

BOOK TRADE DISTRIBUTION by Simon & Schuster, a division of Simon and Schuster,
Inc., 1230 Avenue of the Americas, New York, New York 10020

05 04 03 02 01   10 9 8 7 6 5 4 3 2 1

Printed in the United States of America

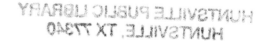

Dedication

To my son Samuel, with whom I look forward
to sharing many reading adventures; and to
the authors and illustrators of outstanding picture books,
with gratitude for the high standards you uphold
and the generations of readers you have inspired.

Acknowledgments

A mother of five children, two of whom are a toddler and a baby, who home-schools her children and writes books in her "free time" either goes without sleep or has help from some very fine people! Sleep indeed eludes me at times, but my accomplishments are possible only because of the following people, to whom I wish to express my gratitude.

The Bible says, "Let us not become weary in doing good, for at the proper time we will reap a harvest if we do not give up" (Gal. 6:9). Meeting the demands placed on me isn't easy, and I thank the Lord for His love, His sacrifice, and the strength He gives me to do the job I'm called to do.

To my husband, Wayne: Your contentment with what we have has allowed me to stay home to raise our children. I sincerely appreciate the sacrifices you make on our behalf. One day, honey, you'll golf again!

To my older children, Andria, Emily, and Joshua: Thanks for keeping up with your schoolwork and chores and for helping out with the little ones. You're growing into fine young people, and I'm so very proud of you.

To the little ones, Johanna and Samuel: Thanks for keeping us laughing. Seeing the world through your eyes makes each day precious.

To my mother, Irene McGeorge; my mother-in-law, Betty Kuffner; and our summer baby sitter, Paulina Gabinska: Few mothers have the luxury of locking themselves away to take a bath, never mind write a book. Your help allowed me to shut out the world from time to time, and I'm grateful to you all.

To my friend, Joy Francescini: I like to think we help each other out, but it seems to me that you've been doing more than your share. Thanks for your selflessness; we love and appreciate your whole family.

To the librarians at the Fraser Valley Regional Libraries, especially the Terry Fox Branch: Thank you for the hundreds of books you've pulled for me over the past few years. Your help is invaluable to me, both as a writer and as a lover of good books.

To my publisher, Bruce Lansky: Thanks for believing in me and allowing me to write about my passion.

To the staff at Meadowbrook Press: Thanks for your help each step of the way. This book wouldn't be possible without your expertise and experience. I appreciate everything you do.

Art Credits

Contents

Picture Book Activities

Appendixes

Indexes

Introduction

The man who doesn't read good books has no advantage over the man who can't read them.

—Mark Twain

Reading good books is one of the greatest pleasures in my life, and it has been as far back as I can remember. Long before I became a mother, I looked forward to the day when I would share my favorite picture books with a sweet-smelling, pajama-clad child or two cuddled on my lap. When my husband and I were finally blessed with a baby, a bookshelf was an essential part of the nursery. It was soon filled with many children's classics just waiting to be shared. My best memories of my daughter's early years were the hours we spent snuggled together reading Ludwig Bemelmans's *Madeline,* P. D. Eastman's *Are You My Mother?,* and Robert McCloskey's *Blueberries for Sal.*

Our family grew, and life changed in many ways. I had worked part-time after our first child was born, but I didn't return to work when our second daughter was born seventeen months later. We were soon blessed again with a son, and the leisurely hours I spent reading—to myself and to my children—began to dwindle. How does one effectively or enjoyably

read to a preschooler while caring for a fussy baby and trying to keep a toddler out of mischief? I still read to my children as much as I could, but I also learned the value of songs, games, crafts, and other activities during the long hours I was alone with the children each day.

Life continued to change with each passing year. My love for reading walked hand-in-hand with a gift for writing, so I used what I was learning about children and children's activities to write a book on the subject. Then I became a teacher as our family embarked on a wonderful journey called home-schooling. Home-schooling allowed us to continue our habit of reading good books together every day. Picture books gave way to novels, and together we adventured on the prairie with Laura Ingalls Wilder, in the far north with Farley Mowat, in coon country with Wilson Rawls, and in Narnia with C. S. Lewis.

Our family continued to grow. A baby was born; I wrote another book; another baby was born; and suddenly I was back in the world of picture books. How I had missed them! How good it was to share characters such as Ferdinand, Frederick, Mike Mulligan, and Noisy Nora with my little ones again. And what a joy it was to see my older children fall back into the magic of picture books as they listened to me or read the books themselves to their young siblings.

Although it has taken me a little over a year to write *Picture Book Activities,* I trace its beginnings to my childhood, when I first discovered the joy of books. The pure pleasure I get from reading a good picture book, my respect for the authors and illustrators of children's books, and my desire to share my love of books with children and to encourage others to do so has made writing this book a privilege and a delight. Finding the time to write wasn't always easy, and neither was immersing myself in great books and calling it "work"! But the result is a book that I trust will help you discover—or rediscover—the joy of children's books, encourage you to pass that joy on to your own child, and inspire a lot of fun along the way.

While many of the picture books and activities described in this book will continue to be enjoyed by your children long after the preschool stage, most are suitable for children between the ages of three and six. The abilities of preschoolers vary greatly, so one book or activity may be too advanced for a three-year-old, while another may be too easy for a five- or six-year-old. Simply choose the books and activities that best fit your child's abilities and interests. And if a book or activity doesn't go over well, don't write it off. Try it again in a week, a month, or a year, or adapt the experience to make it more meaningful and interesting for your child.

Reading aloud to my children and thereby passing on my love of good books has always been one of my priorities as a parent. What a delight it has been to discover that in addition to the pleasure it gives us, reading aloud provides many other benefits. Reading aloud helps young children learn about written language and prepares them to succeed as readers. It also leads to discernment, emotional growth, and an appreciation for the wider world. "Good books have always been the doorway to learning," says Jane Claire Lambert, author of *Five in a Row* (Five in a Row, 1996), and good picture books can be the doorway to a reading adventure that will enrich the lives of children and the adults who lead them. I hope you and your child will share many happy hours of reading, playing, growing, and learning with the best of the best in children's books.

Children and Books

It has always seemed clear to me that a good book for children must be a good book in its own right.

—John Rowe Townsend

Discovering the Joy of Reading

I don't know when I discovered the joy of reading. I do clearly remember the day I learned to read: I rushed home from school to the house on Twelfth Avenue, waited patiently on the couch for my mom to finish her telephone conversation, then followed my finger as I read aloud from the first page of my Dick and Jane reader. Learning to read was exciting.

But discovering the joy of reading—feeling the sheer pleasure of holding a good book in my hand and anticipating the world to which it would take me—I don't know when that happened. I don't even know who to thank for it. My parents? A teacher? A librarian? Maybe good books were just something I happened upon. Until I became a parent, I never thought much about the joy of reading. But as a brand-new mother I read in Gladys Hunt's *Honey for a Child's Heart* (Zondervan, 1989) that "[c]hildren don't stumble onto good books by themselves; they must be introduced to the wonder of words put together in such a way that they spin out pure joy and magic." I learned that in most cases, children learn to love books when significant adults in their lives take the time to share their own enjoyment of books and reading. Reading to my children and passing on my own love of books became one of my priorities as a parent.

Why is reading good books to children so important? For starters:

- Reading aloud to a preschooler prepares her to succeed as a reader.
- A child may learn new ideas from books that are read to her.
- Reading helps instill a family's or society's values in a child.
- Reading is a good way to spend time with a child.
- Reading may calm a child and be a vital part of a bedtime routine.

These are all great reasons to read to your child, but none is as important as this: Reading good books to your child helps her discover the pleasure they can give and thereby helps her develop a love of books.

Zena Sutherland says it this way in

Children and Books (Addison-Wesley, 1997): "Young children are naturally receptive, responding with enthusiasm to new stimuli and experiences. The pre-school years are ones during which it is first possible to instill a joy in books, to lead children to the realization that books and reading are sources of pleasure. Through the sharing of our own enjoyment of books, we can not only help prepare children for learning to read but can also help them take the first steps toward the habit of reading, a habit that will provide lifelong pleasure."

Helping Your Child Develop the Reading Habit

As parents, teachers, or caregivers, we can and should actively help the children in our lives take their first steps in developing the habit of reading. There's no sure-fire formula that guarantees your child will learn to love reading, but you can provide two very effective tools.

The first tool is time: Adults must be willing to invest the time it takes to read to the children in their lives. A busy schedule is the enemy of reading, so parents and caregivers must be willing to turn off the TV, slow down the hectic pace of activities and outings, and read to their children every day.

Adults willing to invest time in reading to their children must also invest effort in finding good books. Just as a steady diet of junk food hampers a body's ability to thrive, poor-quality books hamper the development of a love of reading. Read only the best books to your child. Children can discover the pleasure of reading and learn to recognize quality in books only by exposure to good books.

Choosing Books for Children

The Biblical wise man Solomon said, "There is no end to the writing of books" (Eccl. 12:12). Solomon wrote that about 3,000 years ago, but he could have been talking about children's books in the twenty-first century! With about 40,000 children's books in print and roughly 4,000 new books published each year, choosing books to read to your child may seem like an overwhelming task. Don't despair; it's not as difficult as it may seem. Here are a few general guidelines to help you:

- The best way to determine which books your child will enjoy is to read children's books—lots of them.
- Choose books *you* enjoy, and trust your judgment.
- Avoid books that are too cute, too boring, too preachy, or too condescending or those with explicit themes. Implicit themes are more effective and more memorable. In *Choosing Books for Children* (Delacorte, 1990), Betsy

Hearne writes, "In general, the less a moral shows through, the better."

- Read many different kinds of books to your child and don't expect her to enjoy every book you choose. In *American Library Association Best of the Best for Children* (Random House, 1992), Denise Perry Donavin quotes Maurice Sendak: "'Why would any one book be good for all children? That's silly. No grown-up book is good for all people.'"
- Read old classics as well as new treasures. Books give young children a picture of their world, so as Alice Dalgleish says in *First Experiences with Literature* (Charles Scribner's Sons, 1932), "We need to keep the best of the old, and add to it the best of the new, for literature must reflect life and to reflect it truly it must keep pace with our ever-changing world."
- Hundreds of books receive special recognition each year. Appendix C describes several prominent North American and international awards. Award-winning books usually hold to a high standard of literary and artistic excellence, but don't limit the books you choose to award winners. Many excellent books for children are runners-up or receive no special mention at all.
- Read books about children's books. For in-depth study, read Zena Sutherland's *Children and Books,* the leading textbook on the subject. Other favorites include *The Read-Aloud Handbook* by Jim Trelease (Penguin Books, 1995) and *Honey for a Child's Heart* by Gladys Hunt. Other resources about reading and children's books are listed in Appendix E.
- Make the children's room of your library your second home. Get to know the librarians and ask for recommendations. Popular books are usually checked out as soon as they are returned, so reserve books if you can. If you have Internet access, you may be able to reserve books from home—a lifesaver if you have an infant or toddler! Alternatively, you could schedule an afternoon or evening to visit the library without children in tow to spend some time familiarizing yourself with the best in old and new children's books.
- Visit your local bookstore and browse the shelves of the children's section. Be cautious when asking for recommendations. Many clerks aren't experts on children's books and may simply recommend what everyone else is buying. That's not necessarily a bad thing, but bear in mind that today's buying trends tend to be based more on advertising and popular culture than on quality.

Evaluating Picture Books

A true picture book has little or no text and contains only pictures of objects a child may recognize and point to. A picture book is also understood more broadly as one that tells a story, but in which the picture is the dominant feature on each page. Children should be able to "read" a picture book simply by looking at the illustrations.

Good picture books maintain high literary and artistic standards. When evaluating picture books for your child, keep in mind the traits that distinguish a truly good picture book:

- A good picture book has brief text written in a simple and direct style.
- A good picture book retains a child's interest after many readings.
- A good picture book has solid characters.

- A good picture book combines action, wordplay, humor, and poetry.
- A good picture book includes few concepts and only those a child will comprehend.
- A good picture book contains high-quality art that perfectly complements the text in mood and subject matter. A picture book's illustrations are very important, because young children usually pay more attention to its pictures than to its words.
- A good picture book stands the test of time. It continues to be loved long after its publication.

Ultimately, a good picture book is one that children will read and enjoy. Knowing how to evaluate and choose picture books for your child will help her learn to love books and develop a lifelong habit of reading for knowledge and pleasure.

Before You Begin

Wear the old coat and buy the new book.

—*Austin Phelps*

About *Picture Book Activities*

Picture Book Activities provides ideas to enrich a preschooler's experience with fifty of the best picture books available. Some of these books have won awards, while others have not; some are best-sellers, and others are not; some are funny; some are sad; some are silly; and some are serious. Despite their differences, each of these books will be enjoyed by most children and the adults who read to them.

For each picture book featured in *Picture Book Activities,* you'll find discussion questions, six activities, and many additional ideas to enrich your child's experience with the book. The six activities include detailed suggestions for arts and crafts, cooking and baking, snacks, rhymes and finger plays, music and movement, games, drama and imaginative play, outdoor and community experiences, and activities to help develop prereading and premath skills. Many of the activities don't fit neatly into one category. For example, making a book

with your child may involve arts and crafts, prereading and premath skills, and so on. I've placed activities like this in what seem to be the most appropriate categories. For each picture book you'll also find up to ten enrichment activities, which include suggestions for additional reading, crafts, games, snacks, and outings.

Because the purpose of *Picture Book Activities* is to encourage adults to provide young children with enriching book experiences, I've designed the discussion questions and activities to draw on the literature as much as possible. The discussion questions help children relive important episodes in the book and draw parallels between situations or characters in the book and those in children's lives. The activities relate as much as possible to the literature, although sometimes the literary connections are tenuous. For example, prereading and premath activities do more to help develop important skills like sorting; matching; counting; calendar reading; telling time; color, shape, and letter recognition; printing; and so on than to enhance a child's literary experience.

Picture Book Activities favors the relaxed approach to reading and activities usually found in family settings, but its suggestions are also suitable for preschools, daycares, and other group situations.

Using the Multiple-Readings Approach

The ultimate goal in reading to your child is his enjoyment. A child usually enjoys a good picture book even more at a second reading than at the first, so read a particular book as many times as your child requests it.

Jane Claire Lambert, author of *Five in a Row* (Five in a Row, 1996), advocates reading a picture book at least five days in a row. She writes, "The technique of reading the same story for at least five days in a row is one that I have tested in teaching for more than eight years. I continue to be amazed at the effectiveness of this technique! Each book will become very special to the children. They will remember more and more about the story, but more importantly, they will begin to think more critically (even four-year-olds!) as they begin wondering how certain portions of the story came to be, or how the characters solved a certain problem. These results could never be achieved in just one reading."

It's easy to implement the multiple-readings approach at home: Simply choose a book for the week and read it every day. Follow each reading with one or two activities that you think your child will enjoy. A preschool that runs a two- or three-days-a-week program could choose a book for the week, read the book two or three times each day, then implement two or three activities each day. A play group that meets once a week could read its chosen picture book at the start, middle, and end of the program and do activities between the readings.

Planning Your Activities

How and when you read to your child and do activities together will depend on your schedule. Some parents prefer running errands in the morning and reading in the afternoon, while others prefer the reverse. Working parents will likely read to their children in the evening and carry out a simple activity when time permits.

Keep in mind that reading picture books and doing simple activities each day is an excellent alternative to preschool, especially if you are considering home-schooling your children. Spending an hour or so in the morning reading and doing activities helps establish a school-like routine and develop your child's attention span and skills.

If you're planning activities for your preschooler as a parent at home, be sure to consider any other children in your household. While most of the activities in this book are appropriate for children ages three to six, some are suitable for and fun to do with children of all ages. On the other hand, some of the cooking and craft activities are best done when babies and toddlers are napping or otherwise occupied.

If you're planning activities for children in a preschool, daycare, or play group, keep the children's varying abilities in mind. Young children have short attention spans and lots of energy, and they often lack social skills. Also, their fine motor skills are still developing, which limits their ability to participate in some finger plays, crafts, and other activities. Choose books and plan activities that fit the personalities and skills of your unique group of children.

Providing a child with many different experiences helps develop a wide range of skills, but it's equally important to let him repeat the experiences he enjoys. In *More Things to Do with Toddlers and Twos* (Telshare Publishing Company, 1990), Karen Miller says that allowing a child to fully explore an activity "encourages the development of concentration and experimentation, both elements of creativity." If your child really loves to paint, always do a painting activity with whatever book you're reading, whether I've suggested it or not. For example, you could paint blue pictures for *Blueberries for Sal,* pink pictures for *Geraldine's Blanket,* a snowy scene for *The Snowman,* a windy scene for *Gilberto and the Wind,* a house for *The Little House,* a chair for *A Chair for My Mother,* and so on.

Consider planning a birthday party around a picture book. Use your child's favorite book as the theme for invitations, decorations, games, songs, crafts, food, and so on. Or instead of basing the party on one book, plan a more general party complete with book-shaped invitations, decorations incorporating pictures and characters from some of your child's favorite books, and guests dressed as their favorite picture book characters. See *Storybook Parties* by Liya Lev Oertel and Penny Warner (Meadowbrook Press, 2001) for many more great ideas.

As a mom at home with five children, I know there are days when a parent just doesn't have the energy to keep little ones occupied or spend a great deal of time on crafts or other activities. On days like these, taking a walk or visiting friends will lift your spirits. Treat yourself to lunch at a fast-food restaurant with a play area. If your kids travel well, go for a long drive in the country. Or as a special treat, let your child watch a videotape or TV program while you take a break.

Three-Day Schedule	
Day 1 morning	• Introduce the book, read it, and talk about it. • Make stick puppets to represent George and Martha.
Day 1 afternoon	• Read the book a second time. Your child may enjoy playing with his stick puppets as you read. • Do the "Five Little Hippos" finger play. • Play dentist together.
Day 1 evening	• Have a water play session in the bathtub. • Read the book before bed.
Day 2 morning	• Read the book. • Make some split pea soup together and eat it for lunch.
Day 2 afternoon	• Read the book after lunch. • Make a friends poster.
Day 3 morning	• Read the book again. • Snack on chocolate chip cookies and tea. • Make a silly picture of yourself and tape it to the bathroom mirror.
Day 3 afternoon	• Visit the library and look for more George and Martha books or other funny books by James Marshall.

Sample Schedules

Because I've provided many discussion questions, activities, and enrichment ideas for each picture book featured in *Picture Book Activities,* it's possible (and advisable) to read each book many times and accompany each reading with a different activity. You can do this over two or three days if you like or stretch the experience out over five days. Above are sample three-day and five-day schedules for James Marshall's *George and Martha.* (See pages 74–77 for complete descriptions of the activities.)

Not every parent will want to or be able to create a plan and stick to it. When and how you read to your child and do activities together will be influenced by the time and energy you have, the needs of other family members, and your personal approach to life.

Five-Day Schedule	
Day 1	• Introduce the book, read it, and talk about it. • Make stick puppets to represent George and Martha. • Read the book a second time. Your child may enjoy playing with his stick puppets as you read.
Day 2	• Read the book. • Do the "Five Little Hippos" finger play. • Play dentist together.
Day 3	• Read the book. • Make a friends poster. • Have a water play session in the bathtub.
Day 4	• Read the book. • Make some split pea soup together and eat it for lunch. • Make a silly picture of yourself and tape it to the bathroom mirror.
Day 5	• Read the book. • Snack on chocolate chip cookies and tea. • Visit the library and look for more George and Martha books or other funny books by James Marshall.

Getting Started

The books we read should be chosen with great care, that they may be, as an Egyptian king wrote over his library, "The medicines of the soul."
—Paxton Hood

If you've read the previous chapters, I hope you're now convinced of the importance of reading good books to your child. I also hope I've helped you develop the enthusiasm and confidence you need to evaluate and choose picture books for your child. I trust that you're looking forward to some great literature-based experiences with your child. Let's take a look at how to read aloud, discuss a story with your child, and implement the suggestions in *Picture Book Activities.*

Before You Read

Before you begin reading a story to your child, allow her time to get ready to hear it. Let her settle down and get comfortable. Some children like to cuddle while listening to a story; others prefer to lie on the floor and draw or play quietly. Because the illustrations are a vital part of any picture book, your child should be close enough to see the pictures.

Begin by introducing the book. Show your child the cover and tell her what the book is about—not the entire story, just a brief, general comment on the setting,

main character(s), or problem. If you've previously read your child a similar book or other books written or illustrated by the same author or illustrator, mention this before you begin reading.

As You Read

For some of the books featured in *Picture Book Activities,* you'll find a section titled "As You Read." In this section are suggestions for things you or your child might say as you read the book. For example, in the chapter on *Blueberries for Sal,* I suggest that you encourage your child to make the *kuplink, kuplank, kuplunk* sound effects as you read the story. This section may also suggest actions to accompany the reading, such as shaking your finger at the monkeys as you read *Caps for Sale,* and things to notice as you read, such as how the expression on George's face changes from one page to the next in *Curious George.*

Some picture books may contain words, phrases, or concepts that are unfamiliar to your child, such as the code *S O S* in *Little Toot*. If my children ask a question pertaining to a book while I'm reading it, I'll always answer the question as best I can. However, I try not to interrupt myself while reading aloud to avoid disrupting the flow of a story. If I think my children won't understand something, I explain it beforehand or after I've finished reading. Sometimes explanations are unnecessary; the meanings of words or phrases you think your child won't understand are clear from the context in which the words or phrases are used.

Let's Talk about It

Well-formulated discussion questions enrich your child's experience with a book you've read. Questions should help your child relive important episodes of a story and encourage her to compare the events and characters with those in her own life. In *Children and Books* (Addison-Wesley, 1997), Zena Sutherland writes, "Questions beginning with *why, what,* and *which* usually lead to a more open discussion than the sorts of questions beginning with *when* and *where*."

The questions you'll find in "Let's Talk about It" are simply suggestions. Some require a simple answer; some are more complex. You needn't ask all the questions in one sitting; casual discussions about a book may take place in the course of your regular activities over one or several days.

Some children and adults prefer not to discuss a book formally at all; they would rather let the words and illustrations speak for themselves. I favor this approach with my children. I sometimes ask them to retell a story, ask them what their favorite part of a story was, or talk about the book with them later, when we're playing, walking, or driving together. And often situations occur or questions come up that naturally lead our conversation to some aspect of a book we're reading.

Try to avoid trite questions and comments about a story. Picture books aren't necessarily written to teach, and most don't require an adult's interpretation. Children should be allowed to reason through stories and draw their own conclusions. Richard Jackson points out in his article "Alone in the Crowd: Breaking the Isolation of Childhood" (*School Library Journal,* November 1995) that "Half the fun of art—book, poem, painting, play, or song—is inference. Children may be shortchanged of that fun too often by the adult urge to explain, document, hit home, and send signals. As a publisher, I'm more for illumination than instruction. What we infer, we make our own. The most satisfying books leave some possibilities up to readers and lookers."

Act It Out

Children of all ages love to pretend. A toddler enters the world of make-believe by engaging in activities she sees around her and by putting herself in another person's place. As she grows older, her play develops more structure. She acts out favorite stories, creates original situations from life experiences, and imagines herself in fantasy worlds where anything is possible. If she's encouraged in this kind of play at home, she becomes ready for creative drama by the time she enters school.

The activities you'll find in "Act It Out" include role-playing (in which one assumes the qualities of a character from a story), story theater (in which a narrator reads a story while others pantomime the action), and creative dramatics (in which actors perform the action and speak the dialogue in a story, with or without props). These activities provide valuable opportunities for children—especially the very young, who can respond physically but cannot yet easily respond verbally—to interact with literature.

Many stories are quite easy and fun to act out, and because of the value of drama to your child's development, you should try to act them out with your child whenever you can. Involve your child in making or gathering costumes and props, too. However you choose to implement the suggestions in "Act It

Out," remember that drama, whether rehearsed or impromptu, should be fun for everyone.

Arts and Crafts

Because arts and crafts are so important for young children, I've included at least one arts-and-crafts project for every book featured in *Picture Book Activities* and have often suggested several more in "Enrichment Activities." The arts-and-crafts activities range from painting and drawing to sculpting with play dough and clay to creating collages and working with papier-mâché. Appendix A provides recipes for many of the materials you'll need for these activities.

Arts-and-crafts projects provide great opportunities for creative play. Through well-chosen arts and crafts, your child will learn to think creatively and will develop skills in drawing, painting, sculpting, designing, concentration, coordination, organization, and manipulation. Arts-and-crafts activities promote a sense of achievement and are fun and exciting for children of all ages.

An old phone book can be very useful when your child is coloring, painting, or gluing. Just open the phone book and place your child's paper on the first page. For the next project, simply turn the page and—voilà!—your child will have another clean surface to work on. If you use this technique, you'll never have to hunt for scrap paper to protect your kitchen table and you'll spend a lot less time cleaning paint and glue off it, too.

What can you do with all the arts and crafts your child creates? Here are a few suggestions:

- Keep an eye out for creative ways to use your child's art, such as for gifts or gift-wrap.
- Display your child's art all over your house, not just on your refrigerator. Visit an art framing shop and ask the shop to save its mat scraps for you. You may get some great pieces for mounting or framing your child's art.
- Make a calendar of your child's art for her grandparents and/or other relatives. Save your little artist's masterpieces throughout the year. As a new year approaches, collect free calendars from local businesses. Glue your child's art over the pictures so a new masterpiece will be displayed each month.
- Create a portfolio. You can save some of your child's outstanding creations in a three-ring binder with plastic page protectors. Be sure to label each work of art with the date or your child's age. For an extralarge or three-dimensional creation, take a photo or two for the portfolio. The artwork itself will have to go eventually!

Remember that arts and crafts should be fun for both you and your child. Don't take on a messy project when you're tired, rushed, or otherwise unable to devote yourselves fully to the activity. With the right attitude, you and your child will have a wonderful time exploring the world of art.

Cooking and Baking

I've suggested cooking or baking activities wherever possible in *Picture Book Activities* for a number of reasons:

- Parents at home naturally spend time each day preparing meals, and their children usually want to be with them, either to "help" them or join in the "fun."
- For a young child, a kitchen is a stimulating environment full of irresistible things to see, hear, touch, taste, and smell.
- With a bit of effort and a lot of patience, you can make your kitchen a wonderful classroom for your child. In it she can practice premath skills like counting, measuring, weighing, and sorting, as well as learn scientific concepts like how cornstarch thickens a sauce, how yeast makes bread rise, and how the heat in an oven turns a pan of batter into a cake.
- Cooking and baking activities provide children with practical experience that will serve them well as they grow older.
- I know from experience that parents who take the time and exercise the

patience to train little hands in kitchen skills reap great rewards. At age eleven, my oldest daughter is adept at baking cakes, cookies, and bars, preparing lunch for her younger siblings, and even cooking the family dinner occasionally.

Consider assembling a box of unbreakable kitchen tools for your child to use when she helps you in the kitchen. Include items like cookie cutters, oven mitts, measuring spoons and cups, wooden spoons, mixing bowls, and baking pans. Store your child's "baker's box" in a kitchen cupboard that's low enough for her to reach. She can use her tools either for play or for doing some real cooking or baking with you.

You might also make or buy your child her own recipe box and fill it with her favorite recipes explained with simple words, pictures, and symbols. Add some simple no-cook recipes that she can make with little supervision.

Remember that the kitchen is a hazardous place for unsupervised children, so you'll need to be safety conscious. Infants and toddlers should be occupied elsewhere when you're doing a cooking or baking project with your preschooler. Keep dangerous objects well out of reach and make a rule that only an adult can use sharp tools and hot appliances like the oven.

Rhymes and Finger Plays

You can enjoy rhymes and finger plays just about anytime and anywhere. Use them to liven up a walk or drive with your child and to amuse a toddler at changing time or a preschooler waiting for her meal. Say rhymes and do finger plays while cuddling in a rocking chair or giving your child a bath.

To learn the words of a rhyme, try these helpful hints:

- Memorize two lines at a time, reciting those lines throughout the day until you know them by heart. Then add another two lines and continue in this way until you've memorized the whole rhyme.
- Post one or two unfamiliar rhymes near your baby's changing table, on the wall next to your rocking chair, or in the kitchen where you cook, eat, or clean up. You'll know them well after reading and saying them to your child several times.

Some of the rhymes and finger plays included in *Picture Book Activities* are traditional, while others are completely new. None are violent or aggressive, a common criticism of traditional nursery fare.

Fun and Games

The activities you'll find in "Fun and Games" include ideas for indoors and outdoors and for one child or a group of children. Some of the games require props, and others can be played anywhere, anytime with no supplies at all.

As often as possible, I've suggested games that are closely related to the stories, such as blowing bubbles like Gilberto in *Gilberto and the Wind* or having a pretend fox hunt for *Harquin.* Occasionally I've included a game more for fun than to enhance your literary experience. Examples of the latter are the card game Pigs that accompanies *The Three Little Pigs* and the paper airplane games suggested for *"Could Be Worse!"*

Let's Pretend

"Let's Pretend" activities provide opportunities for your child to exercise her mind, body, and imagination by creating situations based on picture books you've read together. Whereas an "Act It Out" activity retells a story (or part of it), a "Let's Pretend" activity encourages your child to create and dramatize an original situation, such as working in or visiting a restaurant or toy store or having a birthday party or sleepover. "Let's Pretend" activities draw substantially on your child's imagination and are essential for her full development. Pretending is how your child rehearses for life.

Ernie Coombs, well known to Canadian children as the title character on the long-running TV program *Mr. Dressup,* visits his "tickle trunk" during every episode and creates a make-believe situation with the clothes and props he finds there. Why not start your own tickle trunk? It not only will come in handy for "Let's Pretend" activities, but also will keep your child occupied and foster spontaneous imaginative play at other times. Fill a trunk, toy box, large plastic container, or cardboard box with adult clothes, shoes, hats, scarves, gloves, and costume jewelry. Old suits are great, as are Hawaiian shirts, vests, baseball hats, bridesmaid dresses, nightgowns, wigs, boots, slippers, and purses. Keep your eyes open at garage sales and thrift shops or stock up at post-Halloween costume sales.

Young children may have trouble with zippers and small buttons, so consider replacing these with Velcro. You could also enlarge buttonholes and replace small buttons with large ones.

Music and Movement

Music is an essential part of a child's general education. Through the study of music, a child acquires knowledge, skills, and attitudes that influence her throughout her life. Children who participate in musical activities not only learn to enjoy music for its own sake, they also learn coordination, goal setting, concentration, and cooperation. Finally, children who study music may become better listeners and develop high musical intelligence.

The first music your child hears will probably come from you. Don't worry if you can't carry a tune; no matter how your voice sounds, it's the most beautiful one your child hears. Sing to your infant, toddler, or preschooler as you rock her, take her for walks, carry her, change her, bathe her, and play with her. If you'd like to learn more songs, borrow a few children's audiotapes or CDs from the library or buy some for your own collection.

The activities you'll find in "Music and Movement" include singing, dancing, listening to music, and moving to music. These are the best musical activities for young children and should be part of every day for you and your child.

Out and About

As a busy home-schooling mom, I sometimes need to remind myself to get outside for a simple walk in the neighborhood. When my three oldest children were preschoolers and toddlers, however, getting out was a very important part of each day. I think it often saved my life and theirs!

Daily outdoor play is essential for children of all ages and the adults who care for them. Whether they're playing in the snow, stomping in puddles, picking flowers, or crunching fallen leaves, toddlers need to be outdoors in all kinds of weather to master their newfound skills in walking, running, climbing, and jumping. And preschoolers, with their seemingly endless energy, will always find something entertaining to do outdoors. Sandboxes, wading pools, swings, slides, and other outdoor venues are not only fun, they're great places for a preschooler to blow off some steam. Short daily walks also benefit both parent and child, whether you push a stroller, pull a wagon, or walk with your child at her pokey pace.

"Out and About" activities include suggestions for walks, outdoor games, other kinds of outdoor play, and outings in the community. Some activities aren't practical for every situation; for example, you can't go berry picking in the winter, of course, or play in the snow if you live in a warm climate, or visit the countryside if you live there. But you'll be able to do most of the activities regardless of the season or your place of residence.

Play and Learn

The activities in this category teach pre-math and prereading skills like counting, sorting, matching, sequencing, number and letter recognition, calendar skills, telling time, and printing. Because these activities are designed mainly to teach basic skills, they may not always enhance your child's literary experience. I've included them in *Picture Book Activities* to help you incorporate basic skills development in your daily routine. You probably know that children who start school already familiar with the letter names and sounds as well as basic math concepts are better prepared to succeed than those who do not.

"Play and Learn" activities make use of ordinary objects found in most homes. The only special material you'll need is a set of number and object flash cards that you can easily and affordably buy or make. If you choose to make flash cards, all you need are twenty-two index cards and a marker or a package of small stickers. On half the cards, write the numbers zero through ten (one number per card). On the remaining cards, draw groups of objects (or attach small stickers) in amounts from zero through ten. For example, you could draw one ball on the first card, two leaves on the second card, and so on.

Here are some additional tips to help you help your child develop prereading and premath skills:

- Don't push academics. Young children must spend lots of time developing their motor skills in order to make academic learning possible and productive. Some activities that develop large motor skills are running, jumping, hopping, dancing, and playing with balls, pull toys, push toys, riding toys, climbing toys, swings, and slides. Some activities that develop fine motor skills are filling and emptying boxes and containers and playing with nesting and stacking toys, simple wooden jigsaw puzzles, shape sorters, and blocks.

- Read aloud to your child; it's the best way to prepare her for success as a reader. When children are read to, they almost automatically understand written language. They learn that the words in a particular book are always in the same order and always on the same pages. They may also learn that print is read from left to right, that words are made up of letters, that each letter has at least two forms (capital and lowercase), and that spaces separate words.

- Tap into your child's natural curiosity to help her learn prereading skills. While reading to your child, you'll have many opportunities to answer her questions about the names, sounds, and shapes of letters. Preschoolers are very observant and often focus on trademarks and logos that include or resemble letters of the alphabet. Pointing out such symbols is an easy way to begin helping your child recognize letters. For example, you could note that the Golden Arches sign at McDonald's looks like an *m*.

- Remember that children often learn premath skills through play. For example,

DUPLO and LEGO toys are great tools for learning basic math skills; a child can sort pieces by color or size, build towers, compare constructions, count pieces, make patterns, and so on.

- Teach your child that math is a vital part of everyday life. Shopping, traveling, gardening, meal planning, cooking, eating, and even laundry are all ways in which people apply math to their daily routines.
- Watch TV programs like *Sesame Street* with your child. Such programs can help her learn letters, sounds, numbers, colors, and shapes, among other things. If you watch with her, you can enhance her learning by discussing the letter (or number or shape or color) on TV and point out all the other places it appears.

Snack Time

Where I haven't suggested a cooking or baking activity to accompany a particular picture book, I've tried to provide a "Snack Time" suggestion instead. For many children, food is as much a plaything as something to eat, so whenever possible, I've suggested hands-on snacks that your child can create (or help you create). These include quick treats like sandwiches, fruit, no-bake cookies, popcorn balls, and crackers with homemade butter.

Enrichment Activities

In addition to the six main activities for each book featured in *Picture Book Activities,* I've offered suggestions for more things to do, see, or read to enrich your child's literary experience. Videotapes, for example, can often enhance a child's understanding of a book. (I suggest watching a videotape after you've read the book on which it's based.) Other enrichment activities are perfect for when you're driving, walking, or eating lunch together. For example, when you're taking a walk after reading *Blueberries for Sal,* you might ask your child, "What would be good and bad about sleeping all winter?"

Because computer software and web sites become obsolete fairly quickly, I've avoided recommending any computer-related enrichment activities. But of course there are thousands of great games and learning tools available to those who have computers and software budgets. Those who have Internet access and some time on their hands may also enjoy looking for web sites related to the books they're reading.

If you like, you can use many of the enrichment activities, such as finding Australia on a map, reading a simple nonfiction book on ocean life, or learning about the custom of bullfighting, to gently introduce your child to home-schooling. A goal of many home-schooling parents is to help their children develop a love of learning, and using literature-based units that encompass many fields of study is a great way to keep learning lively.

Whenever a picture book is related to another book in *Picture Book Activities* —for example, *The Happy Lion, Madeline,* and *Mirette on the High Wire* are all set in Paris—I mention the related book(s) in "Enrichment Activities."

One Last Thought

The child who is exposed naturally, as part of a happy home life, to the work of good writers, is fortunate indeed.

—Frank Eyre

While listening to a radio discussion about raising better readers, I heard an "expert" advise parents to stop reading aloud to their children once the children could read on their own. He reasoned that children would then be forced to read for themselves.

I was horrified! Some of the best times I share with my older children are when we're immersed in a reading adventure together. Although my children are all excellent readers and love to read on their own, they still enjoy and benefit from hearing good books read aloud. I believe that reading aloud is a priceless, irreplaceable family activity that's often overlooked and undervalued in our hurried world, and I encourage you to keep doing it as long as you like.

I also urge you to hold to high standards when choosing books for your children and to continue doing so long after they're reading independently. Too often I hear parents say, "I don't care what they read, as long as they're reading." Don't forget that although we can't remember everything we read, what we read changes us. It feeds our minds and nourishes our souls. Good books help us grow and add to our inner stature. I pose to you the challenge Gladys Hunt so eloquently makes in *Honey for a Child's Heart* (Zondervan, 1989): "A young child, a fresh uncluttered mind, a world before him—to what treasures will you lead him? With what will you furnish his spirit?"

Alexander and the Terrible, Horrible, No Good, Very Bad Day

Written by Judith Viorst
Illustrated by Ray Cruz
(Atheneum, 1972)

Adults often remember childhood as a fun-filled, carefree time. While it's true that children don't have many pressing responsibilities, it's not always easy to be a child. In *Alexander and the Terrible, Horrible, No Good, Very Bad Day,* Judith Viorst takes a humorous look at some of the everyday problems children face.

Both you and your child will relate to the injustices Alexander experiences, such as not getting a prize in his cereal box and getting scolded for being dirty after his older brother makes him fall in the mud. And although, like Alexander, you may sometimes want to move far away from your problems, you know that "some days are like that. Even in Australia."

As You Read

- Alexander's rambling, childlike descriptions make this a delightful book to read aloud. (After borrowing it from the library, I knew we'd enjoy reading it again and again, so I bought a copy.) Have fun conveying Alexander's emotions with your voice.
- Allow plenty of time for your child to look at each picture. She'll enjoy noticing how Alexander's poses and expressions show his emotions.
- After you've read the book, read it again and pause each time you reach the words *Australia* or *terrible, horrible, no good, very bad day.* Your child will enjoy "reading" these words herself.

Other fun-to-repeat phrases are *they can't make me wear them, I hate lima beans,* and *I hate kissing.*

Let's Talk about It

Ask your child:

- What are some of the terrible things that happen to Alexander?
- Do you like Alexander's family? Why or why not?
- Why do you think Alexander's teacher doesn't like his picture of the invisible castle?
- Have you ever had a terrible, horrible, no good, very bad day? What happened?
- What was your favorite part of the story? What do you remember about it?
- Do any of the people in the book remind you of people you know?

Arts and Crafts

Sparkle Paint

If Alexander's teacher had taught him how to make sparkle paint, his artwork might have been a little more creative!

Flour	*Small containers*
Water	*Liquid tempera paint*
Salt	*Poster board or cardboard*
	Plastic squeeze bottles

1. Mix equal parts flour, water, and salt to make a thin paste.

2. Divide paste into small containers and add liquid tempera paint in desired colors to each. Mix well.
3. Pour paints into plastic squeeze bottles. Squeeze paint onto poster board or cardboard to make pictures.
4. Let dry and admire how the salt makes the pictures sparkle.

Cooking and Baking

Jellyroll

Alexander suffered through a treatless lunch while his friends enjoyed sweets like jellyroll. A jellyroll is easy to make, so let your child do as much of this recipe as she can.

3 eggs	*1 teaspoon*
1 cup white sugar	*baking powder*
5 tablespoons	*¼ teaspoon salt*
cold water	*Powdered sugar*
1 teaspoon vanilla	*or shredded*
1 cup sifted	*coconut*
cake flour	*Jam*

1. Preheat your oven to 375°F.
2. Beat eggs until thick, then gradually beat in sugar.
3. Add water and vanilla.
4. Sift flour, baking powder, and salt together, then add to the batter and beat just until smooth.
5. Pour the batter into a greased baking sheet or jellyroll pan and bake it for 12–15 minutes.

6. Remove from oven. Loosen the edges of the cake and immediately turn it upside down onto a dishtowel sprinkled with powdered sugar or coconut.
7. Spread the cake with jam and roll it up, starting on a long side.
8. Let the cake cool and cut it into slices.

Fun and Games

Bath Paints

Most kids can count on having fun in the tub, but Alexander even has a miserable bath. It might've been better if he'd had bath paints to play with. If your child's skin is delicate, use a shaving cream for sensitive skin. And be warned that if you have ceramic tile in your bathroom, the food coloring may stain your grout.

Shaving cream
Muffin pan
Food coloring
Spoon
Paintbrushes or sponges

1. Squirt shaving cream into the muffin pan sections.
2. Add a few drops of food coloring to each section and mix with a spoon.
3. Let your child paint the walls, the tub, and herself with paintbrushes, sponges, or her hands. Older children will enjoy mixing colors to create new ones.

Let's Pretend

Office

Alexander wreaks havoc in his father's office. Let your child wreak havoc in a make-believe office of her own.

1. Gather as many of the following materials as you can: unopened junk mail, unneeded return envelopes, stickers from magazine and record clubs, pads of paper, inexpensive stationery, pencils, tape dispenser, stapler, rubber stamps, ink pad, play telephone.
2. Play office with your child or let her play alone or with siblings or friends.

Music and Movement

The Wheels on the Car

Sing a song describing Alexander's car ride to the tune of "The Wheels on the Bus." You can sing the verses below or make up your own.

The wheels on the car go round and round,
　round and round, round and round.
The wheels on the car go round and round
　all the way to school.

The wipers on the car go swish...
The horn on the car goes beep...
Alexander in the back gets scrunched...
Alexander in the back gets smushed...
Alexander in the back gets sick...
Alexander has a terrible time...

Play and Learn

Shoe Trail

Having to buy shoes he doesn't want is one bad part of Alexander's day. Maybe he'd have a better day if he played with shoes instead!

Empty laundry basket	Pen
Shoes	Markers (optional)
Paper	Stickers (optional)

1. Have your child fill a laundry basket with shoes.
2. Make a trail of shoes around the house, lining them up heel to toe.
3. Follow the trail together. Keep a tally as your child counts how many shoes each family member owns, how many shoes of each color there are, or how many shoes there are in total.
4. Help your child make a simple chart to record the information collected. For example, if you're counting shoes by color, list the colors down the left side of a sheet of paper (perhaps using a brown marker to write the word brown and so on). Next to each color, have your child place the same number of stickers as shoes counted.
5. Help your child put the shoes away.

Enrichment Activities

- Locate Australia on a map or globe, then point out where you live. Ask, "Why do you think Alexander wanted to go to Australia?"
- Encourage your child to write a "terrible, horrible, no good, very bad day" story featuring herself as the main character and describing real or imaginary events.
- Sometimes, like Alexander, lots of unpleasant things happen to us in one day. Other times, we may have a bad day just because we see things from a negative point of view. Reread the book and challenge your child to find positive things in Alexander's day. For example, she might say, "It's a good thing Alexander didn't break his leg when he tripped on his skateboard."
- Watch a videotape of *Alexander and the Terrible, Horrible, No Good, Very Bad Day.* (See Appendix D for more information.)
- Judith Viorst has written two other books about Alexander and his family: *Alexander, Who Used to Be Rich Last Sunday* and *Alexander, Who's Not (Do you hear me? I mean it!) Going to Move.*

And to Think That I Saw It on Mulberry Street

Written and Illustrated by Dr. Seuss
(Vanguard, 1937)

What discussion of picture books would be complete without mention of Theodor Seuss Geisel (better known as Dr. Seuss)? Although an art teacher told him he couldn't draw well, and his first book was rejected thirty times, Dr. Seuss went on to create a distinctive style of illustration and become a best-selling author of children's books. He received the Wilder Award in 1980 for his contribution to children's literature.

And to Think That I Saw It on Mulberry Street was Seuss's first children's book. Its rhyming verse tells of a boy on his way home from school who, seeing only a horse and wagon on Mulberry Street, spins a fantastic yarn to tell his father. The book is filled with the zany Seuss illustrations that generations of children have loved and is, as Zena Sutherland says in *Children and Books* (Addison-Wesley, 1997), "only a sample of more and better nonsense to come."

As You Read

Marco's not too excited about seeing a horse and wagon, which would thrill most children today. You might introduce this book by explaining that it was written when horses and wagons were common.

Let's Talk about It

Ask your child:

- What do you think Marco's dad means when he tells Marco to "stop turning minnows into whales"?
- Why do you think Marco turns the horse and wagon into a fancy make-believe parade?
- What happens when Marco's father asks him what he's seen? Do you think his father would believe his story of the parade? Why or why not?
- Have you ever made up a story and pretended it was true? Did you tell anyone? Did anyone believe you?

Arts and Crafts

Drawing

Fortunately, Dr. Seuss wasn't discouraged by criticism of his drawings. Follow Seuss's lead and teach your child to focus on the process, rather than the product, of each artistic endeavor.

Drawings are probably the first artworks your child will create. For preschoolers, drawing is not only a creative exercise, but also one that develops small muscles and hand-eye coordination. Because drawing requires minimal supplies, it can be done anywhere and anytime. The following tips will help you encourage your child's drawing efforts:

- Provide your child with a variety of drawing tools: crayons, pencils, pens, chalk, and markers.
- Offer a variety of papers, including construction paper, newsprint, fine sandpaper, and grocery bags.
- Cut paper into shapes like circles, triangles, and stars.
- Provide three-dimensional drawing surfaces like boxes and rocks.
- Give your child a small notebook or sketchbook in which to draw.
- Let your child draw while you read a book to him.
- Encourage your child to draw pictures in shades of one color.
- Encourage your child to draw with wet chalk on dry paper or with dry chalk on wet paper.
- Challenge your child to draw while blindfolded.

Cooking and Baking

Peanut Butter–Oat Bars

Marco must have been hungry after all his imagining. Perhaps he helped his mother make these delicious bars, which would have impressed even his stern father!

½ cup butter, softened
1 cup brown sugar, lightly packed
½ cup corn syrup
1 teaspoon salt
2 teaspoons vanilla
4 cups oats
½ cup peanut butter
½ cup chocolate chips
1½ teaspoons butter

1. Preheat the oven to 350°F.
2. Cream butter and sugar.
3. Add corn syrup, salt, vanilla, and oats. Mix well.
4. Spread the mixture evenly in a greased 9-by-13-inch pan. Bake it for 15 minutes and let it cool slightly.
5. Spread peanut butter evenly on top.
6. Melt the chocolate chips and butter together until smooth. Drizzle over the peanut butter.
7. Cool to set the chocolate, then cut into squares.

Fun and Games

Nonsense Words

Dr. Seuss is well known for his imaginative nonsense words. Have fun making up some nonsense of your own!

- Make up and use nonsense names for everyday objects. For example, you might call a piano a "plink-a-plunk." You could also borrow words from Dr. Seuss.
- Think up a nonsense word for an object or action and challenge your child to guess its meaning.
- Recite a familiar story or rhyme. Substitute a few words with nonsense words and have your child say "Beep!" as he hears each one.
- Sometimes young children invent words without realizing it! Our oldest daughter always called the vacuum cleaner "babikesh," and our second daughter's blanket was always a "beeda." Tell your child about funny words he used to say.
- Write and illustrate your own silly story full of nonsense words. Staple sheets of paper together inside a construction paper cover or follow the directions in Appendix B.

Music and Movement

Marching Song

In Marco's parade the band rides on a wagon, but most parades include a marching band. Pretend you are part of Marco's parade and march around the room singing the following song to the tune of "Twinkle, Twinkle, Little Star."

See the brass band in the street,
Hear the marching of their feet;
They are singing as they go,
Marching, marching, to and fro.
See the brass band in the street,
Hear the marching of their feet.

Out and About

Tall Tales

Marco is known for "turning minnows into whales," or telling tall tales that blatantly exaggerate the facts. You and your child will enjoy telling tall tales based on your daily experiences.

1. If possible, take a walk in your neighborhood. (Telling tall tales is also fun on long car or bus rides or while waiting for a meal in a restaurant. If you can't get out, just look around your house or yard.) Observe your surroundings.
2. Choose one of the things or people you see and make up a tall tale about it. You might start with an animal like a cat and say it weighs 3,000 pounds, wears a church bell on its collar, sleeps in a blanket-lined swimming pool, and drinks 20 gallons of milk for breakfast.
3. Take turns adding elements to the story. If you get stalled, ask yourselves questions like "What did it

look like?" "What else did you see?" or "What happened next?"

4. End your tale with "And to think that we saw it on _____ Street!"

Play and Learn

Counting

And to Think That I Saw It on Mulberry Street is rich with objects to count: flowerpots on the wagon, musicians in the band, police officers on motorcycles, and so on. After you've read the book once, reread it and count some of the objects you see. To make the flash cards mentioned below, see "Getting Started: Play and Learn" (page 18).

Number flash cards (optional)
Object flash cards (optional)

• As you look at each page, say, "Let's count the _____ in this picture. How many _____ do you see?" Point to each object as you count it: "One, two. There are two people on the sled." You might then say, "What else do you see in this picture?" and go on to count other objects.
• If you like, use number flash cards as you count. When your child counts two objects, ask him to find the card that has the number two on it.
• If your child is not yet able to recognize numbers, use object flash cards. When your child counts two objects, ask him, "Can you find the card that

has two stickers on it?" To help him learn to associate numbers with groups of objects, show him the card with the number two and explain that the number two means "two things."

Enrichment Activities

• Decorate a bike or wagon and have a pretend parade.
• Write and illustrate one of the tall tales you made up. (See page 28.) Turn your tale into a book by stapling sheets of paper together inside a construction paper cover or following the directions in Appendix B.
• Read other books by Dr. Seuss, such as *The 500 Hats of Bartholomew Cubbins, How the Grinch Stole Christmas!, Horton Hears a Who!,* and *If I Ran the Zoo.* Dr. Seuss has also written books for beginning readers, such as *The Cat in the Hat* and *Green Eggs and Ham.* These books contain limited vocabulary but still make great read-alouds.
• If your child enjoys Dr. Seuss, he might also enjoy books by Bill Peet. Try *Buford the Little Bighorn* and *Smokey.*

Blueberries for Sal

Written and Illustrated
by Robert McCloskey
(Viking, 1948)

Several generations of children have loved this Caldecott Honor Book. I especially enjoy the way the deep blue illustrations of the characters' clothing, their car, their kitchen wood stove, and the products in their cupboards depict a bygone era.

Blueberries for Sal describes the excursion of Little Sal and her mother to Blueberry Hill. As the two collect blueberries—*"kuplink, kuplank, kuplunk"*—for canning, Little Bear and his mother search on the other side of the hill for berries "to store up...for the long, cold winter." The adventure that ensues when Little Sal and Little Bear wander away from their mothers is sure to delight your child and keep her listening intently to the very last page.

As You Read

While listening to the story, your child will enjoy making its many sound effects: *"kuplink, kuplank, kuplunk"* as the berries hit the bottom of the pail; *"caw, caw, caw"* as the crows fly away; *"munch, munch," "gulp,"* and *"swallow"* as Little Bear's mother stores up food for the winter; and *"garumpf"* as she discovers Little Sal is not her child.

Let's Talk about It

Ask your child:

- Why are Little Sal and her mother picking blueberries? Do you think Little Sal is enjoying herself? How do you know?

- What are Little Bear and his mother doing on Blueberry Hill?
- In late summer and autumn, both people and animals store up food for the winter. What's the difference between the ways Little Sal's mother and Little Bear's mother store up food?
- How do Little Bear and Little Sal and their mothers get all mixed up with each other?
- Look at the pictures in which the mothers discover the mix-up. How do the mothers look? How do Little Bear and Little Sal look?
- What do you think Little Sal and her mother do when they get home from picking blueberries?

Arts and Crafts

Blueberry Bubble Prints

Newspaper
Liquid dishwashing detergent
Shallow dish
Blue or purple tempera paint
Straw
Paper
Clear contact paper (optional)

1. Cover your child's work surface with newspaper.
2. Pour ¼ cup liquid dishwashing detergent into shallow dish.
3. If you're using powdered tempera, mix the paint with a small amount of water.
4. Add the paint to the dishwashing liquid until the color is intense.
5. Place one end of the straw into the paint mixture and blow until bubbles almost spill over the edge of the dish.
6. Gently place a sheet of paper on the bubbles and hold it in place until several bubbles pop.
7. Repeat steps 5 and 6 as needed until your blueberry print is complete.
8. Let the print dry, then display it or cover it with clear contact paper and use it as a place mat.

Cooking and Baking

Blueberry Muffins

If you use frozen blueberries, do not defrost them. Defrosted berries will discolor the batter.

2 eggs
¼ cup butter or margarine, melted
1 cup milk
1 teaspoon grated lemon rind (optional)
2 cups all-purpose flour
¾ cup sugar
1 tablespoon baking powder
½ teaspoon baking soda
½ teaspoon salt
1½ cups fresh or frozen blueberries
½ cup chopped walnuts (optional)

1. Preheat the oven to 400°F and grease a muffin pan.
2. In a large bowl, combine eggs, melted butter or margarine, milk, and grated lemon rind. Mix well.

3. In a smaller bowl, combine flour, sugar, baking powder, baking soda, salt, blueberries, and chopped walnuts. Mix well.
4. Add the dry ingredients to the wet ingredients and fold them together gently until they're just mixed.
5. Spoon the batter into the muffin pan and bake for 25 minutes.
6. Remove the muffins from the pan and let them cool on a rack.

Fun and Games

Blueberry Hunt

Scissors
Blue or purple construction paper
1 small bucket or plastic margarine or yogurt tub for each player

1. Cut large "blueberries" (2–3 inches in diameter) from the paper.
2. Hide the blueberries around your house or play area.
3. Give each player a small bucket or plastic tub and have the players hunt for the blueberries.
4. If you are playing this game with only one child, you may enjoy telling her she's "hotter" as she nears a hidden berry and "colder" as she moves away from it.

Music and Movement

The Bear Went over the Mountain

Sing the familiar song "The Bear Went over the Mountain" with your child. If you like, make up your own words about Little Sal and her mother.

The bear went over the mountain,
The bear went over the mountain,
The bear went over the mountain,
To see what he could see.
And what do you think he saw?
And what do you think he saw?
The other side of the mountain,
The other side of the mountain,
The other side of the mountain,
Was all that he could see.

Out and About

Visit a Blueberry Farm

- If you live in or near an agricultural area and it is early summer to midsummer, visit a blueberry farm to pick fresh blueberries.
- If visiting a blueberry farm is not possible, see if your local garden center has a blueberry bush you can look at. Then visit your grocery store and purchase some fresh or frozen blueberries.
- Back at home, talk about how you are storing up food like the characters in *Blueberries for Sal* when you can fresh berries, make jam, or freeze

berries to use later in baking muffins, pancakes, or other blueberry treats.

Play and Learn

I'm So Blue

- Go on a color hunt in your house, yard, or neighborhood. Ask your child, "How many blue things do you see here?"
- Draw a picture using crayons in various shades of blue.
- Cut blue pictures from magazines or catalogs. Glue the pictures to separate sheets of paper, then staple the sheets together. Add a blue construction paper cover to make a blue book.
- Sculpt blueberries from blue play dough.
- Have a blue day: Wear blue clothes, paint with blue paint, drink blue juice, make blueberry pancakes, and so on.

Enrichment Activities

- Read a simple nonfiction book about bears to learn where they live, what they eat, what they do in the winter, and why they hibernate.
- Ask your child to pretend she's a bear who's been eating and eating and eating. Now winter has arrived and it's time to hibernate. Ask your child, "What would be good and bad about sleeping all winter?"
- Watch *Blueberries for Sal* on videotape. (See Appendix D for more information.)
- Read other picture books about bears, such as *Little Bear* by Else Holmelund Minarik or *Bear's Bargain* by Frank Asch.
- Read other books by Robert McCloskey, such as *Make Way for Ducklings* (a Caldecott winner), *One Morning in Maine,* and *Lentil.*

Bread and Jam for Frances

Written by Russell Hoban
Illustrated by Lillian Hoban
(HarperCollins, 1964)

Bread and Jam for Frances is the first of several books about Frances the badger. Frances, like many children, is reluctant to try anything new. Rather than eat the mouthwatering meals her mother prepares, Frances prefers to stick with bread and jam. She says, "I always know what I am getting, and I am always pleased." Children and parents alike will enjoy Lillian Hoban's attractive illustrations, the gentle humor in the dialogue, and the wise way in which Frances's parents handle the dilemma.

As You Read

- The phrase "bread and jam" is repeated many times throughout this book. When you first read the book, pause before reading the phrase, then emphasize it slightly. Your child will catch on quickly and will soon be chiming in with "bread and jam" each time you pause.
- Notice how Frances's enthusiasm for bread and jam wanes as she eats more and more of it. Her face looks sad and worried, her skipping slows down, she's unable to finish her snack, and finally she cries when she's served bread and jam for dinner.

Let's Talk about It

Ask your child:

- What was Frances's favorite food? Why did she get tired of it?
- Do you like the way Frances's parents act? What else could they do?

- What would be good and bad about always eating bread and jam? (Some good aspects might be: You'd never have to decide what to eat; you'd always know what it would taste like. Some bad aspects might be: It might get boring after a while; your body wouldn't get all the nutrients it needs; jam at every meal would be bad for your teeth.)
- Would you rather eat bread and jam than eggs, veal cutlets, or any of the other foods that Frances's mother serves? Would you like to eat bread and jam at every meal?
- What would you choose if you were allowed to eat your favorite food at every meal?

Arts and Crafts

Favorite Foods Collage
If, like Frances, your child could choose one meal to eat all the time, what would it be? Encourage your child to create a collage of his favorite foods.

Scissors
Old magazines
Glue
Paper plate, tape, and pipe cleaner or construction paper and clear contact paper

1. Help your child cut pictures of his favorite foods from old magazines.
2. Arrange the pictures to make a collage.

3. For a wall hanging, glue the pictures onto a paper plate and tape a pipe cleaner hook on the back for hanging. For a place mat, glue the pictures onto a sheet of construction paper and cover the collage with clear contact paper.

Cooking and Baking

Bread Sculpture
This activity combines baking and art. Use the bread dough to create sculptures that can be baked and admired, then eaten.

1 cup water
1 teaspoon sugar
1 tablespoon or 1 package dry yeast
2 cups flour plus additional flour for kneading
1 tablespoon oil
1 teaspoon salt

1. Preheat your oven to 400°F.
2. Mix water, sugar, and yeast in a bowl for 2–3 minutes until the yeast softens.
3. Add 1 cup flour and beat with a wooden spoon until smooth. Mix in oil, salt, and second cup of flour to make a thick batter.
4. Pour the batter onto a floured surface and slowly add more flour while kneading. Keep the dough coated with flour to prevent sticking.

5. Knead for about 5 minutes. The dough should be smooth and elastic and should bounce back when poked. Place the dough in an oiled bowl and cover with a clean towel. Set the dough in a warm place and let it rise for about 45 minutes.
6. Punch down the risen dough and work it into a smooth ball. If necessary, divide the dough into portions for each child or for different parts of your sculpture.
7. Sculpt the dough into any shape you like. Use a knife, fork, or toothpick to add interesting details.
8. Bake your sculpture(s) for 15–20 minutes or until they're golden brown. (Large sculptures may take longer.)
9. Cool your sculpture(s) on a wire rack. Eat them plain or with jam.

Fun and Games

Taste Test

Frances prefers the predictable taste of bread and jam to other foods her mother prepares. Can your child identify foods by their taste?

Blindfold
Various food items

1. Blindfold your child and challenge him to identify some of his favorite foods (for example, ice cream, pickles, yogurt, cereal, and cookies) by taste and smell.

2. Ask your child to describe the different tastes, smells, and textures.
3. Ask your child to group the foods into these categories: sweet, salty, bitter, sour, spicy, or tangy.

Let's Pretend

Bread and Jam Restaurant

Table
Table linens
Centerpiece, such as vase of flowers
Candle
Homemade menu listing different kinds of bread and jam
Bread and jam (real or pretend)

1. Set a table with linens, a centerpiece, a candle, and a homemade menu to create a make-believe restaurant that serves only bread and jam.
2. Decide who will play the server and who will play the customer.
3. Take turns playing each role. The server might pretend to take the customer's coat, show the customer to his seat, give him a menu, take his order, and deliver his food. The customer might pretend to ask questions about the menu selections, eat the food, and ask for the server's assistance.

Music and Movement

Skipping Song

Frances likes to make up songs about the situations she finds herself in. In *Bread and Jam for Frances,* she sings a skipping song about jam while she waits for the school bus.

- Sing Frances's song with your child to the tune of "Twinkle, Twinkle, Little Star."
- Skipping rope is tough for most preschoolers, so your child can chant Frances's song while he jumps, hops, walks, or swings.
- Make up your own silly songs as you eat, play, walk, or drive with your child.

Out and About

Fruit Picking

If you live in or near an agricultural area and it is summer or early autumn, visit a fruit farm to pick fresh fruit. (Tip: Strawberries are easy for young children to pick, as they grow near the ground, are easy to see, and have no thorns.)

1. Find a farm that will let you pick your own fruit. Go early in the day, before it gets too hot, and bring sunscreen, insect repellent, and hats if necessary.

2. A half-hour of fruit picking is a long time for a preschooler, so bring a snack, juice, and some books or toys for your child to enjoy in the shade when he tires.

3. Back at home, your child can help you wash and hull the fruit. Enjoy the fruit as a snack or serve it with ice cream or whipped cream.

4. If you've picked a large amount of fruit, use some of it to make a batch of jam.

Enrichment Activities

- Look for pictures of real badgers and read a simple nonfiction book about them. Discuss how they live and what they really like to eat.
- Serve your child a breakfast of poached eggs on toast and orange juice.
- Read other books about food, such as *The Very Hungry Caterpillar* by Eric Carle.
- Check your bookstore or library for other books about Frances, such as *Bedtime for Frances, A Baby Sister for Frances, Best Friends for Frances,* and *A Birthday for Frances.*

Caps for Sale

Written and Illustrated
by Esphyr Slobodkina
(Addison-Wesley, 1940)

This timeless folktale is one your children will surely want to hear again and again. It's about a peddler who walks up and down the street balancing caps on his head and calling, "Caps! Caps for sale! Fifty cents a cap!" One fine day when he can't sell any caps, the peddler sits under a big tree to rest. He falls asleep and upon waking finds all his caps gone. He spots his caps up in the tree, each one on the head of a mischievous monkey. Children and adults alike will love the way the peddler finally—unwittingly—gets the monkeys to return his caps.

As You Read

- *Caps for Sale* provides wonderful opportunities for your child to participate in the reading process. Whenever you approach the dialogue "Caps! Caps for sale! Fifty cents a cap!" pause and let your child say it with you.
- As you read about the peddler shaking his finger and fist and stamping his feet, demonstrate these actions.
- Encourage your child to act like a monkey mimicking the peddler's actions and saying "Tsz, tsz, tsz."
- After a few readings, your child will be able to tell you the order in which the peddler stacks his caps: "first his own checked cap, then the gray caps, then the blue caps..." and so on.

Let's Talk about It

Ask your child:

- What is the peddler's job?
- Why does the peddler sit down to rest? What happens while he sleeps?
- How does the peddler try to get the monkeys to return his caps? What do the monkeys do?
- How does the peddler finally get his caps back?
- What do you think the peddler will do next time he wants to rest?

Act It Out

Caps for Sale

However you choose to act out this story, be sure to provide plenty of caps for the peddler to wear.

- If you're reading this book to just one child, she can act out the peddler's and the monkeys' actions as you read the story. Alternatively, your child could play the peddler while you play the monkeys or vice versa.
- If you're reading this book to a group of children, have them take turns acting out the parts of the peddler and the monkeys.

Arts and Crafts

Peddler Picture

Pen or pencil
Paper
Scissors

Crayons or colored construction paper
Glue stick

1. Draw or trace a picture of the peddler walking down the road or leaning against the tree. Omit the caps stacked on his head.
2. Cut 17 cap shapes from paper and have your child color them as follows: 1 checked cap, 4 gray caps, 4 brown caps, 4 blue caps, and 4 red caps. (If you like, use colored construction paper instead.)
3. Challenge your child to glue the caps onto the picture so they appear stacked on the peddler's head in the proper order.

Fun and Games

Pin the Cap on the Monkey

Crayons or markers
Large sheet of paper or poster board
Tape
Scissors
Construction paper
Scarf for blindfolding

1. Draw a monkey on a large sheet of paper or poster board using a picture from *Caps for Sale* as a guide.
2. Tape the monkey drawing to a wall so that a preschooler can reach it easily.
3. Cut 1 cap for each player from construction paper.
4. Fasten a loop of tape (sticky side out) to the back of each cap.

5. One at a time, blindfold the players and let them take turns trying to stick their caps on the monkey.

Let's Pretend

Hat Store

Table or desk
Hats (real or paper)
Bags from your recycling bin
Play money
Play purse or wallet (optional)
Small box (optional)

1. Set up a pretend hat store at a large table or desk with real hats from your own closets or with play hats made from paper. Grab a few bags from your recycling bin to use as shopping bags.

2. Assemble play money in 50-cent denominations. You can use store-bought play money, cut your own from paper, or use different-colored lids from plastic milk and juice jugs.

3. If you like, provide a play purse or wallet and a small "cash box" to hold the play money.

4. Take turns playing the clerk and the customer. If you want to reinforce math skills while you play, require the customer to ask for hats by color and quantity: for example, "I would like two red hats, please." The customer should take care to pay the right amount of money, and the clerk should be sure to count the money.

5. You can also use this game to reinforce good manners by requiring (and if necessary, modeling) courteous dialogue between the clerk and the customer.

Play and Learn

Caps to Count and Sort

Pencil
1 sheet white construction paper
Scissors
Black marker or crayon
4 sheets each gray, brown, blue, and red construction paper

1. With a pencil, draw a cap on white paper. Cut out the cap and draw a checked pattern on it with a black marker or crayon.

2. Trace the checked cap to draw caps on the remaining 16 sheets of construction paper. Cut out the caps or let your child do this if she's able.

3. Ask your child to count the caps. She may also enjoy sorting the caps by color.

4. Ask your child to lay the caps on the floor or on a table in the same order as described in *Caps for Sale.*

Snack Time

No-Bake Banana Cookies

Everyone knows monkeys love bananas. And your little monkey will adore making these easy banana cookies!

3 graham crackers
1 banana

1. Seal the graham crackers in a Ziploc bag and crush them with a rolling pin.
2. Slice a banana into small pieces.
3. Shake a few banana pieces at a time in the bag to coat them with cracker crumbs.
4. Place the cookies on a plate with small forks for spearing them.

Enrichment Activities

- Read a simple nonfiction book or watch an educational videotape about monkeys. Find out where and how they live and what they eat.
- Visit a zoo with a monkey exhibit. Watch the monkeys at play.
- Play follow the leader in which the leader pretends to be a monkey and the followers imitate her sounds and actions. Take turns being the leader.
- Listen to an audiotape or watch a videotape of *Caps for Sale*. (See Appendix D for more information.)
- Read other picture books about monkeys, such as H. A. Rey's *Curious George.*
- Read other folktales, such as *Tikki Tikki Tembo* by Arlene Mosel or *Why Mosquitoes Buzz in People's Ears* by Verna Aardema.

A Chair for My Mother

Written and Illustrated
by Vera B. Williams
(Greenwillow, 1982)

A Chair for My Mother is the first in a series of three books about a young girl named Rosa and her mother and grandmother. This Caldecott Honor Book tells a heartwarming story about Rosa's family's struggle to save enough money to buy a comfortable chair. Day by day they save coins in a big glass jar to replace the chair that's been burned up, along with everything else the family owned, in a terrible fire.

I especially enjoy the closeness apparent in Rosa's family and community: how relatives and neighbors care for the family after the fire; how Rosa shows concern for the comfort of her mother and grandmother; and how Rosa's aunt and uncle pick up the chair right away because they know Rosa's family can't wait for it to be delivered.

Let's Talk about It

Ask your child:

- What does Rosa do with the money she earns at the diner? Why do you think she saves it for her family instead of spending it on something fun? Why is it important to save money?
- Where does Mama put all the change from her tips? What is a tip?
- What sad thing has happened to the family? Has anything like this ever happened to someone you know?
- How would you feel if everything you own were burned up in a fire? How do

Rosa's family act after the fire? Do they act angry and sorry for themselves or thankful and eager to rebuild their lives? What do they have to be thankful for?

- If you had a jar full of coins saved up, what would you spend them on?

Arts and Crafts
Coin Bank

Scissors
Paper
Small can with plastic lid
Stickers and/or markers
Glue
Clear contact paper

1. Cut a piece of paper that will completely cover the curved outside of the can.
2. Decorate the paper with stickers and/or markers.
3. Glue the decorated paper onto the can and cover it with clear contact paper.
4. Cut a small slit in the plastic lid and place it on the can.

Rhymes and Finger Plays
Fire Engine

This is a fire engine,
(Fold your arms across your chest.)
This is a hose.
(Extend your left arm and put your right hand on your left elbow.)

They work hard when the siren blows.
(Wave the "hose" about.)

Up goes the ladder,
(Extend both arms as if holding a ladder and move your hands upward.)
On goes the hose.
(Pretend to turn on a water faucet.)
The fire goes out as the water flows.
(Wipe your forehead and sigh with relief.)

Fun and Games
Waterfall
Before Rosa and her family spend their coins, they might use them to play this fun game.

Bowl, cup, or other container
Water
Pennies

1. Fill a container almost to the top with water.
2. Give each player a supply of pennies.
3. Take turns dropping pennies one at a time into the container.
4. The game ends when one player drops the penny that makes the water overflow.

Out and About
Neighborhood Walk
Take a walk in your neighborhood.

1. Rosa and her mother enjoy looking at everyone's tulips as they walk. On your walk, observe the flowers growing wild and in gardens.

2. Notice the fire hydrants as you walk. Walk by a fire station and look at the fire engines. If possible, arrange to met the firefighters and get a close-up look at one of their trucks.
3. Stop at a furniture store and try out the chairs.
4. Have a drink or snack at a diner. Watch the servers work and discuss why Rosa's mother comes home tired. Leave a tip for your server—he or she may be saving tips in a jar at home!

Play and Learn

Count the Coins

The following activities will help your child practice sorting, matching, and counting. To make the flash cards, see "Getting Started: Play and Learn" (page 18).

Object and number flash cards
Bowl full of different kinds of coins
Pen or marker
Egg carton
Flat surface

- Lay out object flash cards and ask your child to place the same number of coins on each card as there are objects pictured on the card.
- Lay out number flash cards and ask your child to place the appropriate number of coins on each card.

- Write the numbers one to twelve inside the sections of an egg carton (one number per section). Give your child a bowl full of coins and ask him to fill each section with the right number of coins.
- Dump a handful of coins onto a flat surface. Sort the coins by heads and tails, then count the number of coins in each group.
- Dump a handful of coins onto a flat surface. Sort the coins into groups of pennies, nickels, dimes, and quarters.

Snack Time

Peanut Butter Pennies

18 ounces peanut butter
6 tablespoons honey
Nonfat dry milk
Cocoa powder (optional)

1. Mix the peanut butter and honey in a bowl, adding dry milk gradually until the mixture has the consistency of bread dough.
2. Add cocoa if you like.
3. Shape the dough into small balls and flatten into "pennies." Eat up the pennies!
4. If you prefer, use chocolate cookie dough instead and bake the cookies before eating them.

Enrichment Activities

- Draw a picture of the new apartment after the neighbors and relatives bring furniture and other household items.
- Rosa may have lost every material thing in a fire, but she is surrounded by a close and loving family. Help your child appreciate his family by making a family album together. Staple sheets of paper together inside a construction paper cover or follow the directions in Appendix B. Glue pictures of family members into your homemade album.
- Even a preschooler can be encouraged to save a little money. Explain to your child the importance of learning to save allowance money, gift money, or money earned through doing chores.
- Start a family savings jar. Identify something your family would like to purchase. Get in the habit of putting loose change and savings from good bargains into the jar. Encourage each family member to contribute whenever possible. Watch how the money adds up over time. When your jar is full, roll the coins into paper wrappers and take them to the bank.
- Putting others first is a prominent theme in *A Chair for My Mother.* Challenge your family to think of sacrifices you can make to help others. Perhaps you could donate your Friday pizza-and-movie money to a homeless shelter or give items you were planning to sell at a garage sale to people in your community who need them.
- Watch *A Chair for My Mother* on videotape. (See Appendix D for more information.)
- Read more about Rosa and her family in *Something Special for Me* and *Music, Music for Everyone.*

Chicka Chicka Boom Boom

Written by Bill Martin Jr.
and John Archambault
Illustrated by Lois Ehlert
(Simon & Schuster, 1989)

Unlike the other books featured in *Picture Book Activities, Chicka Chicka Boom Boom* is more of an alphabet rhyme than a story. Beginning with A, B, and C, the letters of the alphabet race up a coconut tree to the rhythm of a lively chant. The refrain "Chicka chicka boom boom! Will there be enough room?" is repeated throughout the story as more letters join the race. The illustrations are bright, bold, and simple. Your child is sure to enjoy this book regardless of whether she recognizes the letters or even understands the concept of the alphabet.

As You Read

- Invite your child to recite with you "Chicka chicka boom boom! Will there be enough room?" and "Skit skat skoodle doot. Flip flop flee."
- If your child knows the alphabet, let her name each letter as you come to it.

Arts and Crafts

Printmaking

Printmaking is creating an impression of an object on another surface. Use the following suggestions to teach your child the basics of printmaking, develop her alphabet skills, and, of course, have fun!

Paring knife
Potatoes
Liquid tempera paint
Shallow pan, paintbrush, roller, or ink pad (optional)
Paper
Scissors
Thin craft foam
Glue
Empty paper towel or toilet paper rolls
Sponges
Clothespins

- **Potato prints:** With a paring knife, cut a few potatoes in half. On each half, carve a relief sculpture of a letter in your child's name. Remember to carve the letters backward so they will print forward. Dip each letter into a shallow pan of liquid tempera paint, paint it with a brush or roller, or press it onto an ink pad, then press the letter firmly onto paper.

- **Roller prints:** Cut letters from thin craft foam. Glue the letters onto empty paper towel or toilet paper rolls. Paint your homemade rollers with a brush or pour liquid tempera paint into a shallow pan big enough to fit your rollers and dip the rollers into the paint. Then roll them on paper.
- **Sponge prints:** Cut letters from small, thick sponges. On the back of each letter, cut 2 slits about ¼ inch deep and ¾ inch apart. Clip a clothespin into the slots to make a handle. Dip each letter into a shallow pan of liquid tempera paint, paint it with a brush or roller, or press it onto an ink pad, then press the letter firmly onto paper.

Cooking and Baking

Coconut-Oatmeal Cookies

When your child tastes these delicious coconut cookies, she'll understand why the letters in *Chicka Chicka Boom Boom* are so eager to climb up the coconut tree.

½ cup margarine
½ cup brown sugar, firmly packed
½ cup white sugar
1 egg
1 cup all-purpose flour
½ teaspoon baking powder
½ teaspoon baking soda
½ teaspoon salt
½ cup rolled oats
½ cup shredded coconut

1. Preheat your oven to 350°F.
2. Cream the margarine with both sugars.
3. Add the egg and mix well.
4. Sift the flour with the baking powder, baking soda, and salt. Add the dry mixture to the wet mixture.
5. Mix in the oats and coconut.
6. Roll the dough into about 30 small balls and place them on greased baking sheets.
7. Bake the cookies for 7–10 minutes.

Fun and Games

Beanbag Toss

Large sheet of paper and markers or
  scissors and construction paper
Beanbag

1. Draw several large letters in different colors on a large sheet of paper or cut letters out of construction paper. Lay the sheet or cutouts on the floor.
2. Have your child stand a few feet away and toss a beanbag onto the letters. Ask her to identify the color and/or letter the beanbag lands on.

3. As your child becomes more skilled, ask her to aim for a certain letter with each toss.

Out and About

Shopping List

Play this word game with your child as you run errands or take a walk together.

1. Say to your child, "I went to the store and I bought carrots, cabbage, and cream. What else did I buy?" Your child must add items to the list that begin with the same sound as the items you've named.

2. You may want to tell a younger child the rule, but an older preschooler should be able to figure it out for herself. If she tries to add an item that doesn't begin with the right sound, tell her, "No, that wasn't on my shopping list."

3. Your child will probably guess the rule after a few tries, but if she has trouble, keep adding items to your list until she understands.

Play and Learn

Alphabet Fun

The following ideas will help your child learn to recognize—and perhaps print—the alphabet.

Sand, salt, or sugar	*Play dough*
9-by-13-inch pan	*Scissors*
Broad-tip marker	*3 coffee mugs*
Paper	*Raisins*
Clear contact paper	*Toothpicks*

- **Alphabet sand:** Pour a thin layer of sand (or salt or sugar) into a 9-by-13-inch pan. Show your child how to write letters in the sand with her finger.

- **Play dough letters:** With a broad-tip marker, write large letters on sheets of paper (1 letter per sheet). Cover each sheet with clear contact paper. Roll play dough into ropes and let your child shape the play dough to match the letters.

- **Touch and guess:** Follow the directions above to make play dough letters. Challenge your child to close her eyes, feel each letter, and identify it by shape.

- **Find the letter:** Cut out paper circles small enough to hide beneath coffee mugs. Write a different letter on each circle. Place 3 coffee mugs on the table and hide a circle under 1 of them. Let your child guess where the circle is and identify the letter when she finds it. Take turns hiding the circles.

- ***Xs* and *Os*:** Print a letter at the top center of a sheet of paper. Below the letter, randomly write many letters of the alphabet, spreading them all over the sheet of paper. Have your child circle the letters that match the one printed at the top. Have her draw an X over each letter that doesn't match.

- **Raisin play:** Stick 1 raisin on the tip of each of several toothpicks. (The raisins serve as connectors.) Write large letters on paper and challenge your child to connect toothpicks to create each letter. For older preschoolers, you may not need to write the letters.

Snack Time

Letter Sandwiches

Sliced wheat bread
Peanut butter, jam, or honey
Alphabet cereal

1. Spread each slice of bread with peanut butter, jam, or honey.
2. Help an older preschooler spell her name or a simple sentence like *I love you* by sticking alphabet cereal onto the bread. A younger preschooler may enjoy simply sticking the letters onto the bread in no particular order—or she may not want to combine them at all!
3. Let your child eat her creation(s).

Enrichment Activities

- Look at a photo of a coconut tree. If you live in a tropical area or near an arboretum, you may be able to examine a live coconut tree. Then visit your local grocery store, buy a coconut, and snack on its meat and milk.
- Have alphabet soup for lunch.
- Sing the alphabet song together.
- Use letter-shape cookie cutters to make alphabet cookies from rolled cookie dough.
- Read other alphabet books, such as *Anno's Alphabet* by Mitsumasa Anno, *A Apple Pie* by Kate Greenaway, and *Brian Wildsmith's ABC* by Brian Wildsmith.
- Read other books by Bill Martin Jr. and John Archambault, such as *The Ghost-Eye Tree* and *Knots on a Counting Rope.*

Corduroy

Written and Illustrated
by Don Freeman
(Viking, 1968)

Corduroy is one of several picture books about a stuffed bear who comes to life. In this book we meet Corduroy living in the toy department of a big store, waiting day after day for someone to come and take him home. One day he hears a mother tell her little girl, who wants him very much, that he doesn't look new because he's missing a button from his overalls. That night he hops off his shelf and searches the store for his missing button.

Corduroy's innocent discovery of his world around him is sure to charm you and your child. Corduroy thinks the escalator is a mountain and says, "I think I've always wanted to climb a mountain." He thinks the furniture department is a palace and says, "I guess I've always wanted to live in a palace." Your child will especially enjoy the ending, when Corduroy discovers both a friend and a home.

Let's Talk about It

Ask your child:

- Why does Corduroy think the escalator is a mountain? How are escalators and mountains similar? How are they different?
- Why does Corduroy think the furniture department is a palace? How are furniture departments and palaces similar? How are they different?
- Why has Corduroy always wanted a home? How would you feel if you lived in the toy department of a big store?

- Could this story really happen? Can toy animals like Corduroy think and move around on their own?
- What would happen if one of your toys came to life? What would it say and do?

Arts and Crafts

Button Necklaces

Large buttons (or construction paper, scissors, and hole punch)
Shoelace, yarn, or ribbon

1. Give your child an assortment of large buttons or cut circles from construction paper and punch 2–4 holes in each circle.
2. Show your child how to make a necklace by threading the buttons onto a shoelace or length of yarn or ribbon.

Cooking and Baking

Button Cookies

1 cup graham flour
1 cup whole-wheat flour
½ teaspoon baking soda
1 teaspoon cinnamon
¼ cup apple juice concentrate
¼ cup vegetable oil
1 banana, sliced
1 teaspoon vanilla

1. Preheat your oven to 350°F.
2. In a medium-size bowl, mix the flours, baking soda, and cinnamon.
3. In a blender, mix the apple juice concentrate, vegetable oil, banana, and vanilla.
4. Pour the wet ingredients into the dry ingredients and stir them until they're well mixed.
5. Roll out the dough on a floured surface.
6. Use a round cookie cutter or a bottle lid to cut small circles from the dough. With a toothpick, make 2–4 holes in each cookie to make it look like a button.
7. Place the buttons on a baking sheet. Bake for about 5 minutes.

Fun and Games

Button, Button

This game is suitable for a group of children.

1. Have the children sit in a circle with their hands cupped in front of them.
2. Choose one child to be the guesser. That child leaves the circle and stands with his back to it.
3. Walk around the circle with a button in your cupped hands, pretending to drop the button into each child's hands. You'll give the button to only one child, but each child should close his hands as you pass so no one can tell who has the button.
4. The guesser stands in the center of the circle. As the other children chant "Button, button, who's got the button?"

the guesser walks around the circle looking at each child.

5. The guesser tries to guess which child has the button. With each guess, the chosen child opens his hands to show whether he has the button.

6. If the guesser chooses correctly, he sits down in the circle. The child with the button becomes the guesser, and the game starts over.

7. If the guesser chooses incorrectly, he guesses again as the other children chant "Button, button, who's got the button?"

Let's Pretend

Toy Store

Table or desk
Toys
Bags from your recycling bin
Play money
Play purse or wallet (optional)
Small box (optional)
Price tags (optional)

1. Set up a pretend toy store at a large table or desk with toys from your own house. Grab a few bags from your recycling bin to use as shopping bags.

2. Assemble play money. You can use store-bought play money, cut your own from paper, or use different-colored lids from plastic milk and juice jugs.

3. If you like, provide a play purse or wallet and a small "cash box" to hold the play money. Older preschoolers may enjoy making a price tag for each item.

4. Take turns playing the clerk and the customer. To reinforce math skills, the customer should take care to pay the right amount of money, and the clerk should be sure to count the money.

5. You can also use this game to reinforce good manners by requiring (and if necessary, modeling) courteous dialogue between the clerk and the customer.

Music and Movement

Teddy Bear, Teddy Bear

Act out the movements in this rhyme as you chant it with your child. If you like, sing it to the tune of "Twinkle, Twinkle, Little Star" or make up your own melody, new verses, and/or new actions.

Teddy bear, teddy bear, turn around.
Teddy bear, teddy bear, touch the ground.
Teddy bear, teddy bear, shine your shoes.
Teddy bear, teddy bear, read the news.
Teddy bear, teddy bear, go upstairs.
Teddy bear, teddy bear, say your prayers.
Teddy bear, teddy bear, turn out the light.
Teddy bear, teddy bear, say good night.

Play and Learn

Button Play

Buttons (or construction paper button shapes) of many sizes and colors
Flat surface
Glue and paper plate (optional)

Place the buttons on a flat surface.

- Count them.
- Sort them into groups by color.
- Sort them into groups by size.
- Line them up from smallest to largest.
- Group them in twos, threes, fours, and so on.
- Pick out your favorite and least favorite buttons.
- If you like, glue buttons onto a paper plate to make a collage.

Enrichment Activities

- Eat teddy-bear-shaped crackers for a snack.
- Visit the toy department of a large store.
- Hide buttons around the house or yard. Have each player hunt for the buttons and collect them in a paper bag or plastic container. If you like, award a small prize to each player who finds any buttons or exchange the buttons for a special snack.
- Watch *Corduroy* on videotape. (See Appendix D for more information.)
- Read other books about Corduroy, such as *A Pocket for Corduroy, Corduroy's Day, Corduroy's Party,* and *Corduroy's Toys*.
- Read other books about teddy bears, such as *Ira Sleeps Over* by Bernard Waber.

"Could Be Worse!"

Written and Illustrated
by James Stevenson
(Greenwillow, 1977)

James Stevenson is well known for his syndicated political cartoons as well as for the many books he has written and illustrated for children and adults.

"Could Be Worse!" is the tale of two children, Mary Ann and Louie, and their grandfather. The children think nothing interesting ever happens to Grandpa. He always eats the same breakfast, follows the same routine, and—no matter what one says—replies the same way: "Could be worse!"

Imagine the children's surprise when one morning at breakfast Grandpa says something different! He begins, "Guess what?" then goes on to tell an incredible tale of adventure that enthralls (and worries) his grandchildren.

Stevenson's droll illustrations and storytelling combine to create a very funny, very readable book.

As You Read

- Encourage your child to join you each time you read "Could be worse!"
- Before you read the page on which Grandpa overhears the children's conversation, take turns making up situations that might elicit Grandpa's comment "Could be worse!"
- After you've read the book twice, let your child "read" it to you by looking at the pictures and telling the story as she remembers it.

Let's Talk about It

Ask your child:

- What does Grandpa do the same way every day?
- What does Grandpa say no matter what happens?
- Why do the children think Grandpa never says anything interesting?
- What happens when Grandpa hears the children say that nothing interesting ever happens to him?
- Do you like Grandpa? Why or why not? Is he like anyone you know?
- What do you do the same way every day? What's good and bad about always doing things the same way?

Act It Out

Could Be Worse!

Act out Grandpa's tale with props and costumes if you like—or just use your imagination.

1. If there are only two of you, one can play the part of Grandpa while the other plays the parts of all the other characters. In a larger group, one child can play Grandpa while the other kids play the remaining characters. Take turns playing the part of Grandpa.
2. Read the book aloud as the actors dramatize it or let them perform the story without a narrator.

Arts and Crafts

Papier-Mâché Something-or-Other

After hearing about the giant something-or-other that squishes Grandpa, your child will enjoy making her own papier-mâché something-or-other! A group of children may enjoy working together on a large something-or-other.

Cardboard boxes, oatmeal containers, ice-cream containers, egg cartons, and juice cans
Wide masking tape or duct tape
Flour
Water
Large plastic bucket or tub
Newspaper
Tempera paint and paintbrushes or fabric, tissue paper, and glue

1. Build an animal or make-believe creature with cardboard containers. Use wide masking tape or duct tape to hold your creature together.
2. Mix ¼ cup flour with 1 cup water. Stir this mixture into 5 cups lightly boiling water. Gently boil and stir for 2–3 minutes. Let the paste cool until it's not too hot to touch. Pour it into a large plastic bucket or tub.
3. If your creature is large, tear the newspaper sheets in half. If your creature is small, tear the newspaper into strips. Soak the newspaper briefly in the paste. Squeeze out the excess paste.

4. Press the newspaper onto the card-board creature. Smooth out the wrinkles with your bare hands or a damp towel.
5. Continue adding paste-soaked news-paper until your creature is completely covered.
6. Let your something-or-other dry for a day or so, then finish it with tempera paint, fabric, and/or tissue paper.

Cooking and Baking

Pigs in a Blanket

Pigs in a blanket would be a nice change of pace from Grandpa's toast and mar-malade! Young children can help mix, pour, and roll the pancakes.

Vegetable oil for greasing
Breakfast sausages
1¼ cups all-purpose flour
2 tablespoons sugar
2 teaspoons baking powder
¾ teaspoon salt
3 tablespoons vegetable oil
1⅓ cups milk
1 egg, slightly beaten

1. Preheat a griddle or skillet and grease it lightly with vegetable oil.
2. Fry the sausages until they're cooked. Keep them warm on a paper towel–lined plate.
3. Mix the flour, sugar, baking powder, and salt with a fork in a large bowl. Add the vegetable oil, milk, and egg

and stir just until the flour mixture is moistened.
4. Pour 5-inch circles of batter onto the griddle or skillet. Cook until the tops of the pancakes bubble and the bot-toms are golden.
5. Flip the pancakes with a spatula. When both sides are golden, remove the pancakes from the heat.
6. Roll a pancake around each sausage. Serve with syrup, ketchup, or cottage cheese.

Rhymes and Finger Plays

Grandfather's Breakfast

This rhyme is a variation of a finger play called "Grandmother's Glasses." Act out the words as you say them.

This is Grandfather's breakfast.
This is Grandfather's cup.
Grandfather eats his toast like this
And drinks his coffee up.

This is Grandfather's paper.
He reads each line and verse.
No matter what you say to him,
He'll tell you, "Could be worse!"

Fun and Games

Paper Airplanes

In Grandpa's tale, he flies home on a paper airplane. You can play the follow-ing paper airplane games with one child or a group.

Paper in as many colors as there are players
Empty box or laundry basket

Fold several paper airplanes of each color. Let each player choose a color.

- Place an empty box or laundry basket about 5 feet away from the players. Take turns throwing paper airplanes into the box or basket.
- If you like, give each child lots of airplanes. Set a timer and see how many airplanes each child can throw into the box or basket in 1 minute.
- Let each child throw her airplanes as far as she can, then run to pick them up.

Out and About

Wild Adventures
The following game is fun to play while walking, riding in a car or bus, or waiting in a doctor's office.

1. Start by saying to your child, "Guess what!" Then make up a tale about a wild adventure you've had. Make your adventure as exciting as you can— and also obviously made-up.
2. End your tale with "Now, what do you think of that?"
3. Hopefully your child will reply, "Could be worse!"
4. Take turns making up wild adventures until you tire of the game.

Enrichment Activities

- Your child may want to learn more about some elements of Grandpa's tale. Look for simple nonfiction books or videotapes on mountains, deserts, weather, and marine life.
- Have toast and marmalade for breakfast.
- Write and illustrate a wild adventure you've made up. (See "Out and About.") Turn it into a book by stapling the pages together inside a construction paper cover or following the directions in Appendix B.
- Enjoy more of Grandpa's imaginative tales in *Grandpa's Great City Tour, What's under My Bed?, We Can't Sleep, Worse Than Willy!, The Great Big Especially Beautiful Easter Egg,* and more.
- Read other story-within-a-story books, such as *And to Think That I Saw It on Mulberry Street* by Dr. Seuss, *Where the Wild Things Are* by Maurice Sendak, and *One Monday Morning* by Uri Shulevitz.

Curious George

Written and Illustrated
by H. A. Rey
(Houghton Mifflin, 1941)

This book needs no introduction; millions of people around the world know and love the little monkey named George. *Curious George* is the first of more than twenty books about George's insatiable curiosity, which gets him into many funny situations.

Some elements of this book, which was written more than sixty years ago, wouldn't be seen in more recent children's books. I don't condone taking animals from their natural habitats, smoking pipes, throwing naughty monkeys (or children) in prison, or glibly packing animals off to the zoo, but I think it's important to realize that *Curious George* isn't really about any of these things. Children adore George because they can empathize with him; like George, children often get into trouble inadvertently while discovering the world around them. With your guidance, your child will surely benefit from exposure to this classic character without any ill effects.

As You Read

- Notice how George's facial expressions change from page to page.
- After hearing the story several times, your child will be able to end some of the sentences.
- Let your child make the sounds of the telephone *(ding-a-ling-a-ling)* and the fire engine *(ding-dong-ding-dong)*.

Let's Talk about It

Ask your child:

- How does George meet the man with the yellow hat? Where does the man take George?
- How does George's curiosity get him into trouble on the boat?
- How does George end up in prison? How does he get out of prison?
- Do you like the way the story ends? Why or why not?
- What does it mean to be curious? Have you ever been curious about something? What happened?

Arts and Crafts

Balloon Painting

George gets into trouble at one point because "He felt he MUST have a bright red balloon." Children of all ages love balloons, too. Following is one great way to have fun with a balloon.

Remember that deflated or burst balloons pose a choking hazard for young children. Supervise your child closely whenever he's around balloons.

Balloons
Liquid tempera paint
Shallow dish
Paper

1. Blow up a balloon and tie the end.
2. Pour some liquid tempera paint into a shallow dish.

3. Holding its tied end, dip the balloon into the paint and blot it onto a sheet of paper.

Binoculars

The man with the big yellow hat used binoculars to see George in the jungle. Your child will have lots of fun with these toy binoculars he can make himself.

2 empty toilet paper rolls
Tape
Markers, crayons, and/or stickers
Colored cellophane (optional)

1. Tape 2 empty toilet paper rolls together side by side.
2. Decorate the toy binoculars with markers, crayons, and/or stickers.
3. If you like, cover the ends with colored cellophane.
4. Take your binoculars with you on a walk or a car or bus ride and use them to spot interesting things.

Rhymes and Finger Plays

Five Little Monkeys

Five little monkeys jumping on the bed.
    (Hold up five fingers.)
One fell off and bumped his head.
    (Lightly tap your forehead with the palm of your hand.)
Mama called the doctor and the doctor said,
    (Hold one fist to your ear like a telephone receiver.)
"Send that monkey straight to bed!"
    (Wag your index finger.)

Repeat the verse, changing it each time to say "four little monkeys," then "three little monkeys," and so on. You might also want to change the last line each time to offer Mama your own advice. Then say:

No little monkeys jumping on the bed.
  (Hold up fingers shaped into an *O*.)
None fell off and bumped his head.
  (Shake your head.)
Mama called the doctor and the doctor said,
  (Hold one fist to your ear like a telephone receiver.)
"Good night!"
  (Place the palms of your hands together and pillow your head on your hands.)

Fun and Games

Monkey See, Monkey Do
Monkeys are well known for their tendency to copy actions they see. You and your child will have a ball playing the following copying games.

- **Animal charades:** Have your child pretend to be George imitating other animals he sees. Place several stuffed animals in a pillowcase. Close your eyes while your child takes one out, looks at it, and puts it back. Have him act out the animal while you try to guess what it is. Take turns being George.
- **Follow the leader:** Pretend to be a monkey. Challenge your child to follow you through the house, imitating your sounds and actions. Take turns being the leader.
- **George says:** In this adaptation of Simon says, the leader is called George. George performs various actions while commanding the other players to do the same. The players follow George's actions only when he precedes a command with the phrase *George says.* They stay still when a command isn't preceded by *George says.* This is a good game for a group of children and is great fun when played quickly. Have the players take turns being George.

Play and Learn

Colors, Counting, and More
The illustrations in *Curious George* are full of opportunities to practice color skills, counting, and more.

- Challenge your child to identify colors by asking him "What color is the man's hat?...the water?...the fire engine?...the balloons?" and so on.
- Every page offers an opportunity to count. Count leaves and flowers on the tree in the first picture. As the story progresses, count fish, seagulls, sailors, firefighters, fire engines, balloons, people, cars, animals, and so on.
- Ask your child to name all the animals in the zoo picture, tell the color of each, and demonstrate the sound each one makes.

Snack Time

Banana Pops

Banana
Popsicle stick
Lemon juice
Water
Crushed cereal or graham crackers
Wax paper

1. Cut a banana in half. Insert a Popsicle stick into each half.
2. Dip each banana half into a mixture of 1 part lemon juice and 1 part water.
3. Roll the banana half in crushed cereal or graham crackers, place it on wax paper, and freeze it.

Enrichment Activities

- Find Africa on a map. Ask your child, "Why does George travel from Africa on a boat? Could he travel any other way?"
- Make up a new ending for the story. For instance, you could describe what might happen to George if he weren't rescued from the top of the traffic light or an adventure he might have in the zoo. Draw a picture to go with your ending.

- Read a simple nonfiction book about monkeys. Learn how and where they live, what they eat, and so on. If possible, watch a videotape about monkeys or African wildlife.
- If possible, visit a zoo and watch some real monkeys at play.
- Discuss telephone etiquette with your child. Let him answer the phone only when he's learned to do so courteously. If he uses the phone improperly, revoke the privilege until he can demonstrate appropriate telephone behavior.
- Watch a videotape of *Curious George.* (See Appendix D for more information.)
- Read other books about monkeys, such as *Caps for Sale* by Esphyr Slobodkina.
- Read more about George in any of the many Curious George books, including *Curious George Flies a Kite, Curious George Plays Baseball,* and *Curious George Rides a Bike.*

Fortunately

Written and Illustrated
by Remy Charlip
(Simon & Schuster, 1964)

Fortunately is a wonderfully funny story in which a boy named Ned receives a letter inviting him to a surprise party. Good and bad fortune vie with each other as the story unfolds. Fortunately Ned gets the invitation, but unfortunately the party's in Florida. (Ned's in New York.) Fortunately Ned's able to borrow an airplane, but unfortunately its motor explodes...and so on. Your child will listen with great anticipation, knowing as you turn each page that Ned's luck is about to change again.

As You Read

- After you've read a few pages, your child will realize that something bad always follows something good and vice versa. Before you turn each page, ask your child what she thinks will happen next.
- Notice that the "fortunately" pictures are always in color, while the "unfortunately" pictures are black-and-white.

Let's Talk about It

Ask your child:

- What does the word *fortunately* mean? What does *unfortunately* mean?
- Why is it unfortunate that the party's in Florida?
- What's your favorite part of the story? Why?
- Could this story really happen? How do you know?

- Have you ever had a fortunate-unfortunate day like Ned's?
- Do you like the story's ending? Why or why not?

Act It Out

Ned's Adventures

This book is packed with action: Ned falls from an airplane, lands on a haystack, runs from tigers, digs a tunnel, and finds himself in many more exciting situations.

1. Encourage your child to act out the part of Ned as you read the book. If you're reading to more than one child, the additional children can play the parts of the sharks, tigers, and partygoers.
2. If time permits, reread the book until each child has had a chance to play the part of Ned.

Arts and Crafts

Fortunately-Unfortunately Book

Pencil or pen
White paper
Paint, crayons,
   or markers
Stapler
Construction paper

1. Have your child dictate a series of fortunate and unfortunate events. Write 1 event on a separate sheet of white paper. Offer ideas if your child asks for help.

2. Let your child draw pictures to accompany her story. She might want to copy the technique used in *Fortunately,* drawing her fortunate pictures in color and her unfortunate pictures in black-and-white.
3. Staple the pages together inside a construction paper cover or follow the directions in Appendix B.
4. If you don't have time to make a homemade book or your child doesn't want to do so, simply invent a fortunately-unfortunately story together while you take a walk or ride in the car or bus.

Cooking and Baking

Birthday Cupcakes

1 egg
1 cup milk
1 teaspoon vanilla
1¼ cups white sugar
½ cup margarine, melted
1¾ cups flour
2½ teaspoons baking powder
½ teaspoon salt
Frosting

1. Preheat the oven to 350°F.
2. Mix the egg, milk, vanilla, sugar, and margarine in a large bowl with an electric mixer at medium speed.
3. Add the flour, baking powder, and salt. Mix the batter at high speed for 2 minutes.

4. Pour the batter into paper-lined muffin pans. Bake the cupcakes for 20 minutes.
5. Let the cupcakes cool, then have your child frost them with a butter knife or Popsicle stick.

Let's Pretend

Surprise Party
Throw a pretend surprise party for Ned. You or your child may play Ned, or Ned can simply be an imaginary person.

Tableware (real or pretend)
Party snacks and drinks (real or pretend)
Wrapped gifts (old or new)
Cupcakes and candles (optional)

1. Set a table with real or pretend tableware, snacks, and drinks.
2. Gift-wrap a few small objects, such as your child's toys or books or inexpensive new trinkets.
3. If you've made the cupcakes described in "Cooking and Baking" (page 63), serve them with a candle in each one.
4. Sing "Happy Birthday" to Ned.

Music and Movement

If You're Happy and You Know It
Ned surely experienced a wide range of emotions as he tried to reach Florida: happiness, sadness, fright, and so on. Sing this familiar song about emotions and do the actions it describes. Feel free to make up as many new verses as you like!

If you're happy and you know it, clap your hands.
If you're happy and you know it, clap your hands.
If you're happy and you know it,
Then your face will surely show it.
If you're happy and you know it, clap your hands.

If you're sad and you know it, cry "Boo-hoo!"...

If you're scared and you know it, cover your eyes...

Play and Learn

Opposites

Pairs of objects that are opposite in some way (big/small, hot/cold, short/long, old/new, and so on)

1. Explain to your child that in this book, good things (the parts that start with the word *fortunately*) are always followed by bad things (the parts that start with the word *unfortunately*). Point out that good and bad are opposites. Explain that opposite words each mean exactly what the other doesn't mean. Most children understand the concept of opposites without lengthy explanations.
2. Tell your child that you're going to play a game about opposites.

3. Hold up one of the pairs of objects, such as a large book and a small book, and ask your child, "How are these books the same? How are they different?" Your child may use words like *big* and *small, heavy* and *light, thick* and *thin,* and so on.

4. After your child has gotten the hang of comparing opposite pairs, hold up just one object from a pair, such as an old penny and a new penny. Say, "This penny is old. The opposite of old is what?" Challenge your child to say the opposite word and find the opposite object.

5. Look for opposites in your daily routine, such as a noisy child and a quiet one, a hard floor and a soft rug, and so on.

Enrichment Activities

- Find Florida and New York on a map of the United States. Ask your child, "How else could Ned travel to Florida?" (He could walk, ride a bike, take a boat, swim, and so on.)

- Think up a different ending for the story. For example, what might happen if Ned's tunnel were to lead him into the monkey cage at the zoo or onto the stage of a theater where a ballet is under way?

- If any of the objects or animals in the story—airplanes, parachutes, sharks, tigers, or whatever—spark your child's interest, look for simple nonfiction books or videotapes about them.

- Read other books by Remy Charlip, such as his excellent nonfiction books *Handtalk* and *Handtalk Birthday.*

- If your child enjoys improbable yet hilarious stories, she'll surely enjoy *Imogene's Antlers* by David Small, the Amelia Bedelia series by Peggy Parrish, or *Pigs* by Robert Munsch.

Frederick

Written and Illustrated by Leo Lionni
(Pantheon, 1967)

One of Leo Lionni's many books for children, *Frederick* was named a Caldecott Honor Book in 1968. Lionni's collage-style illustrations, which often depict mice, appeal to many youngsters. In *Children and Books* (Addison-Wesley, 1997) Zena Sutherland suggests, "Mice, as small, helpless beings chased by everyone, are easily identified with by small children."

Frederick tells of a family of field mice living near an abandoned farm. As winter approaches, the mice work night and day to store up nuts and grains. But one member of the family is different: Frederick simply sits and gathers sun rays, colors, and words for the long, cold, gray days ahead. Readers may anticipate a lesson like "If you don't help with the work, you don't share in the harvest." But when winter arrives and the mice take to their hideout, Frederick shares in the food he has not helped put away. And now it's his turn to be helpful. He uses the words he's stored up to warm the hearts of his family in the winter darkness.

Let's Talk about It

Ask your child:

- Why do the mice scurry about collecting food? Do mice really do this? What other animals store up food for the winter?
- How is Frederick different? How does his family react as he sits around gathering sun rays, colors, and words while they collect food?

- What happens when winter comes and the mice take to their hideout?
- Does Frederick remind you of anyone you know? Do his brothers and sisters remind you of anyone?
- What's your favorite part of the story? Why?
- Could this story really happen? Why or why not?

Let's Pretend

Indoor Picnic

Like Frederick, you can brighten the coldest, grayest day by filling your hearts with sunshine. Have a picnic indoors!

Tablecloth
Picnic food
Plastic dishes or paper plates
Summer clothing
Photos or videotape of a recent summer vacation

1. Spread a tablecloth on the floor of your living room or family room.
2. Serve your favorite picnic food on your brightest outdoor dishes or on paper plates.
3. Wear summer clothing, such as swimsuits or shorts and T-shirts, and don't forget your sunglasses.
4. Finish your picnic with ice cream, Popsicles, or another summer treat.
5. Look at photos or watch a videotape of a recent summer vacation. Or talk about what you'll do next summer.

Arts and Crafts

Paper Collage

Look closely at the illustrations in *Frederick* and ask your child to choose his favorite. Help him make a similar picture using torn or cut paper.

Scissors
Construction paper in various colors
Glue
Crayon or marker (optional)

1. Tear and/or cut construction paper into the shapes you'll need.
2. Glue the shapes onto a sheet of white construction paper.
3. If you like, use a crayon or marker to add fine details.
4. If your child enjoys this activity, he may want to write a story and illustrate it with collages. For information on binding homemade books, see Appendix B.

Cooking and Baking

Cheddar Cheese Cookies

Frederick and his family would surely enjoy having these cookies to spice up their winter diet!

¾ cup flour
⅔ cup margarine
⅓ cup brown sugar, firmly packed
1 teaspoon vanilla
1 egg
½ teaspoon cinnamon

½ teaspoon baking powder
½ teaspoon salt
1½ cups oatmeal
1 cup shredded cheddar cheese
¾ cup raisins
1 cup apple, peeled and chopped

1. Preheat your oven to 375°F.
2. Place the flour, margarine, brown sugar, vanilla, egg, cinnamon, baking powder, and salt in a medium-size bowl and mix them well.
3. Mix in the oatmeal, cheese, raisins, and apple.
4. Drop 24 tablespoons of dough onto ungreased baking sheet. Bake the cookies for 15 minutes or until they're golden brown.

Rhymes and Finger Plays

The Poet Mouse
Make up actions as you recite this rhyme about Frederick and his family.

Five mice lived in an old stone wall.
The days grew colder, for it was fall.
Winter was coming; they could not play.
The mice worked hard to put food away.

One mouse gathered up some wheat.
Another found corn for all to eat.
Two put nuts and straw away.
But one little mouse just sat all day.

He soaked up colors and bright sun rays.
He stored up words for the long, cold days.
When winter came and the food was gone,
And the dreary days seemed very long...

He cheered the mice with words he spoke,
He warmed their souls and gave them hope.
He helped them through the cold and dark
By bringing joy to each one's heart.

Fun and Games

Rhyme Time
Like Frederick's family, children enjoy the rhythm and rhyme of good poetry. Read poems—especially exciting and funny ones—to your child often. And have fun creating your own! Play the following word games when you're out driving or walking to help your child learn to enjoy language.

- Say a word and challenge your child to say a rhyming word. Begin with simple one-syllable words, then try more difficult words.
- When you recite familiar nursery rhymes to your child, pause and let him say the rhyming words, for example: "Little Miss _____ sat on a _____."
- Make up a simple poem in which the last word of every line rhymes. Say the first two lines, pause at the last word of the second line, and let your child finish the rhyme. When your child is ready, say only the first line and let him say the second line.

- Memorize and recite simple poems with your child. Our children have enjoyed the poetry of Robert Louis Stevenson. Start with short, simple poems like "Rain" and work toward longer poems like "The Moon."

Play and Learn

Seasons Collages

Scissors
Old catalogs, magazines, greeting cards, and/or calendars
Glue
Construction paper or poster board
Clear contact paper (optional)
Small index cards (optional)

1. Discuss the weather and what people and animals do in each season.
2. Cut pictures of seasonal items and activities from old catalogs, magazines, greeting cards, and/or calendars.
3. Sort the pictures by season. Glue them onto separate sheets of construction paper or poster board to make 4 collages. If you like, cover the collages with clear contact paper and use them as place mats.
4. If you like, make a set of playing cards by gluing seasonal pictures onto small index cards. Play go fish or old maid by matching the seasons.

Enrichment Activities

- Read a simple nonfiction book or watch a videotape about mice.
- Have your child close his eyes as you describe colorful things, such as "the warm, red sunset," using lots of adjectives. Ask, "Can you see the colors in your mind?" Close your eyes and let him describe colors to you.
- Sing or say songs and rhymes about mice, such as "Hickory Dickory Dock" and "Three Blind Mice."
- Leo Lionni's illustration style is similar Ezra Jack Keats's and Eric Carle's. Look at books by all three and compare their pictures.
- Read other books by Leo Lionni, such as *Fish Is Fish* and *Alexander and the Wind-Up Mouse.*
- Read other picture books about mice, such as *If You Give a Mouse a Cookie* by Laura Joffe Numeroff, *Broderick* by Edward Ormondroyd, *Cathedral Mouse* by Kay Chorao, and *Norman the Doorman* by Don Freeman.

Frog and Toad Together

Written and Illustrated by Arnold Lobel
(Harper & Row, 1971)

Arnold Lobel has illustrated many children's books, including the Caldecott Honor Books *Hildilid's Night* by Cheli Durán Ryan and *Frog and Toad Are Friends.* In 1981 Lobel won the Caldecott Medal for *Fables.*

Frog and Toad Together, a collection of five humorous stories of Frog and Toad's friendship, is a Newbery Honor Book. Written for beginning readers, it contains limited vocabulary. Still, it flows smoothly when read aloud.

As You Read

- Pause each time Toad is about to cross an item off his to-do list and challenge your child to tell which item Toad will cross off.

- Your child will enjoy repeating sentences like *Now seeds, start growing!* and *I am not afraid!* with Frog and Toad.

Let's Talk about It

Ask your child:

- What's good and bad about Toad's list?
- What does Frog mean when he says his garden is hard work? How is Toad's hard work different from Frog's? Can you help seeds grow by singing or reading to them?
- What is willpower? Can you think of times when you have used it or might need to use it?

- Do you think Toad is happy with the way Frog fixes the cookie problem? Why or why not?
- What does it mean to be brave? Do you think Frog and Toad are brave? Can you think of times when you have been or might need to be brave?
- In Toad's dream, why does Frog get smaller each time Toad performs? Do you have any friends who are showoffs? How do you feel when someone shows off?
- What are some dreams you've had? When you wake up from dreams, are you glad to know you've only been dreaming, or do you sometimes wish your dreams were real?
- Which is your favorite story in *Frog and Toad Together?* Why?

Act It Out
Frog and Toad Together

Pencil and paper
Box of chocolate chip cookies
String, ladder, seeds, and other props
  (real or pretend)

1. Because *Frog and Toad Together* has only two characters, you and your child can easily act out any of its stories. With more children, simply take turns playing Frog and Toad.
2. If you like, have an adult or older child narrate a story as younger children act it out.

3. Practice acting out the story you've chosen and perform it for friends and/or family.

Arts and Crafts
To-Do List
Help your child make a list, poster, or book of her everyday activities, just like Toad's "list of things to do today."

Markers, crayons, or colored pencils
Writing paper or poster board
Construction paper and stapler (optional)
Stickers (optional)

1. Talk with your child about what she normally does every day: wake up, eat breakfast, play outside, read, watch TV, and so on.
2. Make a list, poster, or book using words or pictures to describe the activities you've discussed. If you're making a book, staple sheets of paper together inside a construction paper cover or follow the directions in Appendix B, then write 1 activity on each page.
3. Let your child decorate the list, poster, or book with crayons, markers, or stickers.

Cooking and Baking
Chocolate Chip Cookies
These delicious cookies will give you a chance to practice your willpower!

1 cup margarine at room temperature
1 cup dark brown sugar, packed
1 cup granulated sugar
2 eggs, lightly beaten
2 tablespoons milk
2 teaspoons vanilla extract
2 cups sifted all-purpose flour
1 teaspoon baking powder
1 teaspoon baking soda
1 teaspoon salt
2 cups quick-cooking oats
1 cup (or more) chocolate chips
1 cup coarsely chopped walnuts

1. Cream the margarine and sugars in a large bowl until light and fluffy.
2. Add the eggs, milk, and vanilla and beat the mixture until it's blended.
3. Sift the flour, baking powder, baking soda, and salt together. Add the dry ingredients to the wet ones and stir them just until they're blended.
4. Stir in the oats, then fold in the chocolate chips and walnuts.
5. Cover the dough and refrigerate it for at least 1 hour.
6. Preheat your oven to 350°F. Grease your baking sheet(s).
7. Shape the dough into balls. Use a teaspoon for small cookies or a tablespoon for large ones. Flatten the dough balls into rounded disks. Place the cookies 2 inches apart on the baking sheet.
8. Bake the cookies for 8–10 minutes or until their edges are slightly browned.

Remove them from the oven and let them cool for 5 minutes before moving them to wire racks.

Rhymes and Finger Plays
My Garden

This is my garden;
  (Extend one hand forward, palm up)
I'll rake it with care.
  (Rake your palm with three fingers.)
And then some seeds I'll plant in there.
  (Plant pretend seeds in your palm.)
The sun will shine,
  (Make a circle overhead with your arms.)
And the rain will fall.
  (Flutter your fingers downward till you're squatting near the floor.)
My seeds will sprout and grow very tall!
  (Stand up straight while extending both hands toward the ceiling.)

Fun and Games
Charades

Pencil and paper
Small container

1. Write several of Frog's and Toad's actions on slips of paper. Place the slips in a small container.
2. If four or more people are playing, divide the players into teams.
3. Take turns choosing slips and performing the actions. (Let a nonreader choose a slip, then whisper the action to her.)

4. If you like, begin each charade by saying which story the situation is from. Act out the situation without saying any words.

Out and About

Gardening

Get a simple children's gardening book or videotape and read or watch it together before you do this activity.

Small pots or containers
Potting soil
Fruit or vegetable seeds
Gardening tools (optional)

1. Fill a few small pots or containers with potting soil.
2. Plant 3–4 seeds about ½ inch deep in each pot.
3. Water the seeds and place the pots in a sunny spot. Watch for green sprouts.
4. If it's the right time of year, transplant your seedlings outdoors.
5. If you like, sow your seeds directly in your garden.
6. Walk around your neighborhood and observe the plants growing wild and in gardens.

Enrichment Activities

- Read a simple nonfiction book about frogs and toads. Compare the pictures. Ask your child, "How are frogs and toads the same and different?"
- Make a garden collage with pictures cut from greenhouse fliers and seed catalogs.
- Read *The Carrot Seed* by Ruth Krauss.
- In the story "Dragons and Giants," Frog and Toad read fairy tales. Ask your child, "Which fairy tales do you think they're reading?" Read these tales together.
- Plan a play date for your child and her best friend.
- Read other books about Frog and Toad, such as *Frog and Toad Are Friends, Frog and Toad All Year,* and *Days with Frog and Toad.*
- Read other books about friends, such as *George and Martha* by James Marshall, *See You in Second Grade!* by Miriam Cohen, and *The Unfriendly Book* by Charlotte Zolotow.

George and Martha

Written and Illustrated
by James Marshall
(Houghton Mifflin, 1972)

In this collection of five funny stories,
George and Martha, two great big hippos
who are great friends, find themselves in
some very silly situations. James Marshall's talent for conveying the ridiculous is
evident in all his George and Martha
books, as well as in the other picture
books he has written and illustrated.
This ridiculousness makes his books
appealing to children while giving adults
a good chuckle, too.

As You Read

- After you've read this book at least
  once, your child may enjoy hearing
  it again while playing the parts of
  George and Martha with stick puppets. (See page 75.)

Let's Talk about It

Ask your child:

- What food do you like least? Have you
  ever tried to hide food so that others
  would think you'd eaten it? Where's
  the funniest place you can think of to
  hide food?
- Martha says, "Friends should always
  tell each other the truth." When might
  it be hard to tell the truth? What can
  happen when we lie?
- Have you ever seen a "flying machine"
  (hot-air balloon) before? If so, where?
  Would you like to ride in a hot-air balloon? Why or why not?
- Do you think Martha's reaction to
  George's looking in at her in the tub is

funny? Why or why not? What is privacy? Why does everyone need it?

- Have you ever lost a tooth? If so, how did you feel when it happened? Did the missing tooth change how you looked?

Arts and Crafts
Stick Puppets

Thin white paper
Pencil
Scissors
Glue
Crayons or markers
Heavy paper
Fabric, feathers, glitter glue, or other items to add texture (optional)
Popsicle sticks, one for each puppet

1. With a pencil and thin white paper, trace 1 picture of George and 1 of Martha.
2. Let your child color the traced pictures, then cut them out.
3. Glue the cutouts onto heavy paper. When the glue is dry, cut out the pictures again.
4. If your child wants to, let him glue decorations onto the pictures to add texture. He might, for instance, add fabric for Martha's skirt, a small feather for Martha's hat, a toothpick for George's cane, and gold glitter glue for George's new tooth.
5. Glue a Popsicle stick to each picture.
6. Use the stick puppets to act out George and Martha stories.

Arts and Crafts
Friends Poster

George and Martha is full of ideas about what friends should and shouldn't do. Help your child make a poster based on these ideas.

Crayons or markers
Poster board

1. Write a title like *Things That Friends Do* or *A Friend Is...* at the top of your poster.
2. Ask your child what he thinks a friend is. He may describe ideas from *George and Martha* or his own ideas on how friends should act.
3. Write your child's ideas on the poster. Leave space for illustrations.
4. Let your child illustrate each friendly behavior.
5. Instead of a poster, you may want to make a small book. Staple sheets of paper together inside a construction paper cover or follow the directions in Appendix B.

Cooking and Baking
Split Pea Soup

Martha loved to make split pea soup. When you try this easy recipe, you'll love it, too!

7 cups water
1½ cups chopped cooked ham
1 16-ounce package split peas
2 carrots, thinly sliced
1 medium onion, chopped
¼ teaspoon whole allspice
¼ teaspoon peppercorns
1 bay leaf
Salt to taste

1. About 1 hour before serving, place the water, ham, peas, carrots, and onion in a large kettle over medium heat. Heat the mixture to boiling.
2. Tie the allspice, peppercorns, and bay leaf in a cheesecloth bag. Add the spices to the soup. Reduce the heat to low, cover the soup, and let it simmer for 1 hour.
3. Discard the spices. Add salt to suit your taste.

Rhymes and Finger Plays

Five Little Hippos
Begin this finger play by holding up one hand with all five fingers extended. Tuck a finger into your palm each time a hippo disappears.

Five little hippos running through a door—
One fell down, and then there were four.
Four little hippos in an apple tree—
One fell out, and then there were three.
Three little hippos stirring up some stew—
One fell in, and then there were two.
Two little hippos having lots of fun—
One ran away, and then there was one.

One little hippo left sitting in the sun—
He went home, and then there was none.

Fun and Games

Tub Time
In the story "The Tub," George disturbs Martha's bath and ends up with a tub on his head. Martha might have a nicer bath if she'd try the following ideas— and if George would respect her privacy!

You can use these ideas not only for fun in the tub, but also for playing in puddles on a rainy morning or for cooling off in a plastic tub or wading pool on a hot, sunny day.

- **Colored ice cubes:** Fill an ice cube tray with water. Place a few drops of food coloring in each section, then freeze. Add the ice cubes to your child's bath, puddle, or pool. Remember that ice cubes pose a choking hazard for young children.
- **Ice blocks:** Fill a clean milk carton with water. Add a few drops of food coloring or drop in a few small plastic toys, then freeze. Tear off the carton and let your child play with the block in his bath, puddle, or pool.
- **Ice balls:** Fill balloons with water, tie them tightly, and freeze them. Cut off the balloons and add the ice balls to your child's bath, puddle, or pool.
- **Bubble fun:** As your child splashes about, blow bubbles for him and challenge him to catch them or pop them with his hands.

- **Fishing:** Place a few corks, plastic worms, Ping-Pong balls, or sponge scraps in your child's bath, puddle, or pool. Encourage your child to scoop them out one by one with his hands, a goldfish net, a slotted spoon, or a small strainer.

Let's Pretend

Dentist

When George's tooth breaks, he visits the dentist to have it replaced. Play dentist with your child, taking turns as the dentist and the patient. Because this activity uses water, it's best played in the kitchen or bathroom.

Chair	Toothpaste
Paper napkin	Cup of water
Flashlight	Bowl
Toothbrush	Small toys

1. The dentist greets the patient and shows him to his chair.
2. The dentist tucks a paper napkin into the patient's collar to protect his shirt.
3. The dentist uses a flashlight to look into the patient's mouth.
4. The dentist brushes the patient's teeth, then advises him to rinse his mouth and spit into the bowl.
5. As the patient leaves, the dentist offers him a small toy as a prize.

Enrichment Activities

- Read a simple nonfiction book about hippopotamuses to learn where and how they live, what they really eat, and so on.
- Snack on chocolate chip cookies and tea.
- Draw silly pictures of yourselves and tape them to the bathroom mirror.
- Read other funny books by James Marshall, such as *George and Martha Encore, George and Martha One Fine Day,* and *George and Martha Rise and Shine.*
- Read other books about friends, such as *Frog and Toad Together* and *Frog and Toad Are Friends* by Arnold Lobel, *Alfie Gives a Hand* by Shirley Hughes, and *Overnight at Mary Bloom's* by Aliki.

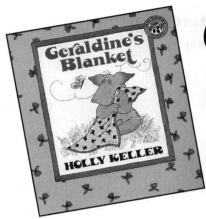

Geraldine's Blanket

Written and Illustrated
by Holly Keller
(Greenwillow, 1984)

This is a charming story about a pig named Geraldine and her beloved pink blanket. Geraldine has had her blanket since she was a baby, and despite her parents' protests, she takes it with her everywhere. She finds many uses for it, and as it becomes tattered and frayed, she loves it all the more. When Geraldine's parents finally come up with a solution to the blanket problem, Geraldine responds with a solution of her own.

If your child has ever been attached to a special blanket, you'll especially appreciate this story. You're sure to recognize your child and yourself in Geraldine and her parents.

Let's Talk about It

Ask your child:

- Why does Geraldine love her blanket so much? How do you think it makes her feel?
- Why do Geraldine's mama and papa get cross about her blanket?
- How do Geraldine's parents try to make Geraldine forget about her blanket? Does it work?
- How does Geraldine handle both Rosa and her blanket? This makes Geraldine happy; how do you think it makes her parents feel?
- What else could Geraldine's parents try to get her to give up her blanket?

- What does the word *compromise* mean? Is Geraldine's solution a good compromise? Why or why not?

Act It Out

Geraldine's Blanket

Blanket
Small doll in a box

1. Encourage your child to act out the part of Geraldine as you read the story. If you're reading to more than one child, additional children can play the parts of Geraldine's mama and papa.
2. Perform the story for friends or family members.

Arts and Crafts

Rosa Picture

Construction paper, heavy paper, or cardboard
Crayons, colored pencils, or markers
Scrap of pink fabric
Scissors
Glue

1. Draw a picture of Rosa on a sheet of construction paper, heavy paper, or cardboard.
2. Have your child color Rosa.
3. From a scrap of pink fabric, cut out a simple dress shape to fit Rosa.
4. Glue the fabric onto the picture of Rosa.

Rhymes and Finger Plays

Piggy Rhymes

This Little Piggy

This little piggy went to market.
> (Wiggle your child's thumb or big toe.)
This little piggy stayed home.
> (Wiggle your child's index finger or second toe.)
This little piggy ate roast beef.
> (Wiggle your child's middle finger or toe.)
This little piggy ate none.
> (Wiggle your child's ring finger or fourth toe.)
And this little piggy cried, "Wee! Wee! Wee!" all the way home!
> (Wiggle your child's pinky finger or toe.)

To Market, To Market

To market, to market, to buy a fat pig;
Home again, home again, jiggety-jig.
To market, to market, to buy a fat hog;
Home again, home again, jiggety-jog.

Fun and Games

Hide Geraldine's Blanket

Small blanket

1. Pretend that you and your child are Geraldine and her mother.
2. Ask your child to leave the room while you hide the blanket. If more than one child is playing, you may want to hide a blanket for each child.
3. Let your child search for the blanket.
4. If you like, provide clues as your child searches. Or for an older child, draw

a simple map showing where the blanket is hidden.

Play and Learn

Pink Hunt
Geraldine is a little pink pig. Do you think Geraldine loves her blanket because it's pink like she is? Go on a color hunt for other pink objects Geraldine might like!

1 child-size hat
1 adult-size hat
Large paper or plastic bag from your recycling bin
Pencil or pen
Paper

1. Put on your hunting hats and grab a large paper or plastic bag from your recycling bin.
2. Tell your child that you're going to hunt for things that are pink. Show her a pink object if necessary.
3. Hunt around your house for pink things and place them in your bag. If you find any pink things that are very large or fragile or can't be put in your bag for some other reason, jot these things down on a sheet of paper.
4. When you're finished hunting, empty your bag and name the items you've found together, for example: pink cup, pink sock, pink pencil, pink nose on your pet rabbit, and so on.

5. If your child enjoys this game, hunt for pink things (without collecting them) at the grocery store or while you're riding in the car or bus together. You could also have a pink theme day during which you wear pink, play with pink play dough, draw pink pictures, drink pink lemonade, and so on.

Snack Time

Pink Toast

2 tablespoons milk
Red food coloring
Small paintbrush
White bread
Toaster
Butter

1. Mix the milk with a few drops of food coloring in a small container.
2. Paint a pink design on the bread with a small clean paintbrush.
3. Toast the bread in a toaster.
4. Eat the toast with butter or use it to make a sandwich.

Enrichment Activities

- Make stick puppets to represent Geraldine, her blanket, her parents, and Rosa. (See "George and Martha: Arts and Crafts," page 75, for instructions.) Use the puppets to tell the story of *Geraldine's Blanket.*

- Draw an outline of Geraldine on a sheet of construction paper or heavy paper. Crumple up small squares of pink tissue paper and glue them onto Geraldine.
- Read a simple nonfiction book about pigs.
- Read other books about pigs, such as *The Three Little Pigs* by Paul Galdone, *Pigs* by Robert Munsch, *Pig Pig Grows Up* by David McPhail, or *Olivia* by Ian Falconer.
- Read other books about Geraldine, such as *Geraldine's Baby Brother, Geraldine's Big Snow,* and *Geraldine First.*

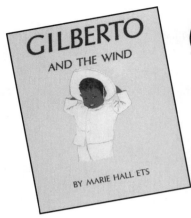

Gilberto and the Wind

Written and Illustrated
by Marie Hall Ets
(Viking, 1963)

This is the delightful story of Gilberto, a little boy who finds a friend in the wind. The wind is a moody playmate: a gentle one that makes Gilberto's balloon float softly through the air; a playful one that romps with umbrellas, kites, pinwheels, and paper boats; and a strong, fierce one that breaks trees and howls at Gilberto's door.

You and your child will enjoy the simplicity of this story and its pencil illustrations. And after reading this book, you may think of the wind just a little differently than you did before.

Let's Talk about It

Ask your child:

- How do you know the wind is there if you can't see it?
- Does the wind really whisper and play? Why might you think you see the wind playing or hear it laughing? What does the wind's whispering, laughing, playing, and so on remind you of? Do you think the wind sometimes acts like a person?
- What's good and bad about wind? For instance, what would happen to a sailboat if there were no wind? What would happen to a sailboat if there were too much wind?
- How is the wind helpful to Gilberto? How does it sometimes cause trouble?

- Has the wind ever scared you? What happened?

Act It Out

The North Wind and the Sun

Read the following fable to your child. Afterward, ask him to tell you the story in his own words. Then take turns playing the parts of the wind, the sun, and the traveler.

The North Wind and the Sun were arguing about which of them was stronger. While they were talking, a traveler came in sight, and they agreed that whoever could make the traveler take off his cloak first should be called stronger.

The North Wind tried his power and blew with all his might, but the stronger he blasted, the more closely the traveler wrapped his cloak around himself. At last the North Wind gave up all hope of winning and called upon the Sun to try her strength.

Then the Sun shone with all her warmth. When the traveler felt the intense heat of the Sun, he loosened his cloak. Soon he threw it aside and hurried to the nearest shade for protection.

Arts and Crafts

Pinwheel

Follow these directions to make a pinwheel like Gilberto's.

Square piece of paper
Crayons, markers, paint, glitter, and/or stickers
Scissors
Tape
Pushpin or thumbtack
Unsharpened pencil with eraser on the end

1. Let your child decorate both sides of a square piece of paper with crayons, markers, paint, glitter, and/or stickers.
2. Mark the center of the square. Cut from each corner toward the center, stopping 1 inch from the center.
3. Fold every other point toward the center and tape the down the points.
4. Poke a pushpin or thumbtack through the center of the pinwheel. Wiggle the pin or tack around a bit to widen the hole. Then poke it into the side of the pencil eraser.
5. Show your child how to blow on the pinwheel, run with it, or face it into the wind to make it spin.

Rhymes and Finger Plays

Tumbleweeds

Tumbleweeds are a familiar sight to prairie dwellers, but urban children may not know what they are. If your child has never seen tumbleweeds, describe them or show a picture of them before you do this finger play.

Tumbleweeds are big and round.
　(Make a large circle with your arms.)
They tumble gaily on the ground.
　(Make a rolling motion with both hands.)

They spin and whirl, bounce and hop,
   (Continue to roll your hands while jump-
   ing up and down.)
But when they hit a fence, they *stop!*
   (Stop jumping and strike the palm of
   your hand with your fist.)

Fun and Games

Bubbles
Mix up a batch of bubble solution and
have fun blowing bubbles with your child,
as Gilberto does with the wind.

2 cups warm water
1 cup liquid dish detergent
¼ cup glycerine
1 teaspoon sugar
Unbreakable household objects like
   funnels, straws, plastic 6-pack
   connectors, and so on

1. Mix the water, dish detergent, glycerine, and sugar.
2. Gather unbreakable household
   objects through which you can blow
   bubbles.
3. Dip the objects in the bubble solution
   and blow through them or wave them
   about.
4. Hold the objects up to the wind or a
   fan and watch the bubbles fly!
5. Store any unused bubble solution in a
   plastic container with a tight lid.

Music and Movement

Autumn Leaves
Sing this song to the tune of "Mary Had
a Little Lamb." Move like slowly falling
leaves during the first verse, then spin
around during the second verse.

Autumn leaves are falling down,
Falling down, falling down!
Autumn leaves are falling down,
Falling on the ground.

Autumn leaves are whirling round,
Whirling round, whirling round!
Autumn leaves are whirling round,
All over town.

Out and About

Walk in the Wind

Balloon
String
Kite (optional)

1. Take a walk on a windy day. Bring a
   balloon on a string with you.
2. Observe the effect of the wind on
   your balloon, clouds, plumes of
   smoke, and/or flags.
3. Ask your child, "How can you tell
   which way the wind is blowing? Can
   you tell how fast the wind is blowing?
   Why is the speed of the wind important to airplane pilots, sailors, and
   even to you and me?"

4. If you live near a lake, river, or ocean, notice how the wind changes the surface of the water.

5. If you live in the country, try to spot a weathervane. Look for windbreaks between fields and discuss why farmers plant them.

6. If you like, fly a kite in an open field.

Enrichment Activities

- Make a paper boat or a boat with a paper sail like Gilberto's.
- Buy or make a windsock and hang it in a place where it will catch the wind.
- Buy a set of wind chimes and hang them outside your door.
- Read poems about the wind, such as Christina Rossetti's "Who Has Seen the Wind?" or Robert Louis Stevenson's "The Wind."
- Read or watch a simple nonfiction book or videotape about weather.
- Read other books by Marie Hall Ets. One of our favorites is *Little Old Automobile.*

The Happy Lion

Written by Louise Fatio
Illustrated by Roger Duvoisin
(McGraw-Hill, 1954)

The Happy Lion is the first in a series of Happy Lion books written and illustrated by the husband-and-wife team of Louise Fatio and Roger Duvoisin. Duvoisin illustrated more than 140 books in his lifetime, including *White Snow, Bright Snow* by Alvin Tresselt, which won the 1948 Caldecott Medal.

The Happy Lion is set in a small town in France. It tells of a lion living contentedly in a house in the town zoo. He has many human friends who greet him as they pass and offer him meat and other tidbits. One day the zookeeper forgets to close the door of the lion's house, so the lion decides to walk out and visit his friends. Your child will be delighted at the excitement and humor that ensues when the happy lion pads down the cobblestone streets of town.

As You Read

- After hearing this story once or twice, your child will enjoy saying the French terms *bonjour* (hello) and *au revoir* (good-bye) as they occur.

Let's Talk about It

Ask your child:

- Why is the lion so happy?
- Why does the happy lion decide to leave his home? What happens next?
- Why are the lion's friends so happy to see him when he's in the zoo, but they faint or run away when they see him in the street?

- How does the happy lion get back to his house at the zoo?
- What's your favorite part of the story?
- Could this story really happen? Why or why not?

Act It Out

The Happy Lion

The Happy Lion is full of fun scenes to dramatize.

- If there are only two of you, read the book aloud as your child acts out the parts of the people as they see the lion first in the zoo, then in the street.
- If you're reading to a group of children, let each play a different character.

Arts and Crafts

Happy Lion Picture

Pencil
Paper
Crayons, markers, or colored pencils
Dark brown or black yarn or construction paper
Scissors
Glue

1. Draw or trace a picture of the happy lion. The illustration on the first page of the story is a good one to copy.
2. Color the happy lion in shades of yellow and gold.
3. Glue on pieces of dark brown or black yarn for the lion's mane. Glue on

shorter pieces for the end of his tail. Or if you prefer, glue on thin strips of construction paper that have been curled around a pencil.

Cooking and Baking

Popcorn Animals

Popcorn is a favorite snack of zoo visitors. And these popcorn animals are bound to become a favorite treat in your family!

¾ cup sugar
1 teaspoon white vinegar
¾ cup brown sugar
½ cup light corn syrup
½ cup water
¼ teaspoon salt
¾ cup butter
8 cups popped popcorn

1. Stir all the ingredients except the popcorn and butter in a pan over medium heat until the mixture is 260°F as measured with a candy thermometer.
2. Reduce the heat to low, then add the butter.
3. Put the popcorn in a large bowl and pour the liquid over it. Let the mixture cool slightly.
4. Butter your child's hands and let her mold the popcorn into animal shapes.
5. Place the shapes on wax paper until they cool and harden.

Rhymes and Finger Plays

Five Big Lions

Begin this finger play by holding up one hand with all five fingers extended. Tuck a finger into your palm each time a lion disappears.

Five big lions waiting at the door—
One ran away; then there were four.
Four big lions looking at the sea—
One swam away; then there were three.
Three big lions going to the zoo—
One joined the circus; then there were two.
Two big lions sleeping in the sun—
One chased a monkey; then there was one.
One big lion chasing you for fun—
He got lost; then there were none.

Music and Movement

Waltzes and Polkas

On summer Sundays, the happy lion loves to listen to the town band play waltzes and polkas at the bandstand.

Recordings of waltzes or polkas
Several pieces (3–4 feet long) brightly colored ribbon (optional)
Empty key chain or plastic shower curtain ring (optional)
Chiffon scarf (optional)

1. Listen to some waltz or polka recordings with your child. If you don't own any, borrow some from your local library.
2. As you listen, encourage your child to physically express how the music makes her feel. For example, she might want to run for fast music, tiptoe for soft music, and hop for happy music.
3. If you like, attach several ribbons to an empty key chain or plastic shower curtain ring. Let your child wave the ribbons to the music as she dances. A chiffon scarf is also a great dance accessory. If the scarf is very long, tie a knot in the middle to make a handle.
4. If you hear about an upcoming outdoor concert that will include waltzes or polkas, plan to attend it.

Out and About

The Zoo

1. A lion's natural habitat is in Africa or India. Find Africa and India on a map. Ask, "Are they far from where you live? How might a lion get from Africa or India to a zoo in France or North America?"
2. Visit a zoo or wildlife sanctuary near you. Spend time with the lions—and/or any other members of the cat family—at your zoo. Ask your child if she sees any relatives of the lion in her everyday life.
3. Compare your zoo and the happy lion's zoo. Find out if your zoo keeps large animals in cages or in more natural enclosures and if it has safety features like moats around the large animal enclosures.

4. Discuss what's good and bad about zoos. For example, you might ask your child, "Should we keep wild animals in zoos? Do you think they would rather be in their natural habitats? Without zoos, would most people ever get to see animals like lions?"

Enrichment Activities

- Learn a few simple French terms, such as *s'il vous plaît* (please), *merci* (thank you), *la mère* (mother), *le père* (father), *le bébé* (baby), and *l'ami* (friend).
- Read or watch a simple nonfiction book or videotape about lions in the wild. Learn how they live, what they eat, and so on.
- *Androcles and the Lion* by Janusz Grabianski is a beautifully illustrated edition of the heartwarming story about a lion in Africa who is captured and kept in captivity, then eventually returned to the wild.
- Read any of the several Happy Lion books by Louise Fatio and Roger Duvoisin.
- Read other books set in France, such as *Madeline* by Ludwig Bemelmans and *Mirette on the High Wire* by Emily Arnold McCully.

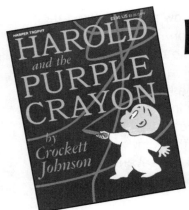

Harold and the Purple Crayon

Written and Illustrated
by Crockett Johnson
(HarperCollins, 1955)

This book tells the story of a boy named Harold and his magical purple crayon. Harold's adventure begins when he decides to go for a walk in the moonlight. There's no moon, so Harold simply draws one with his purple crayon. He then needs something to walk on, so he draws a long, straight path to avoid getting lost. But he gets lost anyway as his purple crayon takes him from one silly situation to another. Your child will be enchanted by Harold's imaginative adventures and comforted when he finally finds his way home and "draws" up the covers before falling asleep.

As You Read

Some children enjoy counting when an illustration shows a number of the same item. While you read *Harold and the Purple Crayon,* for example, your child may want to count the apples on the apple tree or the pies on the picnic blanket.

Let's Talk about It

Ask your child:

- What's special about Harold's purple crayon?
- What happens to Harold as he sets off on his moonlight walk?
- Could this story really happen? Why or why not?
- What's your favorite part of the story?
- What would it be like if everything you drew became real? What would you draw?

Act It Out

Harold and the Purple Crayon

This story is lots of fun to dramatize. All you'll need is one person to read the story, one to play the part of Harold, and a big purple crayon.

- As your child plays the part of Harold, he may either pretend to draw or draw real pictures. If your child chooses the latter, simply cover a wall with a large sheet of paper.
- If you're reading this story to more than one child, the additional children can play the dragon, the moose, the porcupine, and/or the police officer. Read the story several times so each child has a chance to play the part of Harold.

Arts and Crafts

Purple Book

Because Crockett Johnson's drawings are so simple, your child can easily create his own book using *Harold and the Purple Crayon* as a model.

White paper
Purple crayon, marker, or paint (Or choose your child's favorite color.)
Purple construction paper (Or choose your child's favorite color.)
Stapler

1. Encourage your child to draw a series of purple pictures that tell a story.

Your child may invent his own story or simply retell Harold's story and draw interpretations of Crockett Johnson's drawings.

2. Let your child tell you what's happening in each drawing. Write what he says beneath each picture.
3. Staple the pictures together inside a construction paper cover or follow the directions in Appendix B.

String Painting

Here's another great way for your child to interpret Crockett Johnson's simple drawings.

Bowl
Purple liquid tempera paint
Liquid starch or white glue
String
Heavy paper
Pencil (optional)

1. In a bowl, mix equal parts of liquid tempera paint and liquid starch or white glue.
2. Immerse a length of string in the paint mixture and drop or lay it on a sheet of heavy paper. Your child may want to pencil a simple picture on the paper first, then place the string on the lines he's drawn.
3. As the paint dries, the starch or glue will make the string stick to the paper.

Fun and Games

Real or Make-Believe?

Is Harold's crayon really magic, or is he just pretending? You can play the following game at home, while walking, or during a bus or car ride.

- Make up a story for your child. After each sentence, challenge your child to say "real" or "make-believe." Combine real and make-believe elements in your story. For example, the main character could be your child, who of course is real. But perhaps the child in your story does something your child wouldn't do or gets into a situation your child would interpret as make-believe.

- If you like, read some of your child's favorite picture books together. Identify which elements of the story are or could be real and which elements are make-believe.

Out and About

Moonlight Walk

Harold's adventure begins when he decides to take a walk in the moonlight. For young children, an evening walk can be downright magical!

1. Take a family walk on a clear, moonlit evening. For safety's sake, wear light colors and carry flashlights. If you like, bring a stroller or wagon for younger children.

2. In *Harold and the Purple Crayon,* the moon goes wherever Harold goes. Notice how the moon seems to follow you, too.

3. Harold notices that the moon is always in his bedroom window at night. When you get home from your walk, notice which of your windows the moon appears in.

Snack Time

Pie Picnic

Harold's picnic lunch consists of nothing but pie—nine of his favorite kinds!

1. Make or buy your child's favorite pie.

2. If the weather is fair, spread a blanket outdoors. If it's too wet or cold to eat outside, a blanket on your living room floor and a little imagination will do the trick.

3. Have a picnic snack of pie and milk or, if you like, your child's favorite food and drink.

4. Talk about what else you might eat if you could have anything you want at your picnic.

Enrichment Activities

- Harold draws a frightening dragon under the tree to guard the apples. Ask your child if he's heard of dragons or seen pictures of dragons before. Teach your child the song "Puff, the Magic Dragon."

- When Harold can't find his bedroom window, he asks a police officer for help. Talk with your child about what he should do if he ever gets lost.
- Have a "purple day." Wear purple clothes, drink grape juice, paint purple pictures, go for a walk and try to spot purple things, and so on. Of course, you'll want to read *Harold and the Purple Crayon* again, too!
- Harold draws a porcupine to help eat the remains of his picnic. Make a porcupine of your own with purple play dough and toothpicks.
- Read other books about Harold, such as *Harold's Trip to the Sky, Harold at the North Pole,* and *A Picture for Harold's Room.*

Harquin

Written and Illustrated
by John Burningham
(Jonathan Cape, 1967)

John Burningham has written and illustrated many beloved children's books. He was the first artist to win the Kate Greenaway Medal twice—in 1964 for *Borka: The Adventures of a Goose with No Feathers* and in 1971 for *Mr. Gumpy's Outing.*

Harquin tells of a young fox who lives with his family at the top of a hill. He's forbidden to go into the valley, for the hunters might see him and follow him home. But Harquin's bored, so he ventures out while everyone sleeps. One night a gamekeeper sees him and tells the local squire, who arranges a hunt. Luckily, Harquin is clever enough to solve the problem he's created!

You and your child are sure to love Harquin's mischievous antics and Burningham's whimsical illustrations.

As You Read

- The dialogue in this story is British, so try to read it with a British accent.

Let's Talk about It

Ask your child:

- Why do Harquin's parents tell him not to go into the valley? Does Harquin obey them? Why not?
- Why does Harquin go out at night instead of during the day? What happens when he is seen?
- Is Harquin clever? How? Talk about the saying *clever as a fox.*

- Why does the gamekeeper no longer work for the squire at the end of the story? Where do you think he goes?
- Have you ever disobeyed your parent(s)? What happened?
- Have you ever learned a lesson you want to teach to your own kids someday? Do you think they'll listen to your advice? Why or why not?

Arts and Crafts

3-D Nature Collage

Take a walk and collect interesting items to combine in a collage.

White glue
Natural objects like pebbles, bark, leaves, pine needles, pine cones, nuts, seeds, wood shavings, shells, and dried flowers
Piece of wood, paper plate, or cardboard
Clear contact paper (optional)

1. Glue natural objects onto a wood, paper plate, or cardboard base. A very young child may enjoy sticking objects onto a piece of clear contact paper taped sticky side up to a table or highchair tray.
2. When the collage is complete, let it dry overnight.

Rhymes and Finger Plays

Harquin

A family of foxes lived in a den;
    (Hide one hand under the other.)

One little fox was named Harquin.
    (Poke out the hidden hand and wiggle its index finger.)
Sometimes Harquin would sleep all day,
    (Pull your hand back under the other.)
But when night came, he liked to play.
    (Poke out the hidden hand and move it left and right as if it's looking around.)
Out of the hole he'd creep, creep, creep
    (Move your hand forward while making a creeping motion with your fingers.)
While his family was fast asleep.
    (Place the palms of your hands together and pillow your head on your hands.)
Down to the valley Harquin would go,
    (Make a running motion with your fingers.)
Although his parents had told him, "No!"
    (Wag your index finger.)
But when he heard the gamekeeper's gun,
    (Cup your hand to your ear.)
Bang! Back to his den he'd run!
    (Clap your hands, then hide one hand under the other.)

Fun and Games

Fox Hunt

Small stuffed animal
Broom or mop (optional)
Flashlight (optional)
Small treat (optional)

1. Hide a small stuffed animal in your house or yard.
2. Let your child lead a search for the hidden animal. She may want to pretend she's on a fox hunt by galloping

along using a broom or mop as a horse. Bring along a flashlight if necessary.

3. If you like, reward the successful hunter with a small treat.

Music and Movement

The Fox

If you don't know this Colonial American folksong, listen to it on-line at The Mudcat Café, see *The Reader's Digest Children's Songbook,* look for a children's recording that includes it, or just make up your own tune or sing the words to a tune you know.

The fox went out in the chilly night;
He prayed for the moon to give him light.
He'd many a mile to go that night
Before he reached the town-o town-o town-o;
He'd many a mile to go that night
Before he reached the town-o.

He ran till he came to a great big bin
The ducks and the geese were kept therein.
Said, "A couple of you will grease my chin
Before I leave this town-o town-o town-o;
A couple of you will grease my chin
Before I leave this town-o."

So he grabbed a gray goose by the neck
And threw a duck across his back.
He didn't mind their *quack, quack, quack*
And their legs all dangling down-o down-o down-o;
He didn't mind their *quack, quack, quack*
And their legs all dangling down-o.

Then old Mother Flipper-Flopper jumped out of bed,
And out the window she stuck her head;
Said, "Get up, John, the gray goose is gone,
And the fox is in the town-o town-o town-o!"
Said, "Get up, John, the gray goose is gone,
And the fox is in the town-o!"

So John, he ran to the top of the hill
And he blew his horn both loud and shrill.
The fox he said, "I better flee with my kill,
Or they'll soon be on my trail-o trail-o trail-o."
The fox he said, "I better flee with my kill,
Or they'll soon be on my trail-o."

He ran till he came to his cozy den,
And there were his little ones, eight, nine, ten.
They said, "Daddy, you better go back again,
'Cause it must be a mighty fine town-o town-o town-o."
They said, "Daddy, you better go back again,
'Cause it must be a mighty fine town-o."

So the fox and his wife, without any strife,
Cut up the goose with a fork and a knife.
They never had such a supper in their lives,
And the little ones chewed on the bones-o bones-o bones-o;
They never had such a supper in their lives,
And the little ones chewed on the bones-o.

Out and About

Mud

Unlike Harquin's hunters, your child will probably play in the mud quite willingly!

- **Mud bricks:** Mix dirt and water to make a very thick mud. Press mud into sections of a muffin pan or metal ice cube tray. Dry it in your oven at 250°F for 15 minutes. Stick the cooled bricks together with wet mud.

- **Mud handprints:** Mix dirt, sand, and water to make a thick mud. Pour it into a sturdy paper or plastic plate and smooth the surface. Press your child's palm into the mud. Let the handprint dry in the sun.
- **Mud painting:** Mix dirt and water to make a thin mud. Give your child a paintbrush, then let her draw mud pictures or words on the sidewalk.
- **Mud pie:** Mix dirt, sand, and water to make a very thick mud. Press the mud into a pie pan, decorate it with grass or flower petals, and bake it in the sun.

Snack Time

Mud Balls

1 cup peanut butter
¼ cup honey
½ cup dry powdered milk
½ cup raisins or chocolate chips
1 cup crushed graham crackers
Chocolate milk powder

1. Mix the peanut butter, honey, powdered milk, and raisins or chocolate chips.
2. Add crushed graham crackers.
3. Show your child how to roll the mixture into balls.
4. Coat the balls by rolling them in a plate of chocolate milk powder.

Enrichment Activities

- Read a nonfiction book on foxes.
- Find out if fox hunts still occur. Discuss why people hunt foxes.
- Pretend you are horses returning from a hunt. Snack on oatmeal cookies and apples.
- Help your child create a poster about the rules in your house and the consequences of disobeying them.
- Read other books about consequences, such as *The Story about Ping* by Marjorie Flack and *Tikki Tikki Tembo* by Arlene Mosel.
- Read other books about foxes, such as *The Fox Went Out on a Chilly Night* by Peter Spier.
- Read other books by John Burningham, such as *Borka: The Adventures of a Goose with No Feathers, Cannonball Simp,* and *Mr. Gumpy's Outing.*

Harry the Dirty Dog

Written by Gene Zion
Illustrated by Margaret Bloy Graham
(Harper & Row, 1956)

Harry the Dirty Dog has been a favorite among generations of children since it was published in 1956. Harry is a white dog with black spots who likes everything—except baths. One day Harry runs away to avoid a bath. He has a great time playing in dirty places, and soon he is a black dog with white spots rather than a white dog with black spots.

Finally Harry becomes tired and hungry and decides to return home. But his family doesn't recognize him. Poor Harry! You and your child will enjoy Harry's discovery that there are much worse things than bathing, as well as the uncharacteristic way he finally convinces his family that he is indeed Harry.

Let's Talk about It

Ask your child:

- What's the one thing Harry doesn't like? What happens to Harry when he decides to run away instead of taking a bath?
- What makes Harry change his mind about bathing?
- What does Harry do to help his family recognize him?
- Do you like taking baths? What's better than taking a bath? What's worse?
- How would you feel if you came home one day and your family didn't recognize you? What could you do to convince your family that you're you?

Arts and Crafts

Soap Clay

As your child works with this clay, warn him to keep his hands away from his eyes and mouth.

2 cups white detergent flakes, such as Ivory Snow
Food coloring (optional)
2 tablespoons water

1. Measure detergent flakes into a bowl.
2. If you like, add food coloring to the water.
3. Gradually add the water to the detergent while mashing and squeezing the mixture with your hands until it forms a ball.
4. Mold the clay to form different shapes. Add more water if necessary.

Cooking and Baking

Dog Bone Cookies

If you like, you can substitute your favorite rolled cookie dough for the following recipe.

2½ cups flour
1 teaspoon cinnamon
½ teaspoon ginger (optional)
½ teaspoon baking powder
¼ teaspoon baking soda
¼ teaspoon salt
¾ cup butter
½ cup honey
⅓ cup granulated sugar

1 egg
Colored sugar, sprinkles, and/or frosting (optional)

1. Mix the flour, cinnamon, ginger, baking powder, baking soda, and salt in a medium-size bowl. Set the mixture aside.
2. Cream the butter, honey, and sugar in a large bowl until the mixture is smooth.
3. Beat the egg into the butter mixture.
4. Combine the wet and dry ingredients and stir them well. Cover and refrigerate the dough for 1½ hours or until it's firm enough to roll and cut.
5. Preheat your oven to 350°F.
6. Roll about ⅓ of the dough on a well-floured surface. Use a small plastic knife to cut out dog bone shapes. You could also use a bone- or dog-shaped cookie cutter.
7. Repeat step 6 twice, then roll the dough scraps together and cut more cookies. You'll end up with 3–4 dozen cookies.
8. Place the cookies on a lightly greased baking sheet. If you like, decorate the cookies with colored sugar or sprinkles.
9. Bake the cookies for 8–10 minutes or until they're lightly browned and firm to the touch.
10. If you didn't decorate the cookies before baking, you can spread frosting on them when they're cool and

then decorate them with colored sugar or sprinkles.

Rhymes and Finger Plays

Five Little Puppies

Begin this finger play by holding up one hand with all five fingers extended. Tuck a finger into your palm each time a puppy is mentioned.

Five little puppies were playing in the sun.
One saw a rabbit, and it began to run.
One saw a butterfly, and it began to race.
One saw a pussycat, and it began to chase.
One tried to catch its tail and circled round
 and round.
One was so quiet, it never made a sound.

Fun and Games

Find the Scrub Brush

This game can be played indoors or out, depending on the weather.

Scrub brush
Treasure map (optional)

1. Hide a scrub brush in your house or yard.
2. Give your child clues to help him find the brush. For instance, if you've hidden it in the piano bench, you might say, "You could sit on it, but you wouldn't feel it or see it."
3. If you like, tell your child he's getting hotter as he nears the hidden brush and getting colder as he moves away from it.

4. An older preschooler may enjoy using a simple treasure map to help him find the hidden brush. To make one, sketch a simple map of your house or yard and draw an X where the scrub brush is hidden.

Music and Movement

Oh Where, Oh Where Has My Little Dog Gone?

If Harry's family were to notice his absence, they might sing this song. Pretend you're looking for Harry as you sing.

Oh where, oh where has my little dog gone?
Oh where, oh where can he be?
With his ears cut short and his tail cut long,
Oh where, oh where can he be?

Out and About

Where's Harry?

1. Take a walk in your neighborhood. Ask your child, "If Harry were your dog, and he ran away, what are the dirtiest places in our neighborhood where he might play?"
2. As you walk, observe any dogs that are out and about. Make up a silly story about why they're out or pretend they're running away from home like Harry. Ask your child, "Why might these dogs be running away from home?"

Enrichment Activities

- Look through old magazines and cut out all the dog pictures you can find. Glue them onto a sheet of construction paper and cover the collage with clear contact paper to make a place mat.
- Visit a pet store or animal shelter and look at some dogs. Ask your child, "Do you see any that look like Harry?"
- Take a bath! See "George and Martha: Tub Time" (page 76) or "Alexander and the Terrible, Horrible, No Good, Very Bad Day: Bath Paints" (page 24) for some bathtub fun.
- Read *Puddleman* by Ted Staunton, a book about a little boy named Michael who has an experience like Harry's: He comes home so muddy that his mother doesn't recognize him!
- Read more about Harry and his adventures in *No Roses for Harry, Harry and the Lady Next Door,* and *Harry by the Sea.*

A House for Hermit Crab

Written and Illustrated
by Eric Carle
(Simon & Schuster, 1987)

A House for Hermit Crab tells of a little crab that outgrows his first shell and must find another. Hermit Crab finds a bigger shell and enlists neighbors to help decorate it. When the shell is finally perfect, he's outgrown it...and the search for a new house begins anew.

This story is based on the true habits of the hermit crab. Carle combines this science lesson with a message that while new experiences can be scary, change is inevitable—and the future is full of exciting possibilities.

As You Read

- Keep in mind that this story is based on facts. Hermit crabs really do live in discarded shells, sea anemones camouflage them, and spiny sea urchins protect them.

Let's Talk about It

Ask your child:

- Why is Hermit Crab afraid to be out in the open sea?
- Why does Hermit Crab want friends to help decorate his new house?
- Why do you think Hermit Crab asks the sea urchins for help?
- What happens when Hermit Crab's house is finally perfect?
- Why isn't Hermit Crab afraid to leave his shell the second time?
- Do you like the way the story ends? Why or why not?

- Have you ever felt afraid to try something new? What happened?

Arts and Crafts

Undersea Collage

Scissors
Construction paper
Glue
Blue or white poster board or paper

1. Study the shapes that make up Eric Carle's sea anemones, starfish, coral, and sea urchins. Cut out simple construction paper shapes that your child can combine to make her own undersea creatures.
2. Let your child glue the shapes onto poster board or paper to create an undersea scene. If you use a white background, you might add blue crayon streaks to indicate water.
3. If your child wants a hermit crab in her collage, trace one of Carle's illustrations. Cut it out and let your child glue it onto her picture.

Cooking and Baking

Snail Shells

My mom has been making these delicious treats with pastry scraps since I was a little girl. Precise quantities aren't important in this recipe; just use whatever's on hand!

Pastry dough scraps or ready-made pie, bread, or biscuit dough, thawed
Margarine or butter, softened
Brown sugar
Cinnamon

1. Preheat your oven to 350°F.
2. Roll out the pastry dough into a rectangle about ⅛ inch thick. (Roll out bread or biscuit dough slightly thicker.) The short sides of the rectangle should measure at least 6 inches.
3. Spread a thin layer of margarine or butter all over the top of the dough.
4. Sprinkle the dough with brown sugar, then cinnamon.
5. Grasp a long side of the dough rectangle and roll it up tightly.
6. Cut the roll into ½-inch slices with a sharp knife. The spiral-shaped slices will look like snail shells.
7. Lay the snail shells flat on a baking sheet, about 1 inch apart. Bake the snail shells for 10–15 minutes.
8. Remove the snail shells from the oven and let them cool on a wire rack before you eat them.

Rhymes and Finger Plays

Houses

This is a nest for the bluebird.
    (Cup your hands, palms up.)
This is a hive for the bee.
    (Hold your fists together, with palms facing each other.)

This is a shell for the hermit crab,
　　(Make an O with your hands.)
And this is a house for me.
　　(Extend your fingers, fingertips touching,
　　to form a peak.)

Fun and Games

Shell Game

Three seashells
Table
Small treats, such as candy, cereal,
*　raisins, or chocolate chips*

1. Place three seashells on the table.
2. Hide a small treat under one of the
   shells. Ask your child to cover her
   eyes or leave the room while you hide
   the treat. Or if you like, hide the treat
   while your child watches, then slide
   the shells around on the table until
   they are mixed up.
3. Challenge your child to guess which
   shell hides a treat. If she guesses
   right the first time, she gets the treat.
   If her first guess is wrong, give her
   another try. If she guesses wrong
   the second time, you get the treat!
4. Take turns being the hider and the
   guesser.

Out and About

Marine Life

- If you live near an ocean, lake, or
  river, have a picnic lunch there. Walk
  along the shore and see what interesting marine life you can spot. Be sure
  to look under rocks and don't forget a
  shovel and pail for digging in the sand.
- If there's an aquarium in your area,
  take a field trip there. Our local aquarium has everything from whales to
  stingrays to sharks to sloths; visiting
  it is an exciting way to learn about animals that live in and near the ocean.
- If you don't live near a body of water
  or an aquarium, visit a pet store and
  discover the fish and other marine life
  on display.
- If you have access to a swimming
  pool or beach, go swimming!

Play and Learn

Read the Calendar

Hermit Crab looks for a new house in
January, finds the right house in February,
and so on. Use this story as a springboard for learning about calendars.
Calendar reading can help your child
learn not only about the days and months,
but also about ordinal numbers.

Calendar
Markers or stickers
Paper, scissors, old magazines, glue,
*　and stapler (optional)*

1. Read the calendar with your child every day. Say the day, the date, the month, and the year. For example, you might say, "Today is Wednesday. That means yesterday was Tuesday, and tomorrow will be Thursday. Today is the fifteenth of April. That means yesterday was the fourteenth, and tomorrow will be the sixteenth."

2. Let your child place a sticker on or cross off each day after your calendar reading session.

3. If you like, help your child make a book of months. Write each month name on a separate sheet of paper. Have your child cut out magazine pictures that show things she associates with each month, such as snow for January, pumpkins for October, and so on. Staple the sheets of paper together inside a construction paper cover or follow the directions in Appendix B.

Enrichment Activities

- Snack on Goldfish crackers.
- Take a trip to a beach or any large sandy area. Write and draw in the sand with sticks, shells, and your hands.
- Sponge-paint an undersea scene by dipping fish-shaped sponges in white paint, then pressing them onto blue construction paper.
- Read or watch a simple nonfiction book or videotape about hermit crabs and/or other ocean animals.
- Compare the illustrations in *A House for Hermit Crab* to those in *Frederick* by Leo Lionni and *The Snowy Day* by Ezra Jack Keats.
- Read other books by Eric Carle, such as *The Very Hungry Caterpillar*, *The Mixed-Up Chameleon*, *The Very Busy Spider*, and *The Grouchy Ladybug*.

If You Give a Mouse a Cookie

Written by Laura Joffe numeroff
Illustrated by Felicia Bond
(Harper & Row, 1985)

If You Give a Mouse a Cookie is a funny cumulative tale. In cumulative tales, episodes follow each other in a neat, logical pattern. Very young children typically enjoy these simple tales a great deal.

The story begins when a boy innocently gives a cookie to a hungry traveling mouse. Of course, if you give a mouse a cookie, he may want a glass of milk to go with it. Once he has a glass of milk, he may need a straw to drink it...and so on. The tale comes full circle at the end when the mouse needs a cookie to go with his glass of milk. Your child is sure to enjoy this silly story and its funny pictures of a demanding mouse and a worn-out boy.

As You Read

- As you read this story for the first time, your child may enjoy guessing the mouse's demands. For instance, you could read "When you give him the milk..." and then ask your child what he thinks the mouse will want. Turn the page to find out what happens.
- After you've read this story several times, your child will enjoy finishing the lines as you read.

Let's Talk about It

Ask your child:

- How did the boy's troubles begin?
- If you were the boy, what would you say to the mouse?

- How do you think the story ends? Does the mouse ever go away?
- Do you think the boy will ever give a mouse a cookie again? Why or why not?
- What do you like best about the story? What's the funniest part?

Act It Out

If You Give a Mouse a Cookie

Because this story has lots of action and no dialogue, it's very easy for preschoolers to act out.

1. If you and your child are the only players, read the book aloud while your child dramatizes the mouse's actions. Use props if you like, or just pretend to hand the mouse a cookie, a glass of milk, and so on.
2. If two or more children are present, they can take turns playing the parts of the mouse and the boy.

Arts and Crafts

Creative Crayon Drawings

The mouse requests crayons and paper so he can draw a picture. If your child enjoys drawing, try the following ideas to add variety to his coloring routine.

Construction paper, newspaper or newsprint, fine sandpaper, paper towels, paper napkins, and/or grocery bags
Scissors (optional)
Crayons
Clothespin
Tape
Cardboard (optional)
Aluminum foil (optional)
Warming tray or electric griddle (optional)
Oven mitt or thick glove (optional)

- Provide your child with many different kinds of paper.
- Before your child begins drawing, cut his paper into shapes like circles, triangles, and stars.
- Clip a clothespin to a crayon and challenge your child to draw by holding the clothespin.
- Tape two or more crayons together and let your child draw a picture with them.
- Place a cardboard shape, such as a circle, square, triangle, heart, or fruit shape, under a sheet of paper. If you like, tape the corners of the paper to your work surface to keep it from sliding. Show your child how to rub the flat side of a peeled crayon over the shape to make an impression.
- Place a sheet of paper or aluminum foil on a food warming tray or electric griddle set on low. Cover your child's nondrawing hand with an oven mitt or thick glove and tell him to hold the paper still with that hand. With his drawing hand, your child can rub a crayon slowly on the warm paper to make a melted crayon design.

Carefully supervise this activity and remind your child to keep his bare skin off the warming tray or griddle.

Straw Ornament

Scissors
Heavy paper, such as a paper plate or file folder
Hole punch
Crayons, markers, or stickers
Drinking straw

1. Cut a square, circle, or other shape from heavy paper.
2. Punch a hole at the top and at the bottom of the cutout.
3. Decorate the cutout with crayons, markers, or stickers.
4. Thread a drinking straw through the two holes. Let your child use his specially decorated straw to slurp up some milk—with cookies, of course!

Rhymes and Finger Plays

Five Little Mice

Five little mice on the pantry floor—
    (Hold up five fingers.)
This little mouse peeked around the door.
    (Wiggle your thumb.)
This little mouse nibbled on some cake.
    (Wiggle your index finger.)
This little mouse not a sound did make.
    (Wiggle your middle finger.)
This little mouse took a bite of cheese.
    (Wiggle your ring finger.)

This little mouse heard the kitten sneeze.
    (Wiggle your pinky.)
"Achoo!" sneezed the kitten. "Squeak!" the mouse cried.
    (Make a fist on the word *achoo;* extend your fingers on the word *squeak.*)
And the mice found a hole and ran inside.
    (Run fingers behind back.)

Play and Learn

Print Your Name

When the mouse finishes his drawing, he wants to sign his name. Help your child learn to print his name or practice printing his name if he already knows how. For more ideas on helping your child learn to recognize, spell, and print his name, see "Tikki Tikki Tembo: Play and Learn" (page 213).

Paper
Pen or marker
Crayon or washable marker
Clear contact paper
Damp cloth

1. On a sheet of paper, draw two parallel solid lines about 2 inches apart. Draw a dotted line between them.
2. Print your child's name between the solid lines and cover the paper with clear contact paper.
3. Encourage your child to trace his name, then wipe it off with a damp cloth and practice as many times as he wishes.

Snack Time

Milk and Cookies

If time permits, bake a batch of chocolate chip cookies with your child. Use your own recipe or see "Frog and Toad Together: Cooking and Baking" (page 71).

1. Snack on milk and cookies together. *If You Give a Mouse a Cookie* features chocolate chip cookies, but any kind will do.
2. As you eat your snack, pretend one of you is the mouse and the other is the boy. Additional children can pretend to be more mice.
3. If you've made a Straw Ornament (page 108), use it as you drink your milk.
4. After you finish your snack, look in the mirror to see if you have a milk mustache.

Enrichment Activities

- Sing songs about mice, such as "Three Blind Mice" and "Hickory Dickory Dock."

- The next time you sweep and wash the floors, have your child pretend to be the mouse in *If You Give a Mouse a Cookie.*
- Have your child put his stuffed animals to bed in a box with a blanket and pillow.
- Read a simple nonfiction book about mice. Learn how and where they live, what they eat, and so on.
- Read other books about mice, such as *Frederick* by Leo Lionni, *Broderick* by Edward Ormondroyd, and *Norman the Doorman* by Don Freeman.
- Write and illustrate your own cumulative tale.
- Read other cumulative tales, such as *Millions of Cats* by Wanda Gág and *The Elephant and the Bad Baby* by Elfrida Vipont.
- Read other books by Laura Joffe Numeroff, such as *If You Give a Moose a Muffin* and *If You Give a Pig a Pancake.*

Imogene's Antlers

Written and Illustrated
by David Small
(Crown, 1985)

This is a very silly story about a girl named Imogene who wakes up one morning to find she has grown antlers. Imogene's mother is quite distressed by the situation and faints from time to time throughout the story, but Imogene is unperturbed. She seems to enjoy her antlers, except when they complicate common tasks like getting dressed and walking through doorways.

You and your child will be delighted by the funny illustrations of Imogene finding practical uses for her antlers and of her mother trying to hide them. And you'll especially enjoy this story's ridiculous ending.

Let's Talk about It

Ask your child:

- How does Imogene feel when she first discovers her antlers? Why do her antlers make it hard to get dressed and walk through doorways? What makes her think her antlers aren't so bad after all?
- Why does Imogene's mother faint?
- What are some ways Imogene's antlers are useful?
- How does Imogene's mother try to solve the antler problem? Does her plan work?
- What is a milliner? Do you think being a milliner is a very common job?
- What happens when Imogene wakes up on Friday morning? Why is her

family overjoyed to see her...until she comes into the room?

Arts and Crafts

Crazy Hat

Imogene's mother calls in a milliner to hide Imogene's antlers. His efforts result in an outrageous hat. Make your own crazy hat with whatever flotsam you have around the house.

Household flotsam, such as paper plates, toilet paper rolls, egg cartons, fabric and ribbon scraps, gift bows, buttons, and so on
White glue, tape, and/or stapler
2 long ribbons
Paint and paintbrushes (optional)

1. Use a paper plate as a base for your hat.
2. Decorate your hat with whatever household flotsam you like. Fasten items to the hat with glue, tape, or staples.
3. Attach 2 ribbons (long enough to tie comfortably under your child's chin) on opposite sides of the paper plate.
4. If you like, paint your hat.

Make a Book

Crayons, colored pencils, or markers
White paper
Construction paper
Stapler

1. Challenge your child to make up a new ending for *Imogene's Antlers* and explain what happens after Imogene sprouts peacock feathers. Or if your child prefers, let her make up an original story. She might, for example, tell what happened one day when she woke with an elephant's trunk, a giraffe's neck, or a porcupine's quills. Write one or two lines on each sheet of paper.
2. Let your child illustrate her story.
3. Staple the sheets of paper together inside a construction paper cover or follow the directions in Appendix B.

Cooking and Baking

Applesauce-Raisin Doughnuts

Hot oil is quite hazardous for young children, so insist on frying these doughnuts yourself while your child is occupied elsewhere. (For safety's sake, use a sealed deep fryer if possible.) She'll enjoy helping you make the dough and shaking the doughnuts in the coating.

Doughnuts:
4 cups buttermilk baking mix
⅔ cup applesauce
½ cup chopped golden raisins
¼ cup sugar
1 teaspoon vanilla extract
½ teaspoon nutmeg
2 eggs
Vegetable oil

Coating:

1½ cups sugar

1 teaspoon nutmeg (or cinnamon, if you prefer)

1. In a large bowl, thoroughly mix all the doughnut ingredients except the vegetable oil.
2. Turn the dough onto a well-floured surface and knead it about 10 times or until it's smooth.
3. With a floured rolling pin, roll out the dough to a thickness of ¼ inch.
4. Cut the dough into rings with a floured doughnut cutter.
5. Press the dough scraps together, roll them out, and cut doughnuts until all the dough is used. (This recipe makes about 36 doughnuts.)
6. Heat 3–4 inches of oil to 370°F in deep fryer (or large saucepan or Dutch oven over medium heat).
7. Fry 4–5 doughnuts at a time in the hot oil. As soon as they float to the surface, start turning them often until they're golden brown.
8. Drain the doughnuts on paper towels.
9. Combine the coating ingredients in a paper bag.
10. Shake a few doughnuts at a time in the coating.

Rhymes and Finger Plays

I Am a Little Peacock
Imogene might chant this rhyme on Friday morning!

I am a little peacock
With feathers bright and gay.
I strut around and spread my tail;
I'm beautiful all day.

Fun and Games

Doughnuts on Antlers
The object of this game is to be the first player to place all the "doughnuts" on the antlers.

Brown crayon or marker
1 sheet of paper per player
Clear contact paper (optional)
Doughnut-shaped breakfast cereal
Dice

1. Draw a set of antlers on each sheet of paper. If you like, cover them with clear contact paper.
2. Give each player an antlers picture and about 100 pieces of cereal.
3. Players take turns rolling the dice and placing the corresponding amounts of cereal on their antlers.
4. The first player to place all her cereal on her antlers wins the game.

Play and Learn

What Day Is It?
Play this game to reinforce the order of the days of the week. It requires no supplies, so you can play it anywhere, anytime.

1. Say to your child, "Imogene wakes up on Thursday and finds she has

antlers. The next day they disappear. What day is that?"

2. Next ask, "If Imogene's antlers appear on Monday and disappear the next day, what day is that?"

3. Vary your questions, for example: "What if Imogene's antlers stay for two or three days?"

4. Ask what day comes before a specific day, for example: "Imogene's antlers appear on Thursday. The day before, she had an elephant's trunk. What day was that?"

5. See "A House for Hermit Crab: Play and Learn" (page 104) for more calendar activities.

Enrichment Activities

- Make antlers out of play dough.
- Norman consults an encyclopedia and announces that Imogene has turned into a rare form of miniature elk. Look in an encyclopedia for a picture of an elk.

- Ask your child, "What do the words voilà, bravo, and bravissimo mean? The literal translation of voilà is "see there," but it's commonly used to express success or satisfaction. Bravo is used to express approval, and bravissimo is used to express great approval. Just for fun, use these words in your everyday conversation. For example, say, "Voilà!" as you tie your child's shoes and "Bravo!" or "Bravissimo!" when she picks up her toys without being reminded.

- Make a bird feeder by spreading peanut butter on a pine cone and rolling it in bird seed. Hang it in a tree and watch the birds eat.

- Read other silly books, such as Fortunately by Remy Charlip, Purple, Green and Yellow by Robert Munsch, or George and Martha by James Marshall.

- Read other books by David Small, such as Fenwick's Suit and Paper John.

Ira Sleeps Over

Written and Illustrated
by Bernard Waber
(Houghton Mifflin, 1972)

This book tells the story of a boy named Ira and his very first sleepover. Ira is thrilled by the invitiation to sleep at his friend's house, but thanks to his sister, he begins to worry: Should he take his teddy bear? If he does, will his friend think he's a baby?

I like Ira's interaction with his family over this dilemma: both his parents' reassurance and his sister's all-too-typical discouragement. He finally decides to leave his teddy bear at home, only to discover that his friend shares what he thinks is his own unique problem. If your child sleeps with a special something every night, he'll especially love this story's ending.

Let's Talk about It

Ask your child:

- Why is Ira so happy about being invited to sleep at Reggie's house? What does Ira's sister say that makes him worry?
- Why does Ira decide not to take his teddy bear with him?
- If you were invited to a sleepover, would you take something to cuddle? Why or why not?
- What does Ira discover that makes him run home for his teddy bear? What does Ira learn from this?

Arts and Crafts

Paper Chain

Reggie's junk collection included a chain made of gum wrappers. I remember saving colorful Wrigley's gum wrappers and making just such a chain when I was a kid. It required a lot of precise folding, which is tough for preschoolers. Following is a larger, simpler version of the gum wrapper necklace. Although it's a difficult process to describe, it's easy to demonstrate. Be sure to try it yourself before showing your child what to do.

2 sheets of different-colored construction paper (8½ by 11 inches)
Scissors
Table

1. Fold each sheet of paper in half so that the long sides meet. Unfold each sheet.
2. Cut the sheets of paper into strips that are ½–¾ inch wide and 8½ inches long.
3. Take a strip and fold both ends inward so they meet at the middle fold. Now close the middle fold.

4. Repeat step 3 until all your strips are folded.

5. Lay a folded strip (A) on the table so that its middle fold points away from you. Now grab a different-colored strip (B) and hold it so that its middle fold points to the left. Thread the ends of strip B through the ends of strip A. Push strip B all the way to the right, then slide strip B away from you until it catches on the middle fold of strip A.

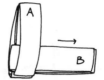 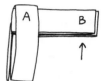

6. Grab another folded strip (C) and hold it so that its folded middle points toward you. Thread the ends of strip C through the ends of strip B and push it all the way up.

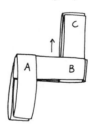

7. Continue weaving strips together to make a long zigzag chain.

Cooking and Baking

Crunch and Munch

Whether you're having a sleepover or not, this delicious snack is the perfect accompaniment to a game of checkers, a good story, or any kind of fun!

½ cup butter or margarine
½ cup honey
1 cup chopped peanuts or other nuts
12 cups popped popcorn

1. Preheat the oven to 350°F.
2. Put the butter or margarine and honey in a small saucepan. Heat and stir them until they're melted and well mixed.
3. Stir in the chopped nuts.
4. Pour the mixture over the popcorn and stir until the popcorn is coated.
5. Spread a thin layer of popcorn on a baking sheet and bake for 12 minutes or until the coating is crisp. Stir the popcorn often to prevent burning.

Fun and Games

TV-Free Fun
When Reggie tells Ira what he's planned for their sleepover, he mentions many activities, none of which requires a TV or computer. Have a TV- and computer-free day or week in your home and do some of the things on Reggie's list:

• Play checkers.
• Have a wrestling match.
• Have a pillow fight.
• Play dominoes.
• Learn a few simple magic tricks.
• Tell stories or read books together.
• Engage in dramatic play with your child: Don silly clothes from your dress-up box, set up a pretend store, or play hospital or office.

Let's Pretend

Sleepover
Your child may be too young for a real sleepover, but a family sleepover is just as fun!

Sleeping bags and pillows
1 teddy bear for each person
Storybooks (optional)
Flashlight
Bedtime snack

1. Have a family sleepover in your living room or family room. If you have a fireplace, lay the sleeping bags in front of it to make your sleepover feel like a campout.
2. Give each person a teddy bear to cuddle.
3. Tell stories or read books by flashlight.
4. If you like, have a bedtime snack. Don't forget to brush your teeth before you go to sleep!
5. If you like, just pretend to sleep on the floor and have everyone go to their own beds to really sleep. This is also a fun activity for a rainy afternoon.

Music and Movement

Teddy Bear, Teddy Bear

As you chant this rhyme with your child, do the actions it describes. If you like, make up additional verses and actions and/or sing the words to the tune of "Twinkle, Twinkle, Little Star."

Teddy bear, teddy bear, turn around.
Teddy bear, teddy bear, touch the ground.
Teddy bear, teddy bear, reach up high.
Teddy bear, teddy bear, touch the sky.
Teddy bear, teddy bear, bend down low.
Teddy bear, teddy bear, touch your toe.

Out and About

Exploring

One of the activities Reggie and Ira plan is to explore outdoors with a magnifying glass.

Magnifying glass

1. Explore your yard, neighborhood, or local park with a magnifying glass. Look closely at common things like tree bark, leaves, and insects. What interesting things can you see with the magnifying glass that you can't see with the naked eye?

2. Have a scavenger hunt. Before you go out, make a list of things to collect, such as a red flower, a pretty leaf, a rock, a piece of wood, something yellow, and so on. Then set out with your list and a paper or plastic bag to hold the items you find.

Enrichment Activities

- Invite one of your child's friends or cousins to a sleepover at your home.
- Your child probably has a junk collection, although he may not think of it as such. Take some time to look at your child's "junk" and let him tell you what makes each item special.
- Read *Ira Says Goodbye,* the sequel to *Ira Sleeps Over,* in which Reggie moves away, or other books by Bernard Waber, such as *The House on East 88th Street* and *Lovable Lyle.*
- Read other books about doing your own thing, such as *The Story of Ferdinand* by Munro Leaf and *William's Doll* by Charlotte Zolotow.
- Read other books about teddy bears, such as *Corduroy* by Don Freeman.

Just Plain Fancy

Written and Illustrated
by Patricia Polacco
(Bantam, 1990)

Just Plain Fancy tells the story of Naomi, a girl who lives in an Amish farming community. Naomi's job is to look after the chickens, and she does it diligently. One day Naomi and her little sister find an abandoned egg in the grass. They place it with the other eggs and wait for it to hatch. When it does and the girls discover what's inside, they try to keep it a secret. But their special chick, Fancy, has ideas of his own. What happens next will not only amuse you and your child, it's sure to warm your hearts, too.

As You Read

- Ask your child to guess what kind of egg Naomi and Ruth find.

- Watch the illustrations for clues about how the Amish live differently from the "English."

Let's Talk about It

Ask your child:

- How do the Amish in this story live differently from the English?
- Why does Naomi want something fancy? Do you think this is wrong?
- What's Naomi's job? Does she do her job well? How do you know?
- Why are Naomi and Ruth worried on the day of the frolic? Why do they think Fancy might be shunned? What does the word shunned mean?
- What does Fancy do that leaves the guests speechless?

- What happens next? Why does Martha say Fancy won't be shunned?
- What's your favorite part of the story? Why?

Arts and Crafts

Eggshell Peacock

Food coloring, hot water, and white vinegar	*Wax paper*
	Rolling pin
	Cardboard
6 hard-boiled eggs	*Glue*
Markers	

1. To make each color of egg dye, mix ¼ teaspoon food coloring, ¾ cup hot water, and 1 tablespoon white vinegar. Soak the eggs in the dye as long as you like, then remove them and let them dry. Or if you like, simply color the eggs with markers.
2. Peel off the eggshells and save the eggs for a salad or sandwich spread. Place the shells on wax paper and crush them into large pieces with a rolling pin.
3. Draw a peacock outline on the cardboard. Spread glue inside the outline and press on eggshell bits.

Cooking and Baking

Shoofly Pie

When you and your child taste this traditional Amish treat, you'll know why it's so popular among Naomi's people!

Filling:
1 cup dark brown sugar
1 cup dark molasses
1 egg, slightly beaten
1 teaspoon baking soda
1 tablespoon flour
2 cups boiling water

Topping:
2 cups flour
1 cup light brown sugar
1 teaspoon baking soda
Pinch of salt
½ cup butter

2 unbaked 9-inch pie shells

1. Preheat your oven to 350°F.
2. Mix the filling ingredients. Chill the filling while you follow step 3.
3. Mix the topping ingredients until they're crumbly.
4. Pour the filling into the unbaked crusts. Sprinkle the topping evenly over both pies. Bake for 35–45 minutes or until the filling is set. Let the pies cool before you eat them.

Fun and Games

Marble Raceway

The Amish resist modern technology, so when it's time for some fun, they sure don't watch TV or play computer games! Amish kids play with simple toys like dolls and marbles. Handcrafted wooden toys from Pennsylvania's Amish country inspired the following activity.

Scissors
2–4 cardboard paper
  towel tubes
Small marble

Wall
Packing tape
Container

1. Slice each tube in half lengthwise to make 2 cardboard troughs.
2. In 1 end of each trough, cut a hole bigger than your marble.
3. Choose a wall that won't be damaged by tape. Tape the rim of 1 trough to the wall so that the hole end inclines gently downward.
4. Tape another trough right below the first to make a sideways V. Again, the hole end should incline gently downward.
5. Repeat step 4 with the remaining troughs to make a cardboard raceway that zigzags down your wall.
6. Place a marble at the top of the raceway and watch it roll down the troughs and drop through the holes until it reaches the bottom.

Music and Movement

I'm a Little Peacock
Sing this fun little rhyme to the tune of "I'm a Little Teapot."

I'm a little peacock, pretty to see.
Everyone likes to look at me.
When I spread my feathers, you'll agree:
Fancy is the name for me.

Play and Learn

Count the Pictures
Patricia Polacco's illustrations are rich with objects to count: people, chickens, eggs, and so on. After you've read the book once, reread it and count some of the objects you see. To make the flash cards mentioned below, see "Getting Started: Play and Learn" (page 18).

Number flash cards (optional)
Object flash cards (optional)

- As you look at each page, say, "Let's count the _____ in this picture. How many _____ do you see?" Point to each object as you count it: "One, two, three. There are three eggs in the basket." You might then say, "What else do you see in this picture?" and count other objects.
- If you like, use number flash cards as you count. When your child counts two objects, ask her to find the card that has the number two on it.
- If your child is not yet able to recognize numbers, use object flash cards. When your child counts two objects, ask her, "Can you find the card that has two stickers on it?" To help her learn to associate numbers with groups of objects, show her the card with the number two and explain that the number two means "two things."

Snack Time

Fresh-Squeezed Lemonade

Naomi and Ruth serve lemonade at the frolic. My kids think lemonade comes from a can, but I'll bet the Amish make theirs fresh!

½ cup sugar
1 teaspoon finely grated lemon peel
½ cup very hot water
½ cup freshly squeezed lemon juice
Ice cubes
Cold water or club soda

1. In a 2-cup jar with a tight lid, shake the sugar, lemon peel, and hot water until the sugar dissolves.
2. Add the lemon juice. Refrigerate the lemon syrup for at least 2 hours.
3. Put ice in 5 12-ounce glasses. Stir ¼ cup lemon syrup and ¾ cup cold water or club soda in each.

Enrichment Activities

- *Just Plain Fancy* takes place in Pennsylvania. Find Pennsylvania on a map of the United States.

- Investigate where the Amish came from, why they formed a separate community, and why they choose a plain lifestyle.
- Discuss what it would be like to live like the Amish. Talk about the benefits and drawbacks.
- Naomi's community comes together to cooperate on various tasks. Ask your child, "Has our family ever joined others to do things like canning fruit or helping someone move? Do you think this is a good idea? Why or why not?"
- Point out the washboards in the illustrations, then say the rhyme "Here's a Little Washboard." (See "Mirette on the High Wire: Rhymes and Finger Plays," page 148.)
- Read *The Rag Coat* by Lauren Mills, another story about a hard-working. simple-living community.
- Many of Patricia Polacco's wonderful books are available on audiotape, read by Polacco herself. We especially enjoy *Mrs. Katz and Tush* and *Rechenka's Eggs*.

Little Bear

Written by Else Holmelund Minarik
Illustrated by Maurice Sendak
(Harper & Row, 1957)

Several generations of children have grown up loving Little Bear and his family since this book was first published. Little Bear's pictures were drawn by Maurice Sendak, a prolific children's illustrator whose books have won many awards. Sendak is probably best known for his book *Where the Wild Things Are,* which won the Caldecott Medal in 1964.

Although *Little Bear* is written for newly independent readers, its limited vocabulary doesn't affect its charm. You and your child will surely enjoy its four stories of Little Bear, his loving and wise mother, his animal friends, and his funny, imaginative play.

Let's Talk about It

Ask your child:

- Has anyone ever forgotten your birthday? Do you think anyone will ever forget it? How would you feel if that happened? Why?
- When Little Bear gets to the moon, he says, "The moon looks just like earth." Why? Does Little Bear really think he's on the moon, or is he just pretending?
- Before Little Bear goes to sleep, he wishes for a Viking boat, a tunnel to China, and a cloud to fly around on. Why can't he have his wishes? What wish can he have?
- How do Little Bear and his mother make each other happy? How do you

make your parent(s) happy? How do(es) your parent(s) make you happy?

Act It Out

What Will Little Bear Wear?
This story is simple to dramatize because it requires only two actors.

Clothes (coat, hat, pants)

- If you're reading with only one child, one of you may play Little Bear while the other plays Mother Bear. If your child isn't able to recite his lines, simply read the story aloud while he dramatizes it.
- If you're reading with two or more children, let each child take a turn playing Little Bear or Mother Bear.
- If your child enjoys this activity, he may want to act out the other stories in *Little Bear* or his own made-up Little Bear stories.

Arts and Crafts

Space Helmet
In "Little Bear Goes to the Moon," Little Bear makes a space helmet from a box and some springs. Encourage your child to make his own space helmet with whatever flotsam you have around the house.

Cardboard box or paper bag that fits your child's head

Household flotsam, such as toilet paper rolls, egg cartons, fabric and ribbon scraps, gift bows, buttons, spools, and wood scraps
White glue, tape, and/or stapler
Paint and paintbrushes (optional)

1. Use a cardboard box or paper bag as a base. Glue, tape, or staple household flotsam onto the base to make a space helmet.
2. If you like, paint the helmet.
3. Encourage your child to wear his space helmet while using his imagination to go to the moon.

Cooking and Baking

Birthday Soup
In "Birthday Soup," Little Bear thinks Mother Bear has forgotten his birthday, so he makes birthday soup from "carrots and potatoes, peas and tomatoes." Use the following recipe to make a pot of soup to enjoy with your little bear.

½ pound lean ground beef
2 teaspoons vegetable oil
1 14-ounce can whole tomatoes, broken up, with juice
10 ounces frozen mixed vegetables
1 cup diced onion
4 cups water
1 tablespoon beef bouillon powder
1 teaspoon salt
¼ teaspoon pepper
¼ teaspoon ground thyme

1. In a saucepan, brown the beef in the oil over medium heat until it's crumbly. Drain any excess fat.
2. Stir in the remaining ingredients.
3. Bring the soup to a boil, then cover it and reduce the heat to low.
4. Simmer the soup for about 20 minutes or until the vegetables are tender.
5. Eat your soup with crackers, crusty rolls, or sandwiches.

Let's Pretend

Birthday Party

Birthday cake or cupcakes
Frosting
Candles
Juice or herbal tea
Small gift-wrapped toys (optional)

1. Bake a cake or cupcakes using a mix or your favorite cake recipe. When the cake is cool, frost and decorate it. Add candles.
2. Throw a pretend birthday party. Your child can play Little Bear, you can play Mother Bear, and siblings, friends, or stuffed animals can play Little Bear's friends.
3. Set a table and bring out the cake or cupcakes and juice or tea.
4. If you like, gift-wrap a few small toys for birthday presents.
5. Light the candles and sing "Happy Birthday" to Little Bear.

Music and Movement

Climb into My Spaceship

Sing the first part of this song to the tune of "Sing a Song of Sixpence" and shout the last two lines. Act out the words as you sing them.

Climb into my spaceship,
We're going to the moon.
Hurry now, get ready,
We're going to blast off soon.
Let's put on our helmets
And buckle up real tight.
Now here comes the countdown,
Let's count with all our might.

Ten! Nine! Eight! Seven! Six! Five! Four!
Three! Two! One! Blast off!

Play and Learn

Count the Candles

Before doing this activity, discuss the concept of birthday candles with your child. Make sure he understands that the number of birthday candles reflects the age of the birthday person. To make the flash cards mentioned in this activity, see "Getting Started: Play and Learn" (page 18).

Birthday candles
Pair of dice
Number flash cards
Object flash cards

• Find the illustration that shows Little Bear's birthday cake. Ask your child, "How old is Little Bear?"

- Ask your child to count out a certain number of candles. For example, you might say, "Please give me five candles."
- Throw a pair of dice and challenge your child to count out the corresponding number of candles.
- Select a number flash card and ask your child to place that number of candles on the card.
- Select an object flash card and ask your child to place the corresponding number of birthday candles on the card.

Enrichment Activities

- Read a simple nonfiction book about bears to learn what they eat, how they live, and how many bears spend the winter.
- Read a simple nonfiction book about the moon to learn what it really looks like. Ask your child, "Does the moon look like Earth? How is it different? How is it similar?"
- Read a simple picture book or nonfiction book about Vikings.
- Find China on a world map. Challenge your child to think of different ways he could get to China.
- Read other picture books about bears, such as *Blueberries for Sal* by Robert McCloskey and *The Biggest Bear* by Lynd Ward.
- Read other books in the Little Bear series, such as *Little Bear's Visit,* or watch a Little Bear videotape. (See Appendix D for more information.)

The Little Engine That Could

Written by Watty Piper
Illustrated by George
and Doris Hauman
(Platt & Munk, 1930)

The Little Engine That Could tells of a train that breaks down while trying to carry toys and food to the children on the other side of a mountain. The toys on board cry out to passing engines for help, but they're repeatedly refused by engines that are too proud, too busy, and so on. Then along comes the Little Blue Engine, who hitches herself to the train and puffs her way up the mountain chugging the now-famous refrain "I think I can. I think I can."

This classic picture book has inspired millions of children around the world with its message of kindness and determination.

As You Read

- Your child will enjoy reciting "chug, chug"; "puff, puff"; "ding-dong"; "I can not"; "I think I can. I think I can"; and "I thought I could. I thought I could."
- Your child may want to pretend she's a train puffing along the tracks.

Let's Talk about It

Ask your child:

- Where is the little train going? What happens to it?
- Why won't most of the engines help the little train? What does the word *proud* mean? What's the difference between being proud of something

you've done and being too proud to help someone?

- Why does the Little Blue Engine decide to pull the train? How have others been kind and helpful to you? How have you been kind and helpful to others?
- Is it easy for the Little Blue Engine to pull the train? What happens? What kind of attitude does the Little Blue Engine have? What might you do that seems difficult? How can a good attitude help?
- How would the story end if the Little Blue Engine weren't willing to help?

Arts and Crafts

Train Collage

Pencil or pen
Construction paper of various colors (or white paper and crayons or markers)
Scissors
Glue stick or white glue
Large sheet of paper
Stickers (optional)

1. Draw several train cars, engines, and cabooses on construction paper of various colors. Or if you prefer, draw on white paper and let your child color in the shapes with crayons or markers. Cut out the shapes.
2. Glue the train cars, engines, and cabooses onto a large sheet of paper to make a train collage.

3. If you like, let your child use stickers to decorate the train cars or fill them with cargo.

Rhymes and Finger Plays

Choo-Choo Train

Start this action rhyme with your arms hanging at your sides.

This is a choo-choo train
(Bend your arms at the elbows so your hands point forward.)
Chugging down the track.
(Rotate your arms like train wheels.)
Now it's going forward;
(Push your arms forward as you rotate them.)
Now it's going back.
(Pull your arms backward as you rotate them.)
Now the bell is ringing;
(Pretend to pull a bell cord.)
Now the whistle blows.
(Cup your hands at your mouth and say, "Toot, toot!" into them.)
What a lot of noise it makes
(Cover your ears with your hands.)
Everywhere it goes!
(Stretch both arms out at your sides.)

Fun and Games

I Think I Can

1. Read the story to your child several times, until she's very familiar with the Little Blue Engine's actions.

2. Discuss how the Little Blue Engine thinks she can make it up the hill even though it's very hard to do.
3. Challenge your child to try actions that seem hard at first. For example, you might ask your child, "Do you think you could hop on one foot?" Demonstrate the action, then do it together, saying, "I think I can. I think I can."
4. Try playing this game to encourage your child to pick up her toys. For example, you might ask, "Do you think you can put away all your blocks before I pick up these cars?"

Play and Learn

Count the Train Cars

Before doing the following activities, you'll need to draw a few train cars on each sheet of paper, then cut them out. To make the flash cards mentioned below, see "Getting Started: Play and Learn" (page 18).

Pencil
Paper in several different colors
Scissors
Pair of dice
Number and object flash cards

- Sort the train cars by color.
- Choose two train cars of each color and set aside the rest. Mix up the pairs and challenge your child to match them again.

- Lay several train cars in a row and practice counting them with your child.
- Roll a pair of dice. Count the dots on the dice and have your child count out the same number of train car shapes.
- Select a number flash card and ask your child to count out that number of train cars.
- Select an object flash card and ask your child to count out the corresponding number of train cars.

Music and Movement

The Wheels on the Train

Sing this song to the tune of "The Wheels on the Bus." Make up appropriate actions as you sing.

The wheels on the train go *chug, chug, chug*
Chug, chug, chug…chug, chug, chug.
The wheels on the train go *chug, chug, chug*
All along the tracks.

The engine on the train goes *puff, puff, puff…*
The engine on the train just will not go…
All the other engines come steaming by…
The toys on the train call, "Help us, please!"…
All the other engines say, "No, not me!"…
The Little Blue Engine comes chugging by…
The toys on the train call, "Help us, please!"…
The Little Blue Engine says, "I think I can."…
The toys on the train cry, "Hurray, hurray!"…
The Little Blue Engine says, "I thought I could."…

Snack Time

Apples, Oranges, and Milk

The little train's cargo includes apples, oranges, and milk for the children on the other side of the mountain. Your child will enjoy eating this snack as a passenger on a pretend train.

Apples
Oranges
Milk

1. Line up chairs or cardboard boxes like a train. If there are only two of you, fill the extra chairs or boxes with dolls or stuffed animals.
2. Encourage your child to find a seat on the train while you prepare the snack.
3. Peel the apples if you like and cut them into wedges. Peel the oranges and separate them into sections.
4. Serve the fruit with a glass of milk to the passenger(s) seated on the train.

Enrichment Activities

- If you're reading this book to a group of children, they may enjoy acting out the story as you read. Let them take turns playing the various engines and toys.
- Sing train songs, such as "I've Been Working on the Railroad" and "Down by the Station," with your child.
- If you live near a train track, find out when trains usually go by. Visit the track when a train is expected and from a safe distance; count the cars as they pass.
- If possible, take a ride on a train. In a city, you may be able to ride a commuter train or a train at a zoo or amusement park. In a rural area, you may be able to ride a passenger train between two neighboring towns. Tourist trains are available in some scenic areas.
- Read or watch a simple nonfiction book or videotape about trains. Good books include *The Big Book of Real Trains* by Walter Retan and *The Train* by David McPhail.
- If your child enjoys *The Little Engine That Could,* she'll probably also enjoy *Little Toot* by Hardie Gramatky and *Smokey* by Bill Peet.

The Little House

Written and Illustrated
by Virginia Lee Burton
(Houghton Mifflin, 1942)

The pictures in this 1943 Caldecott Medal winner make me yearn for a country cottage surrounded by apple trees, green grass, and white daisies. The book tells of a little house built "way out in the country." She's built strong so she'll live to see her builder's "great-great-grandchildren's great-great-grandchildren living in her." But the builder doesn't foresee the changes that come as the city creeps ever closer.

The Little House watches with fear, sadness, and loneliness as the city envelops her. Soon she's surrounded by high-rise buildings, trolley cars, and subways. You and your child will breathe a sigh of relief when the builder's great-great-granddaughter discovers her and moves her back out to a quiet, peaceful life in the country.

Let's Talk about It

Ask your child:

- What does the Little House like about the country? What does she see as the seasons change?
- What happens to the Little House's peaceful country life?
- Why is the Little House sad and lonely in the city? What does she dislike most there? What does she miss most about the country?
- What happens to make the Little House happy again? Why is she so happy to be back in the country?

- Would you rather live in the city or the country? What's good and bad about where you live right now?

Arts and Crafts
Little House Picture

Scissors
Colored construction paper
Pencil
Large sheet of white paper
Glue stick
Crayons, markers, or paint

1. Cut the Little House's parts—red chimney; white windows; black roof, shutters, door, and steps; and so on—from colored construction paper.
2. If you like, pencil an outline of the house on the white paper. Let your child glue on the cutouts to make a picture of the Little House.
3. Use crayons, markers, or paint to add details like trees, grass, and flowers or cars, trains, and buildings. Look at the illustrations in the book for ideas.
4. If your child doesn't want to draw the details, cut them from construction paper instead and let your child glue them onto his picture.

Rhymes and Finger Plays
Five Red Apples
The Little House enjoys watching apple trees, and you'll enjoy doing this finger play about apples together! Begin by holding up one hand with all five fingers extended. Bend a finger down each time an apple disappears. Fill in the blanks with the names of your child's friends and family.

Five red apples in a grocery store—
_____ ate one, and then there were four.
Four red apples on an apple tree—
_____ ate one, and then there were three.
With three red apples, what did _____ do?
Why, she ate one, and then there were two.
Two red apples ripening in the sun—
_____ ate one, and then there was one.
One red apple—and we're almost done.
I ate it up, and now there are none.

Let's Pretend
Little House

Old bed sheets
Rope and clothespins (optional)
Indoor table or yard with trees, shrubs, fence, and/or lawn furniture
Pillow, blanket, flashlight, books, toys, and snack

1. If the weather is bad, drape sheets over a table to make a little house indoors for your child. If the weather is fine, build a little house with sheets, ropes, and clothespins in a corner of your yard. Use trees, shrubs, fences, and/or lawn furniture as supports.
2. Furnish the little house with a pillow, blanket, flashlight, books, toys, and a snack. Let your child "live" there as long as he likes.

Out and About
City and Country

- If you live in the city, try to plan a day trip to the country. As you leave the city behind, notice the changes: Big roads lead to small roads, crowded neighborhoods give way to open spaces, the air becomes fresher, and your surroundings grow quieter. If you're still in the country at night and the sky is clear, look at the sky and notice how much darker it is and how many stars you can see.
- Hunt for old photos of your city or, if you live in the country, a nearby city. Look at the pictures with your child, then visit the areas shown and see how they've changed.

Play and Learn
Count around the House

The Little House is surrounded by things to count: people, animals, trees, flowers, automobiles, trolley cars, train cars, and so on. After you've read the book once, reread it and count some of the things you see. To make the flash cards mentioned below, see "Getting Started: Play and Learn" (page 18).

Number flash cards (optional)
Object flash cards (optional)

- As you look at each page, say, "Let's count the _____ in this picture. How many _____ do you see?" Point to each object as you count it: "One, two. There are two trees in this picture." You might then say, "What else do you see in this picture?" and count other objects.
- If you like, use number flash cards as you count. When your child counts two objects, ask him to find the card that has the number two on it.
- If your child is not yet able to recognize numbers, use object flash cards. When your child counts two objects, ask him, "Can you find the card that has two stickers on it?" To help him learn to associate numbers with groups of objects, show him the card with the number two and explain that the number two means "two things."

Snack Time
Graham Cracker House

Graham crackers
Cardboard milk carton
Ornamental frosting (see Appendix A)
Edible decorations, such as gumdrops, raisins, chocolate chips, hard candy, and cereal

1. Stick graham crackers to the sides of a cardboard milk carton with ornamental frosting. Remember to cover the frosting with a damp cloth when you're not using it.

2. Let the walls set before adding a roof.
3. Add details to your house using frosting and edible decorations.

Enrichment Activities

- Build houses with blocks.
- Look at old family photographs and discuss how hairstyles, clothing, cars, houses, storefronts, signs, and so on have changed over the years.
- Watch the night sky over several days and notice the changes in the moon. Encourage your child to draw the shape of the moon he sees each night. Discuss why the shape changes and how long the moon's cycle is.
- Use white crayons, paint, or star stickers to make a picture of a night sky on black construction paper.

- Ask your child if he can look outside and see any of the seasonal changes the Little House sees: the longer days and warmer weather of spring, the leafy trees and ripe fruit of summer, the cooler weather and brilliant colors of fall, or the short, cold days and snow of winter. Ask him what other signs of the season he can identify.
- Talk about the invention of the automobile and explain why it was called a "horseless carriage." Ask your child, "Do cars make things better or worse for us and our environment?"
- Read other books by Virginia Lee Burton, such as *Katy and the Big Snow* and *Mike Mulligan and His Steam Shovel.*

Little Toot

Written and Illustrated
by Hardie Gramatky
(G. P. Putnam's Sons, 1939)

This book tells the story of "the cutest, silliest little tugboat you ever saw." Although Little Toot comes from a long line of hard-working tugboats, he'd rather play than work. He spends his days gliding through the water, playing at the pier, and blowing big puffs of smoke to make himself feel important. But when the other tugboats make fun of him, Little Toot sets out to work like the others, determined not to be silly anymore. Your child will enjoy the resulting ocean adventure, which makes Little Toot a hero and proves that he has changed.

As You Read

- Give your child opportunities to say "toot-toot-toot" like Little Toot. Encourage her to change the sound to match Little Toot's mood. For example, she may toot happily as Little Toot plays in the river and sadly as he sulks by the wharf.
- Explain that *S O S* means "save our ship." (Some sources claim this while others say the letters were chosen simply because they're easy to transmit.)

Let's Talk about It

Ask your child:

- How does Little Toot like to spend his time? Would you rather work or play?
- Why don't the other tugboats like Little Toot? How does this make him feel? Have you ever felt like that? What did you do?

- What happens when Little Toot decides to stop being silly and start working? Why won't the ships throw him a towline?
- What does Little Toot do to prove that he has changed?
- What's your favorite part of the story?

Arts and Crafts

Tugboat

Hull: milk carton, small shoebox, plastic food container, or Styrofoam block
White glue, tape, and/or stapler
Building and decorating materials: paper, drinking straws, Popsicle sticks, cotton balls, toothpicks, wooden skewers, empty toilet paper rolls, markers, and/or stickers
Aluminum foil or contact paper
String or yarn

1. Choose an object to serve as your boat's hull.
2. Glue, tape, or staple building and decorating materials to the hull. For example, you might make a smokestack from an empty toilet paper roll topped with a cotton ball or a flag from a drinking straw and a slip of paper.
3. Make your boat's hull watertight by covering it with aluminum foil or contact paper.
4. Attach a piece of string or yarn to the bow of your boat with tape and/or staples.

5. Float your boat in the bathtub or in a puddle, pond, or creek.

Cooking and Baking

S O S Pancakes

1¼ cups all-purpose flour
2 tablespoons sugar
2 teaspoons baking powder
¾ teaspoon salt
3 tablespoons vegetable oil
1⅓ cups milk
1 egg, slightly beaten

1. With a fork, mix the flour, sugar, baking powder, and salt in a large bowl. Add the vegetable oil, milk, and egg and stir just until the flour mixture is moistened.
2. Preheat a griddle or skillet and grease it lightly with vegetable oil.
3. Use a spoon to drop the batter in the shapes of the letters *S*, *O*, and *S*.
4. Flip the pancakes with a spatula and remove them from the heat when both sides are golden.
5. Serve the pancakes with syrup, jam, cottage cheese, fruit, or whipped cream.

Rhymes and Finger Plays

Five Little Tugboats

Begin this finger play by holding up one hand with all five fingers extended. Bend a finger down each time a tugboat disappears.

Five little tugboats playing near the shore—
One saw a water snake; then there were four.
Four little tugboats chugging out to sea—
One saw a big blue whale; then there were three.
Three little tugboats on the ocean blue—
One saw an octopus; then there were two.
Two little tugboats having lots of fun—
One saw a lemon shark; then there was one.
One little tugboat floating in the sun—
It saw a giant crab; then there was none.

Fun and Games
Find Little Toot

Markers
Paper
Scissors

1. Draw a picture of Little Toot on a sheet of paper. Let your child color the picture, then cut it out. If you like, make several tugboat cutouts. Or if you've already built a toy tugboat (page 135), you may use it for this game.
2. Hide Little Toot somewhere in your house and challenge your child to find him.
3. As your child searches, tell her she's getting hotter as she nears the hidden tugboat and colder as she moves away from it.

Music and Movement
My Tugboat Sails over the Ocean
Sing this song to the tune of "My Bonny Lies over the Ocean."

My tugboat sails over the ocean.
My tugboat sails over the sea.
My tugboat sails over the ocean.
Oh bring back my tugboat to me.
Bring back, bring back, oh bring back my tug-
    boat to me, to me.
Bring back, bring back, oh bring back my tug-
    boat to me.

Play and Learn
Sink or Float
The water in the ocean is salty, whereas the water in rivers and lakes usually isn't. Play this game to see how objects sink or float depending on the saltiness of the water. If your child has sensitive skin or has any cuts or scrapes on her hands, warn her not to touch the saltwater.

2 ice-cream buckets
Water
2 cups salt
Small objects like corks, Ping-Pong balls, sponge scraps, ice cubes, bar soap, toys, and so on

1. Fill both buckets with water.
2. Add all the salt to one bucket and stir it until it dissolves.
3. Place each object in both buckets to see whether it will float in saltwater

and fresh water. Some objects will always float, some will always sink, and some will float only in saltwater.

Enrichment Activities

- Find the locations mentioned in the story, such as Buenos Aires, the South Seas, the Antarctic, and Asia, on a world map.
- Some of the cargo brought into Little Toot's port, such as hides, copra, and whale oil, may seem strange to your child. Discuss what each of these commodities is and try to find out whether it is still used. (Copra is dried coconut meat from which coconut oil is expressed.)
- Discuss the origins of various objects in your house, such as bananas, books, clothing, and so on, that came from distant lands. Ask your child how these items traveled from their countries of origin to yours.
- Ask your child, "What does a tugboat do? Where would you see a real tugboat?" If you live near a seaport, visit it and watch the tugboats work. If you live near a river with barge traffic, visit it and watch the towboats work.
- Read about the further adventures of Little Toot in *Little Toot on the Thames* and *Little Toot on the Grand Canal.*

Madeline

Written and Illustrated
by Ludwig Bemelmans
(Viking, 1939)

Madeline, the fearless little redhead living in a Paris boarding school, has been a favorite character of several generations. In this Caldecott Honor Book, the first of several books about Madeline's adventures, we meet Madeline and the eleven other girls who live in the care of Miss Clavel at a convent school in Paris. One night bold, brave Madeline wakes crying and is rushed to the hospital to have her appendix removed. Bemelmans's illustrations of the streets of Paris and his rhythmic prose make *Madeline* one of my favorite read-aloud books.

As You Read

- Even toddlers will enjoy adding actions as you read about breaking bread, brushing teeth, smiling, frowning, crying, and so on.
- The rhythm of this story makes it easy to memorize. After a few readings, your child may be able to "read" with you or for you as he looks at the pictures.
- After you've read the story once or twice, read it again and talk about the illustrations. If your family has visited Paris, you may recognize some of the street scenes.
- Your child may not understand why Madeline doesn't live with her family. Explain what a boarding school is.

Discuss where Madeline's family might be and possible reasons for the separation.

Let's Talk about It

Ask your child:

- Where does Madeline live? What does she do each day?
- What happens to Madeline one night? What does Miss Clavel do?
- What do you think the little girls expect when they visit Madeline at the hospital? Are they surprised?
- Why do all the girls want to have their appendixes out, too?
- What does Miss Clavel tell the girls? Do you think this is good advice?
- The girls are jealous of the attention Madeline gets. Have you ever felt jealous? What did you do about it?
- What do you like about Madeline? Does she remind you of anyone?

Arts and Crafts

Bouquet of Flowers

Miss Clavel and the girls bring Madeline flowers when they visit her in the hospital. Make this bouquet of flowers for someone who needs cheering up.

Scissors
Empty cardboard egg carton
Paint, markers, or crayons
Green pipe cleaners
Green construction paper
Glue
Bud vase

1. Cut apart the egg carton sections and let your child paint or color them to look like blossoms.
2. Poke a pipe cleaner through the center of each blossom to make a stem.
3. Cut leaves from green construction paper and glue them onto the pipe cleaners.
4. Place your bouquet in a bud vase to display or give away.

Cooking and Baking

Dessert Crepes

Crepes are delicate pancakes served in many Paris restaurants. As a main dish, they're stuffed with meat, vegetables, fish, or cheese. For dessert, they're stuffed with fruit or sweet sauce or sprinkled with sugar.

⅔ cup all-purpose flour
½ teaspoon salt
3 eggs
1½ cups milk
¼ cup melted butter or margarine
Jam, fresh fruit, and/or cream cheese
Whipped cream, sour cream, ice cream, fruit sauce, and/or chocolate sauce

1. In a medium bowl, beat the flour, salt, and eggs until smooth with a wire whisk or hand beater.
2. Gradually beat in the milk and 1½ tablespoons melted butter or

margarine. Cover the batter and refrigerate it for at least 2 hours.

3. Generously brush the bottom and sides of a 7-inch skillet with melted butter or margarine.
4. Over low heat, cook the batter until the top is set and the underside is lightly browned (about 3 minutes).
5. With a metal spatula, flip the crepe and cook the other side until it's golden (about 1 minute).
6. Slip the crepe onto waxed paper.
7. Repeat steps 3–6 to make about a dozen crepes. Stack them with waxed paper between them.
8. If you don't eat the crepes right away, wrap them in foil and refrigerate or freeze them. (Crepes can be frozen for up to two months.)
9. Fill the crepes with jam, fresh fruit, or cream cheese. Roll them or fold them in quarters. Place them in a baking pan and heat them in the oven or broiler.
10. Top the hot crepes with whipped cream, sour cream, ice cream, fruit sauce, or chocolate sauce. Enjoy!

Fun and Games

Balloon Games
One of the gifts Madeline gets is a balloon. As you play the balloon games below, remember that deflated and broken balloons pose a choking hazard for young children, so supervise your child closely.

Balloons	*Glue*
String or ribbon	*Paper plate*
Plastic baseball bat or golf club, empty gift-wrap tube, or rolled newspaper	*Paint stirrer*
	Marker

- **Bat the balloons:** Inflate several balloons. Attach string or ribbon to each, then suspend the bunch of balloons from the ceiling to hang just beyond your child's reach. Let him bat the balloons with a plastic bat or golf club, cardboard tube, or rolled newspaper.
- **Catch the balloon:** Glue a paper plate to the end of a paint stirrer. Inflate a balloon. Toss it in the air and try to catch it—or just bat it around—with the paper plate.
- **Funny face:** Inflate a balloon and draw a face on it with a marker. Squeeze the balloon at various places to distort the face.

Let's Pretend
Hospital

Pillows and blankets
White clothes
Thermometer (or drinking straw)
Bandages
Medicine measuring spoon
Clean cloth diaper or dishtowel

1. Help your child set up a play hospital room or doctor's office with pillows and blankets.

2. Give the person playing the doctor or nurse white clothes to wear.
3. Have the doctor or nurse take temperatures, bandage arms and legs, and give pretend medicine.
4. Make a sling by folding a cloth diaper or dishtowel into a triangle.

Music and Movement

Frère Jacques

If you don't know this French folksong, see *The Reader's Digest Children's Songbook* or look for a children's recording that includes it.

Frère Jacques, Frère Jacques,
Dormez vous, dormez vous?
Sonnez les matines, sonnez les matines,
Din din don, din din don.

Are you sleeping, are you sleeping,
Brother John, Brother John?
Morning bells are ringing, morning bells are ringing,
Ding ding dong, ding ding dong.

Play and Learn

Count the Girls

- Count the "twelve little girls in two straight lines" each time they appear. Note that after Madeline's operation, only eleven girls are shown—with one exception: One picture after Madeline's operation shows twelve girls. Ask your child if he can find it.

- Ask your child, "What if two girls had their appendixes out? How many would be left in the old house? What if three girls had their appendixes out? Now how many would be left?" and so on. If your child can't subtract in his head, he may need to look at a picture of the twelve girls or use a set of girl-shaped cutouts.

Enrichment Activities

- Visit a local hospital with your child.
- Find Paris on a world map. Ask your child, "Could you walk there from where you live? What could you use to get there?"
- Bake frozen croissants.
- Check your library for other books about Madeline, such as *Madeline's Rescue, Madeline and the Bad Hat,* and *Madeline and the Gypsies.*
- Watch *Madeline* on videotape. (See Appendix D for more information.)
- Read other books set in Paris, such as *The Happy Lion* by Louise Fatio and *Mirette on the High Wire* by Emily Arnold McCully.

Millions of Cats

Written and Illustrated
by Wanda Gág
(Coward-McCann, 1928)

In this Newbery Honor Book, black-and-white pictures accompany the story of a lonely old man and woman. When the woman wishes for the company of a cat, the old man sets out to look for one. You and your child will be tickled by the story that unfolds as the old man brings home not one cat, but "hundreds of cats, thousands of cats, millions and billions and trillions of cats."

As You Read

- Your child will enjoy repeating the phrase *hundreds of cats, thousands of cats, millions and billions and trillions of cats* each time it's read.
- Encourage your child to act the part of the old man as he searches for cats: climbing over hills; trudging through valleys; choosing first one cat, then another; and so on.
- Make stick puppets (page 143) and let your child use them to dramatize the story as you read it.

Let's Talk about It

Ask your child:

- Why does the woman want a cat?
- When the man goes looking for a cat, what does he find?
- Why do all the cats follow the man home?
- When the man and woman realize they can't keep all the cats, what do they do? What happens then?

- What do you think the man and woman would do if they looked out their window and all the cats were still there?
- What would you do if you were surrounded by "hundreds of cats, thousands of cats, millions and billions and trillions of cats"?
- What's your favorite part of the story? Why?

Arts and Crafts

Stick Puppets

Your child can use these puppets to dramatize the story on her own or as you read it aloud.

Scissors
Construction paper
Glue
1 Popsicle stick for each puppet
Markers or crayons
Yarn

1. To make the man and woman, cut 2 circles from construction paper and glue each to a Popsicle stick. Draw facial features with markers or crayons and glue on yarn for hair.
2. To make each cat, cut a circle and 2 small triangles from construction paper. Glue the circle to a Popsicle stick. Draw facial features with markers or crayons and glue on the 2 triangles for ears.

Rhymes and Finger Plays

Little Pussycats

One, then two, then three, then four
 (Extend the fingers of your right hand one by one as you say each number.)
Pussycats came to my door,
 (Wiggle your fingers.)
Looked at me and said, "Good day,"
 (Bend all four fingers on *good* and extend them on *day.*)
Then they all tiptoed away.
 (Walk your fingers across your chest and over your left shoulder.)

Fun and Games

Pin the Tail on the Cat

Large sheet of paper or poster board
Crayons or markers
Scissors
Construction paper
Tape
Scarf

1. Draw and color a cat on a large sheet of paper or poster board.
2. Pin or tape the drawing to a wall at your child's level.
3. Cut a cat's tail from construction paper for each player.
4. Fasten a loop of tape (sticky side out) to each tail.
5. Blindfold the players one at a time and challenge them to stick their tails on the cat.

Let's Pretend

Veterinarian

People who have pets often visit veterinarians. If your child doesn't know what a veterinarian does, here's a fun way to learn. Take turns playing the veterinarian and the pet owners. Your child might even enjoy playing a pet!

Stuffed animals
White clothes
Blankets
Thermometer (or drinking straw)
Bandages
Medicine measuring spoon

1. Help your child set up a play veterinarian's office by laying blankets in a corner of a room.
2. Have the veterinarian wear white clothing as a uniform.
3. Use stuffed animals as patients or let your child pretend to be various animals. Have the veterinarian take temperatures, apply bandages, and give medicine.

Play and Learn

Millions of Cats

If you've already made a set of cat shapes to use with the book *Mittens* (page 153), you can also use them for the following activities.

Pencil and white paper
Several sheets of colored paper
Clear contact paper (optional)
Scissors
Goldfish crackers
Small stickers

1. Draw a page of simple cat pictures on white paper.
2. Photocopy the page of cats onto several sheets of colored paper.
3. If you like, cover the colored pages with contact paper. Cut out the cats.
4. Lay out a row of cats and challenge your child to count them.
5. Ask your child to give you a specific number of cats, for example: "Please give me three cats."
6. Ask your child to place the cats in groups of two, three, and so on.
7. Give your child a handful of Goldfish crackers. Pick up a number of cats and ask your child to count out one cracker for each cat.
8. Make a set of cat-shaped counting cards. On one cat write the number 1; on another place one small sticker. Repeat with the numbers 2 through 10 until you have twenty cards. Have your child match each number cat with the corresponding sticker cat.
9. See "Mittens: Play and Learn" (page 153) for ideas on using cat shapes to practice sorting by color.

Snack Time

Cat Face Sandwich

Peanut butter, honey, or cream cheese
Bread
Raisins
Pretzels or carrot, pepper, or pickle
strips

1. Spread peanut butter, honey, or cream cheese on the bread.
2. Pinch the top corners of the bread to form ears.
3. Add three raisins for eyes and a nose.
4. Use pretzels or thin strips of carrot, pepper, or pickle for whiskers.

Enrichment Activities

- Cut cat pictures from old magazines, greeting cards, or calendars. Glue them onto a sheet of poster board or construction paper to create a cat collage.
- Visit a pet store or animal shelter to look at cats and kittens.
- Snack on animal crackers and milk.
- Sing "Old MacDonald Had a Farm."
- Jump, run, stretch, and curl up like a cat while playing follow the leader.
- *Millions of Cats* is a cumulative tale. In cumulative tales, episodes follow each other in a neat, logical pattern. Very young children typically enjoy these simple tales a great deal. Read other cumulative tales, such as *If You Give a Mouse a Cookie* by Laura Joffe Numeroff, *Ask Mr. Bear* by Marjorie Flack, and *The Napping House* by Audrey Wood.
- Read other books about cats, such as *Mittens* by Clare Turlay Newberry and *All the Cats in the World* by Sonia Levitin.

Mirette on the High Wire

Written and Illustrated
by Emily Arnold McCully
(G. P. Putnam's Sons, 1992)

In this Caldecott Medal Book set about one hundred years ago, beautiful paintings and prose tell the story of Mirette, a girl who lives in Paris with her mother and works hard to help her run a boarding house. One day Bellini, a retired high-wire walker, comes to the boarding house seeking rest and solitude. The next day Mirette sees him "crossing the courtyard on air!" Mirette wants to walk the high wire herself and perseveres despite discouragement from Bellini. When he sees her determination, he agrees to teach her what he knows. And as Mirette helps Bellini in his time of need, her dream of walking the high wire comes true.

Let's Talk about It

Ask your child:

- When does this story happen? How long is one hundred years? Do you know anyone who was alive one hundred years ago?
- Where does Mirette live? What is a boarding house? Why is running a boarding house such hard work?
- What happens when Bellini comes to the boarding house?
- How do you know Mirette is determined to walk the high wire?
- What do the words *nerves of an iceberg* mean?
- What are you afraid of? What do you do when you're afraid?
- How does Mirette help Bellini?

Arts and Crafts

Painting

Emily Arnold McCully enjoys learning to paint in new styles. For this book she taught herself to paint pictures like those Mirette might have seen. Let your child experiment with the painting techniques described below.

- **Starch painting:** Mix 1 part liquid detergent with 1 part liquid starch and pour the mixture onto a sheet of paper or plastic. Sprinkle powdered tempera paint over the starch and let your child experiment with mixing colors.
- **Finger painting:** Wet a large sheet of finger painting paper, then drop a blob of finger paint onto it. Let your child spread the paint across the paper, then draw his fingers through it to make interesting designs.
- **Paint blots:** Fold a sheet of paper in half like a greeting card, then open it. With a spoon, drop different colors of liquid tempera paint onto one of the inside halves of the paper. Refold the paper so the paint is on the inside and roll a rolling pin over it. Open the paper, let the paint dry, then cut out the design or display it as is.
- **Dye dipping:** Fold a paper towel into a small shape. Dip each corner into separate bowls of different-colored dyes, which may be either diluted food coloring or strong watercolor paint. Unfold the paper towel and hang it to dry.

Make a Book

As a child, McCully drew pictures for her favorite stories and put them together to create her very own picture books. Encourage your child to do the same.

Paint, crayons, or markers
Several sheets of paper
Stapler

1. Let your child draw a series of pictures on separate sheets of paper.
2. Have your child tell you what's happening in each picture. Write what he says at the bottom of the picture. If your child doesn't want to create his own story, encourage him to illustrate a favorite story instead.
3. Staple the pictures together inside a construction paper cover or follow the directions in Appendix B.

Cooking and Baking

Buttered Leeks

One of the ways Mirette helps her mother is by chopping leeks. If your child has never had leeks, explain that a leek is a vegetable that looks like a big green onion but has a milder taste.

Make this simple dish so your child can taste leeks—or if your child doesn't like cooked vegetables, add leeks to his favorite soup or salad.

6–12 small leeks
1 teaspoon salt

2 tablespoons butter or margarine
Seasoned pepper

1. Cut the leeks into 2-inch pieces.
2. In a medium saucepan over medium heat, in 1 inch water, heat the leeks and salt to boiling. Cover the pan and let the leeks simmer for 10–15 minutes or until fork-tender. Drain the leeks.
3. Stir in the butter or margarine and a dash of seasoned pepper.

Rhymes and Finger Plays

Here's a Little Washboard
Another job of Mirette's may have been doing the wash. Pretend you are Mirette as you do this finger play together.

Here's a little washboard.
    (Hold your hands with palms down and thumbs touching.)
Here's a little tub.
    (Make a circle with your arms.)
Here's a little cake of soap,
    (Make a circle with your hands.)
And here's the way we scrub.
    (Scrub up and down with both hands.)
Here's a line away up high.
    (Hold your hands horizontally, fingertips touching.)
Now the clothes are drying.
    (Turn your hands palms up.)
Hear the wind come whistling by.
    (Wave your arms.)
See? The clothes are flying!
    (Keep waving your arms.)

Let's Pretend
Boarding House
Mirette and her mother ran a boarding house in Paris. Set up an imaginary boarding house in your home and take turns playing the host and the guest.

Paper	*Blankets*
Pencil	*Towels*
Pillow	*Food (real or play)*

1. The host greets the guest as he arrives at the door, tells him what rooms are available, and asks him to fill out a registration card.
2. The host shows the guest to his room, points out the beautiful view, and provides a pillow, extra blanket, and fresh towels.
3. Meals are included at most boarding houses, so the host should tell the guest what time meals are served.
4. If you like, set up a dining room for your play boarding house.

Music and Movement
High-Wire Walking
Set up a pretend high wire in your playroom or back yard. If you like, play some circus music as you practice.

Rope
Wood plank (about 8 inches by 6 feet)
Magazines or books

1. Stretch a length of rope across the floor or ground. Challenge your child to walk the rope with his arms extended for balance.
2. To add some height to your high wire, use a plank instead. Place the plank on top of two stacks of magazines or books.
3. As your child grows more steady, place one end of the plank on a chair to make a ramp. As he grows even bolder, place the plank across two chairs. Remember: The higher your "high wire," the more supervision your child will need.

Enrichment Activities

- Look for simple picture books in French at the library.
- Make French toast for lunch.
- Sing French folksongs, such as "Frère Jacques" and "Alouette." If you don't know these songs, look for them in a children's song book or on a recording of children's music.
- Find some of the locations mentioned in the book: Paris, Moscow, New York, Niagara Falls, the Alps, Barcelona, and Naples. Ask your child to which of these locations he could travel by air, by sea, or by land.
- McCully was inspired to write this story while researching a real-life daredevil named Blondin who lived about one hundred years ago and crossed Niagara Falls on a high wire. Look at photos of Niagara Falls and ask your child if he thinks Blondin's feat was difficult. Discuss the courage it must take to attempt such a feat.
- Read other books set in Paris, such as *Madeline* by Ludwig Bemelmans and *The Happy Lion* by Louise Fatio.
- Read more about the adventures of Mirette and Bellini in *Starring Mirette and Bellini* and *Mirette and Bellini Cross Niagara Falls.*
- Read other books by McCully, such as *The Bobbin Girl* and *The Amazing Felix.*
- Read Meindert DeJong's *Journey from Peppermint Street,* which was illustrated by Emily Arnold McCully and won the National Book Award for children's literature.

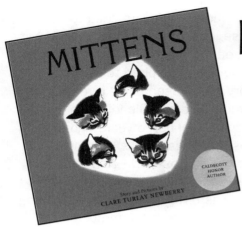

Mittens

Written and Illustrated
by Clare Turlay Newberry
(Harper & Brothers, 1936)

Clare Turlay Newberry wrote and illustrated many charming books about animals, often using her own children and pets as models. All her books have been praised, and four are Caldecott Honor Books. Most were out of print until Smithmark reissued *Mittens, Barkis, Smudge,* and *Herbert the Lion.*

Mittens tells of a tabby kitten with an extra toe on each front paw. He's the adored playmate of a boy named Richard, who is devastated when Mittens disappears. A newspaper ad brings a parade of cats to Richard's doorstep, but none is Mittens. Will Richard and Mittens ever be reunited? The ending will delight children and cat lovers of all ages.

As You Read

- Because *Mittens* has more text than most picture books, a child with a short attention span may get restless waiting to turn the pages.
- Your child will enjoy making the sound effects: "Mew!", "brrrrrrrrrr!", "zzzzzzzzzzzzing!", and so on.

Let's Talk about It

Ask your child:

- Why does Richard name his kitten Mittens?
- When Richard's aunt says kittens are dangerous for children, Richard's mother says children are even more dangerous for kittens. How can kittens

and children be dangerous for each other?

- Many people answer the newspaper ad. Do they all think they've found Mittens, or do some answer for other reasons? What are the other reasons?
- How is Mittens finally found? How do you think Richard feels?
- What's your favorite part of the story? Why?

Arts and Crafts

Clay Cats

4 cups flour
1 cup salt
1 teaspoon powdered alum
1½ cups water
Large bowl
Rolling pin
Cat-shaped cookie cutters, drinking straw, and/or fine wire
Baking sheet
Fine sandpaper
Acrylic paint or markers
Clear acrylic spray or nail polish

1. Preheat your oven to 250°F.
2. Mix the flour, salt, alum, and water in the bowl. If the clay is too dry, knead in 1 more tablespoon water.
3. Roll the clay ⅛ inch thick on a lightly floured surface.
4. Cut the clay with cat-shaped cookie cutters dipped in flour, then make a hole about ¼ inch from the top of each cat with a floured drinking straw. Or if you prefer, mold the clay into cat sculptures no more than ½ inch thick, then insert a loop of fine wire in each cat for hanging.
5. Bake your cats on an ungreased baking sheet for about 30 minutes. Turn the cats and bake them another 90 minutes until they're hard and dry.
6. Let the cats cool, then smooth them with fine sandpaper.
7. Decorate the cats with acrylic paint or markers. Let the cats dry, then seal them with clear acrylic spray or nail polish.

Cooking and Baking

Apple Heart Pizza

If your child ever becomes distressed like Richard, this treat will surely cheer her up! If you like, make the dough ahead of time and store it covered in the refrigerator.

2¼ cups flour
¾ cup butter at room temperature
3 tablespoons plus 1 teaspoon sugar
¼ teaspoon salt
¼ cup cold water
3 medium-size apples
½ teaspoon cinnamon

1. Preheat your oven to 400°F.
2. In a large bowl, mix the flour and butter with your fingers until the flour looks yellowish.

3. Add 3 tablespoons sugar and all the salt, mixing with your hands.
4. Add the water and continue to blend with your hands until the dough forms a ball.
5. Knead the dough on a floured cutting board for 5 minutes. Add more flour if necessary.
6. Shape the dough into a ball. Divide the ball into 4 equal pieces. Roll out each piece to about ¼ inch thick. Sprinkle flour on the dough to keep it from sticking.
7. Shape each piece into a heart. With a spatula, place the hearts on a baking sheet.
8. Core and peel the apples. Quarter each apple, then slice each quarter lengthwise into 6–10 thin slices.
9. Put the slices in a bowl or Ziploc bag with 1 teaspoon sugar and all the cinnamon. Toss or shake the slices until they're evenly coated.
10. Arrange the slices on each heart in a pinwheel or any other design.
11. Bake the pizzas for 15 minutes or until the edges are golden brown. Let them cool before you eat them.

Rhymes and Finger Plays
Kitten Is Hiding

My kitten was hiding under a chair.
   (Hide one thumb under the other hand.)

I looked and looked for her everywhere:
   (Peer about, shading your eyes with one hand.)
Under the table and under the bed.
   (Pretend to look under things.)
I looked in the corner and then I said,
   (Cup your hands to your mouth.)
"Come, kitty, kitty, I have milk for you."
   (Cup your hands to make a bowl.)
Kitty came running and calling, "Mew, mew!"
   (Run your fingers up your arm.)

Fun and Games
Where's Mittens?

1 Mittens (small stuffed cat or cat picture) for each child

1. Have your child leave the room while you hide Mittens.
2. Let your child return and search for Mittens. Give her clues if you like or draw a simple map showing where Mittens is hiding.
3. Sing "Oh Where, Oh Where Has My Little Cat Gone?" while your child searches. (See next activity.)
4. Take turns hiding and searching for Mittens.

Music and Movement
Oh Where, Oh Where Has My Little Cat Gone?
Sing this song to the tune of "Oh Where, Oh Where Has My Little Dog Gone?"

Oh where, oh where has my little cat gone?
Oh where, oh where can he be?
With extra toes, he's got mittens on.
Oh where, oh where can he be?

Play and Learn

Cats to Sort

If you've already made a set of cat shapes to use with the book *Millions of Cats* (page 144), you can also use them for the following activities.

Pencil and white paper
Several sheets of different-colored paper
Clear contact paper (optional)
Scissors
Crayons (optional)
Glue (optional)
Index cards (optional)

1. Draw a page of cat pictures or trace or copy the page labeled "CATS THAT WEREN'T MITTENS."
2. Photocopy the page of pictures onto the sheets of colored paper.
3. If you like, cover the colored pages with contact paper. Cut out the cats.
4. Mix up the cats and challenge your child to sort them by color.
5. Choose two cats of each color and set aside the rest. Mix up the pairs and let your child match them.
6. Choose one cat of each color and set aside the rest. Find crayons in colors that match each cat. Have your child match the cats and crayons by color.
7. Choose two cats of each color and set aside the rest. Glue each cat onto an index card to make a memory game. Place all the cards face-down and take turns trying to find matching pairs.
8. See "Millions of Cats: Play and Learn" (page 144) for ideas on using cat shapes to practice counting.

Enrichment Activities

- Make a puppet by gluing a picture of Mittens to a Popsicle stick.
- Visit a pet store or animal shelter to look at cats and kittens.
- Snack on animal crackers and milk.
- Jump, run, stretch, and curl up like a cat while playing follow the leader.
- Read other books about cats, such as *Millions of Cats* by Wanda Gág and *All the Cats in the World* by Sonia Levitin.
- Read other books by Clare Turlay Newberry, such as *Barkis, Herbert the Lion, Marshmallow,* and *Smudge.*

noisy Nora

Written and Illustrated
by Rosemary Wells
(Dial, 1973)

Rosemary Wells has written and illustrated many beloved picture books. In *Children and Books* (Addison-Wesley, 1997), Zena Sutherland writes, "The stumpy little animal children of her deft drawings appeal both because they capture the essence of children's behavior and because they have marvelously expressive faces."

Your child will easily identify with Noisy Nora, a mouse girl frustrated because her parents are busy with her big sister and little brother. Nora creates disturbances to attract their attention but gets only "Quiet!" and "Hush!" in return. Nora finally leaves, shouting, "I'm never coming back!" The resulting quiet quickly gets her family's attention. You and your child will enjoy their frantic search and Nora's triumphant return.

As You Read

- After several readings, your child will be able to recite the simple dialogue with you.
- Your child may enjoy dramatizing Nora's funny actions as you read.

Let's Talk about It

Ask your child:

- Why is Nora so upset? Have you ever felt overlooked like Nora?
- How does Nora try to get her parents' attention? Does it work?
- How do Nora's parents finally realize something's wrong? What do they do then?
- How do you think Nora feels at the end of the story? Why?

- What's the funniest part of the story? Why?

Act It Out

Noisy Nora

1. If there is only one child, he can play Nora while you read the story aloud. Additional children can play Nora's mother, father, sister, and brother.
2. The dialogue is simple, so let the children say their lines as you narrate the story.
3. If you like, add any appropriate props you have on hand, such as a game, some marbles, baking accessories, a kite, and so on.
4. Practice the play a few times, then perform it for friends and/or family.

Arts and Crafts

Busy Box

Like Nora, most children feel frustrated when their parents are busy and can't attend to them right away. Help your child make a "busy box" he can use whenever he's feeling restless or bored.

Small storage box or plastic crate
Craft supplies your child can use without supervision, such as safety scissors, coloring books, construction paper, cookie cutters, crayons, glue, ink pads, stamps, paper, play dough, stickers, and tape

1. Help your child fill a small storage box or plastic crate with craft supplies. If your child is too young to use craft supplies unsupervised, include sortable items like plastic bottles and lids or stackable items like empty cereal boxes, thread spools, yogurt containers, and individually wrapped rolls of toilet paper.
2. Store your child's busy box in a low kitchen cupboard or any other location he can reach.
3. If you like, vary the busy box contents daily so your child will always find something new to keep him busy and happy.

Cooking and Baking

Apple-Cheddar Muffins

What were Mother and Kate cooking in the kitchen? The illustration shows a muffin pan, and mice love cheese, so maybe they were making these treats! This recipe makes 10–12 muffins.

1 cup all-purpose flour
½ cup whole-wheat flour
1½ teaspoons baking powder
½ teaspoon baking soda
½ teaspoon salt
2 eggs
¼ cup honey or maple syrup
¼ cup oil
½ cup buttermilk or plain yogurt
1 cup (4 ounces) grated cheddar cheese
1 cup peeled, chopped apple

1. Preheat your oven to 400°F and grease a muffin pan.
2. In small bowl, mix the flours, baking powder, baking soda, and salt.
3. In large bowl, mix the eggs, honey or maple syrup, oil, buttermilk or yogurt, cheese, and apple.
4. Add the dry ingredients to the wet ones. Fold the ingredients gently until they're just mixed.
5. Spoon the batter into the muffin pan and bake it for 20 minutes.
6. Remove the muffins from the pan and let them cool on a wire rack.

Rhymes and Finger Plays

I Look in the Mirror

As her story progresses, Nora probably feels a range of emotions—from boredom to frustration to sadness to joy. Say this rhyme about feelings with your child and make an appropriate face to go with each verse. Take turns coming up with new verses and faces. If you like, use a real mirror so your child can see himself.

I look in the mirror
And what do I see?
I see a bored face
Looking at me.

I look in the mirror
And what do I see?
I see a sad face
Looking at me.

I look in the mirror
And what do I see?
I see a happy face
Looking at me.

Fun and Games

Hide-and-Seek

1. Play hide-and-seek with your child.
2. If you like, pretend the hider is Nora and the seekers are Nora's family.

Play and Learn

Marbles

Marbles pose a choking hazard for young children, so carefully supervise this activity—especially if there's a baby or toddler about.

Marbles of varying sizes and colors
Dice
Container

- Sort the marbles by color.
- Sort the marbles by size.
- Count the marbles.
- Sort the marbles into groups of two, three, four, five, and so on.
- Roll a die or pair of dice and count out the corresponding number of marbles.
- Put all the marbles in a container. Pick out a handful of marbles and count them.
- Put all the marbles in a container. Pick out a handful of marbles and line them up in a row. Compare the length of the

row to other objects in your house. Try to find something that is about the same length.

Enrichment Activities

- Ask your child, "Could Nora have found something to do on her own when she was bored?" Together, brainstorm a list of things he can do the next time he feels bored or restless.
- Read a simple nonfiction book about mice to find out where they live, what they eat, and so on. Compare the real mice to the mice in *Noisy Nora.* Ask your child, "How are the mice in *Noisy Nora* different from real mice? How are they the same?"
- Read other books by Rosemary Wells, such as *Stanley and Rhoda, Morris's Disappearing Bag,* and the Max series.

ONE MONDAY MORNING

Text and pictures by Uri Shulevitz

One Monday Morning

Written and Illustrated
by Uri Shulevitz
(Charles Scribner's Sons, 1967)

Uri Shulevitz has written and illustrated many fine picture books for children, including *The Fool of the World and the Flying Ship* by Arthur Ransome, for which he won the Caldecott Medal in 1969.

One Monday Morning tells of a boy living in a dreary New York tenement. One rainy day he invents a world in which "the king, the queen, and the little prince" come to visit him. Finding the boy is out, they promise to return the next day. And they do—with a knight in tow—but again the boy's not home. As each subsequent day passes, the royal entourage returns with another addition and keeps missing the boy...until Sunday comes and they finally meet.

As You Read

- After a few readings, your child may be able to recite the list of visitors with you each time you read it.
- After you've read the story at least once, make a set of stick puppets (page 159) your child can use to dramatize the story as you read it.

Let's Talk about It

Ask your child:

- Could this story really happen? Why or why not?
- The boy uses his imagination to pretend something wonderful is happening on a dull, gray day. What do you do when you're bored or stuck indoors?

- The boy imagines that the royal visitors come while he's out riding the bus, doing laundry, grocery shopping, and so on. Have you ever done any of the things that the boy is doing?
- What's your favorite part of the story? Why?
- Would you like to read other books by this author? Why or why not?

Arts and Crafts

Royal Crowns

Tape or stapler
2 sheets of heavy paper
Scissors
Crayons, markers, or paint
Glue
Ribbons, feathers, glitter, stickers, fake gems, and so on

1. Tape or staple the 2 sheets of paper together (short end to short end) to make 1 long piece.
2. Cut a zigzag pattern (or if you like, any crown pattern shown in *One Monday Morning*) along 1 long side of the paper.
3. Let your child color her crown with crayons, markers, or paint and decorate it by gluing on ribbons, feathers, glitter, stickers, fake gems, and so on.
4. Wrap the crown around your child's head, determine the best fit, trim it if necessary, and staple the ends together.

5. Encourage your child to wear her royal crown when she plays dress-up.

Stick Puppets

Make ten stick puppets to represent the boy and all his royal visitors: the king, queen, prince, knight, guard, cook, barber, jester, and dog. If you like, take your time with this activity and spread the fun over several days!

Pencil and white paper
Crayons or markers
Glue
Heavy paper
Scissors
Glitter, fabric, aluminum foil, feather, pompoms, and/or felt (optional)
10 Popsicle sticks

1. With a pencil and white paper, trace a picture of each character from the book.
2. Let your child color the pictures.
3. Glue each sheet of pictures to a sheet of heavy paper. When the glue is dry, cut out the pictures.
4. If you like, let your child glue textured materials to the pictures. For example, she might use glitter on the crowns, fabric on the clothes, aluminum foil on the knight's armor, a feather on the guard's cap, pompoms on the cook's and jester's outfits, and felt on the dog's fur.
5. Glue a Popsicle stick to the bottom of each picture.

6. Use the stick puppets to dramatize *One Monday Morning* or make up your own story.

Fun and Games

Playing Cards
Did you notice the playing-card look of the royal entourage? Use a deck of cards to play simple games with your child or to reinforce basic math skills like sorting and number recognition.

Deck of playing cards

- Place one red card and one black card faceup on the table. Give your child the remaining cards and challenge her to sort them by color.
- Place all four aces faceup on the table. Give your child the remaining cards and challenge her to sort them by suit.
- Place all the cards of one suit faceup on the table in random order. Help your child arrange them in numerical order. Then give her the remaining cards and challenge her to sort them by number.
- Play simple card games like war, go fish, and snap. If you don't recall how to play these games or want to learn others, look for a book on card games at your local bookstore or library.

Let's Pretend

Royal Dress-Up
If you don't already have a collection of dress-up clothes, now's a good time to start one. See "Getting Started: Let's Pretend" (page 16) for more information.

Dress-up clothes
Royal crown (page 159)

1. Dress up as royalty using whatever clothes you have on hand. Or if you like, visit a thrift store and buy some brightly colored, silky, or otherwise fancy items to add to your collection.
2. Act out *One Monday Morning* or your own made-up story about royalty.
3. Appoint your child "Queen or King for the Day (or Hour)."

Play and Learn

Calendar Math
The king, queen, and little prince first visit on Monday, then return every day until Sunday. Use this story as a springboard for learning about calendars. Reading the calendar each day will help your child learn the names and order of the days of the week.

Calendar
Stickers or markers

1. Read the calendar with your child every day. Say the day, the date, the month, and the year. For example, you might say, "Today is Wednesday. That means yesterday was Tuesday, and tomorrow will be Thursday. Today is the fifteenth of April. That means yesterday was the fourteenth, and tomorrow will be the sixteenth."

2. Let your child place a sticker on or cross off each day after your calendar reading session.

Snack Time

Royal Tea Party

Dress up as royalty (page 160), then serve yourselves a fancy tea.

Fancy tablecloth and napkins
Tea service (real or toy)
Candle, flowers, or other centerpiece
Cookies, sandwich fingers, or other
  treats
Decaffeinated or herbal tea
Milk and sugar

1. Set your table so that it's fit for a king (or queen). Use your best linen and china. (If you're worried about breakage, use a toy tea service.) Add a candle, flowers, or whatever centerpiece you like.
2. Serve treats like fancy cookies or sandwich fingers (crustless sandwiches cut into strips) and tea. For safety's sake, let your child's tea cool and/or dilute it with cold milk before serving it.
3. Nibble, sip, and enjoy each other's company.

Enrichment Activities

- Sing or say the rhyme "Old King Cole" with your child.
- Take a bus ride with your child. As you ride, imagine who might be visiting your house while you're out.
- Leaf through a book with photos of real royalty. Your child may be surprised to learn that they don't walk around all day in their crowns and robes.
- Read *May I Bring a Friend?* by Beatrice Schenk de Regniers. This 1965 Caldecott Medal Book tells of a boy who's invited to tea with the king and queen.
- Read other books by Uri Shulevitz, such as *Dawn* and *Rain Rain Rivers.*

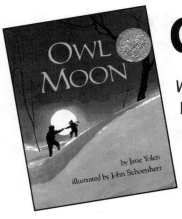

Owl Moon

Written by Jane Yolen
Illustrated by John Schoenherr
(Philomel, 1987)

Jane Yolen is a prolific writer who has won many awards for her work. *Owl Moon* won the 1988 Caldecott Medal for its beautiful illustrations by John Schoenherr.

Owl Moon is the story of a girl out with her father for her first owling adventure. It's a very special night, and as you read Yolen's crisp prose, you'll think you're right there crunching through the snow, feeling the cold air, seeing the shining moon, hearing the soft owl cries, and staring into the owl's golden eyes for "one minute, three minutes, maybe even a hundred minutes."

This book made me cry the first time I read it. The images and feelings it evokes have made it one of my favorite picture books—and one I enjoy even more each time I read it.

As You Read

- Your child may enjoy dramatizing the actions and sound effects—the train whistle's blowing, the dogs' answering, the feet's crunching in the snow, the owl's calling, and so on—as you read the story.

Let's Talk about It

Ask your child:

- Why do you think the girl and her dad go owling at night?
- Do you think the girl is excited about going owling? Why?
- Why do people have to be so quiet when they go owling?
- Why do you think the girl never complains, even when she's cold and tired?

- Do you think the girl really stares at the owl for a hundred minutes?
- Have you ever looked forward to doing a special thing? Or is there any special thing you're looking forward to doing? Why is this thing so special?

Arts and Crafts

Ice Crystal Picture

Spoon
¼ cup hot water
4 tablespoons Epsom salts, table salt, or rock salt
Small bowl
Crayons
Black, purple, or blue construction paper
Paintbrush
Clear contact paper (optional)

1. With a spoon, mix the hot water and salt in a small bowl until the salt dissolves.
2. Use crayons to draw a nighttime forest scene on dark construction paper. Include trees, stars, the moon, and an owl if you like.
3. Brush the drawing with the salt solution. Stir the salt water each time you dip the brush in it to keep it saturated with saltwater and to keep the solution well mixed.
4. Let the painting dry completely. The salt will give a snowy, crystalline effect.
5. The salt crystals will brush off the picture when it's dry, so cover it with clear contact paper if you like.

Rhymes and Finger Plays

Mr. Owl

Mr. Owl sits high in a tree.
    (Bend your arms and hold them close to your body like wings.)
He blinks and blinks his eyes.
    (Blink your eyes.)
He sees and hears most everything;
    (Form eyeglasses with your hands, then cup your hands behind your ears.)
That's why he is so wise.
    (Tap your temple with your index finger.)

Music and Movement

Wise Old Owl

Sing this familiar rhyme to the tune of "This Old Man."

A wise old owl sat in an oak.
    (Bend your arms and hold them close to your body like wings.)
The more he heard, the less he spoke.
    (Cup your hand behind your ear, then hold your index finger to your lips.)
The less he spoke, the more he heard.
    (Hold your index finger to your lips, then cup your hand behind your ear.)
Why aren't we all like that wise old bird?
    (Hold your hands out, palms up, and shrug your shoulders.)

Out and About

Play in the Snow

If you live in an area with cold winters, bundle up and head outdoors for some fun in the snow!

- Run, jump, skip, and dance in the snow.
- Take a walk around your snow-covered neighborhood.
- Build a snow sculpture.
- Make snow angels by lying flat on your back and sweeping your arms and legs back and forth across the snow several times. Get up carefully to avoid ruining your snow angel.
- Have a snowball fight.
- Find a hill with a gentle slope and go sledding.
- Grab a flashlight and take a nighttime walk in the snow.
- Go owling!

Play and Learn

Snowball Counting

Permanent marker
Clear plastic drinking cups
White cotton balls or pompoms
Small box or empty diaper wipe container

1. With a permanent marker, draw 1 dot on the side of a clear plastic cup. Draw 2 dots on another cup, 3 dots on another cup, and so on. Mark as many cups as is appropriate for your child's counting ability.
2. Give your child the "snowballs" (cotton balls or pompoms) and challenge him to drop them into the cups in amounts that correspond with the number of dots on each cup.
3. Store the cups and snowballs in a small box or empty diaper wipe container.

Snack Time

Snow Picnic

Warm clothes
Old blanket
Cookies
Thermos of hot chocolate

1. Dress warmly.
2. Go outside and spread an old blanket on the snow.
3. Eat cookies and sip hot chocolate from a Thermos.
4. If you'd rather snack indoors, spread a blanket on the floor in front of your fireplace or picture window.

Enrichment Activities

- The girl's shadow is much shorter than her father's. Compare shadows with your child. Trace around each other's shadows in the snow or with chalk.

- Read or watch a simple nonfiction book or videotape on owls. Look for information on the great horned owl.
- In *Owl Moon* Yolen uses a literary device called personification (giving human characteristics to things or animals) when she says that trees stand as still as statues and trains and dogs sing out. As you walk or drive with your child, describe the things you see using personification. For example, you might say that flowers are waving cheerfully in the breeze, that the wind is laughing, that raindrops are dancing, and so on.
- Read other books about owls, such as *Owl Babies* by Martin Waddell, *The Owl-Scatterer* by Howard Norman, and *The Man Who Could Call Down Owls* by Eve Bunting.
- Read other winter books, such as *The Snowman* by Raymond Briggs, *The Snowy Day* by Ezra Jack Keats, and *White Snow, Bright Snow* by Alvin Tresselt.
- Read other books by Jane Yolen, such as *The Emperor and the Kite, Sleeping Ugly,* and *Briar Rose.*

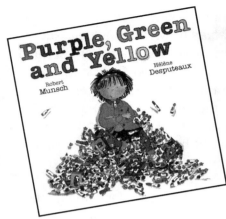

Purple, Green and Yellow

Written by Robert Munsch
Illustrated by Hélène Desputeaux
(Annick, 1992)

Unlike most of the other authors mentioned in *Picture Book Activities*, Robert Munsch hasn't won any major awards. I've included one of his titles because despite his lack of awards, he's one of North America's best-known and most dearly loved storytellers. His stories are crazy, hilarious, and improbable—and kids love them!

Munsch is at his best telling tall tales to young children. In this setting his stories take on lives of their own. *Purple, Green and Yellow*, for example, began at the 1990 Toronto Storytelling Festival when Munsch noticed a girl named Brigid coloring her fingernails with markers. Brigid's adventure with her "super-indelible-never-come-off-till-you're-dead-and-maybe-even-later coloring markers" is sure to delight both you and your child.

As You Read

- Even during your first reading, your child will catch on to Brigid's mother's *Nnnnooos*. After a few readings, she'll be able to recite much of the dialogue with you.
- Your child will enjoy trying to repeat the phrase *super-indelible-never-come-off-till-you're-dead-and-maybe-even-later coloring markers.*

Let's Talk about It

Ask your child:

- How does Brigid get into trouble? Have you ever done anything an adult told you not to do? What happened?
- What happens when Brigid tries to hide her mistake? Have you ever tried

to hide a mistake? Did that make it better or worse? Why?

- Do you think this story could really happen? Why or why not?
- What's your favorite part of the story?
- Would you like to read more books by this author?

Arts and Crafts

Make a Book

Purple, Green and Yellow is a tall tale because of its blatant exaggeration. Help your child write and illustrate her own tall tale.

Several sheets of white paper
Crayons, colored pencils, or markers
Construction paper
Stapler

1. Have your child continue where Munsch leaves off, describing new silly situations Brigid finds herself in. Or if you prefer, help your child make up an original tall tale. Write 1 or 2 lines of your child's tale on each page.
2. Let your child illustrate her tale with crayons, colored pencils, or markers.
3. Staple the pages together inside a construction paper cover or follow the directions in Appendix B.

Marker Play

Most children would rather draw with markers than with anything else. Here are a few suggestions to help your child get the most out of her markers.

Markers	*Coffee filter or paper towel*
Paper	*Paintbrush or sponge*
Water	*Plaster of Paris*
	Small plastic container

- Encourage your child to draw yellow lemons, red roses, and orange oranges like Brigid's.
- Show your child how to dip dried-up markers in water and use them like watercolors. When the tips turn white, throw them away or use them as paintbrushes.
- Let your child draw with markers on a coffee filter or paper towel. The absorbent paper will blur the colors prettily.
- Draw with a thick black marker on a paper towel. Brush water over the picture with a paintbrush or sponge, then watch the colors seep.
- Paint a sheet of paper with water using a paintbrush or sponge. Let your child draw with washable markers on the wet paper and watch the colors run and blend.
- Make a marker holder by mixing plaster of Paris in a small plastic container that's at least as deep as a marker cap. Set the caps in the wet plaster

with the open ends up. Keep the plaster clear of the open ends. When the plaster is dry, press the markers into their tops, which are now imbedded in the plaster.

Cooking and Baking

Painted Cookies

You can bake and glaze these sturdy cookies ahead of time, then paint them with food coloring on a rainy day.

2 cups softened butter or margarine
2 cups granulated sugar
2 teaspoons vanilla
5 cups flour
5–9 teaspoons warm water
6 cups powdered sugar
Food coloring

1. Preheat your oven to 300°F.
2. Beat the butter or margarine, granulated sugar, and vanilla.
3. Add the flour and mix the dough until it's thoroughly blended.
4. Roll out the dough to a thickness of ¼–⅜ inch. Cut out cookies with a floured knife or cookie cutter.
5. Bake the cookies on an ungreased baking sheet for 25–30 minutes or until they are a pale golden color. Let them cool for about 7 minutes, then transfer them to a sheet of aluminum foil.
6. To make the glaze, gradually stir the warm water into the powdered sugar until the glaze is smooth and thick. Glaze the cookies and let them dry thoroughly (8–24 hours) before covering or moving them.
7. If you'll be painting the cookies later, store them at room temperature for up to 4 days. Freeze them for longer storage and thaw them before painting.
8. Paint the cookies with a clean paintbrush and small cups of undiluted food coloring for bright colors or slightly diluted food coloring for lighter colors. Food coloring will run, so let each color dry briefly before adding the next.

Music and Movement

I Like Markers

Sing this song to the tune of "Frère Jacques." For a large group of children, hand out markers and have each child hold up her marker when its color is mentioned. For a smaller group or a single child, give each child several markers and have her hold up each marker when its color is mentioned.

I like markers, I like markers,
How about you? How about you?
Pink and green and yellow,
Red and brown and orange,
Black and blue, purple, too!

Out and About

I Spy

Play this game in your yard, at the park, or as you take a walk together.

1. Tell your child, "I spy, with my little eye, something that is blue."
2. Let your child look around, then count from ten to zero while she runs to touch something that sports the color you've named.
3. Take turns spying and running.

Play and Learn

Color Hunt

1 hat for each player
Paper or plastic bags

1. Don your hunting hats and choose a color to hunt for. If your child is very young, pick up an object of that color, name the color, then put it in a bag. Do this several times until you're sure your child understands.
2. Hunt around your home or yard for objects that match your chosen color. You can either hunt together or race to see who can collect the most objects within a certain time.
3. When your hunt is done, empty your bag(s) and name the items you've collected, for example: blue ball, blue book, blue shoe, and so on.

4. If you like, hunt for colors (without collecting them) at the grocery store or when you're riding in a car or bus.

Enrichment Activities

- Teach your older preschooler how to play simple games like tick-tack-toe with a marker and paper.
- Take turns pretending to be invisible. You might, for example, pretend you can't find your child even when she's right under your nose. Be sure your child understands that you're just pretending. Note that a very young child won't be able to do this activity and that a child may prefer to pretend she has an invisible friend rather than be "invisible" herself.
- Read other books by Robert Munsch. Our favorites are *David's Father, Thomas' Snowsuit, I Have to Go!,* and my personal favorite, *Pigs.*
- Read other books about colors, such as Eric Carle's *My Very First Book of Colors,* Tana Hoban's *Colors Everywhere,* and John J. Reiss's *Colors.*

The Rag Coat

Written and Illustrated
by Lauren Mills
(Little, Brown and Company, 1991)

The Rag Coat tells of Minna, a young girl growing up in Appalachia. Her family is so poor that Papa carries her to church in a burlap feed sack because she doesn't have a coat. Minna yearns to start school, but when Papa gets sick with the miner's cough, she stays home to help Mama, who "stitches day and night on her quilts to try to make some money."

Minna's parents have almost nothing material to give their children, but they and the people in their community pass on priceless lessons on selflessness, resourcefulness, and the value of people. This story will probably make you laugh and cry, and ultimately it will charm you with its message of love and friendship.

Let's Talk about It

Ask your child:

- At first Minna doesn't mind not having a coat. Why?
- Minna's Papa says, "People only need people, and nothing else." What does that mean?
- Why do people wear black when someone dies? Why can't Minna stand everyone's wearing black when her father dies?
- Why does Minna line her coat with the sack her Papa used to carry her in? Why does she add a piece of his work jacket to her coat?
- Minna is sure that if robbers come to her door, the first thing they'll want is

her coat. What makes the coat so valuable to Minna?

- Has anyone ever made fun of you? How did it feel? Have you ever made fun of someone?
- Minna deals with her schoolmates' teasing by remembering that "people only need people." What does she do that helps the children see her and her coat in a new light?
- What do you like most about Minna?

Arts and Crafts

Rag Coat Collage

Pencil or marker   Fabric scraps
Heavy paper   Glue
Scissors

1. Draw an outline of a coat on a sheet of heavy paper.
2. Cut fabric scraps into small pieces.
3. Glue the fabric pieces onto the coat.
4. As you work, talk about where each piece comes from, what the fabric was originally used for, and so on.

Cooking and Baking

Alabama Sour-Milk Biscuits

The Appalachian coal mining region includes part of Alabama. You can make this simple recipe from Alabama using ingredients you probably have on hand.

2 cups sifted all-purpose flour
1 teaspoon baking powder
½ teaspoon baking soda
1 teaspoon salt
¼ cup softened butter or margarine
1 cup thick sour milk or buttermilk

1. Preheat your oven to 450°F.
2. Sift the dry ingredients into a bowl.
3. Cut in the butter or margarine with a pastry blender.
4. Add the sour milk or buttermilk while mixing with a fork to make a soft dough.
5. Turn the dough onto a floured cutting board and knead it about 20 times.
6. Roll the dough to ½ inch thick. Cut out 12–14 biscuits with a floured 2-inch round cookie cutter.
7. Bake the biscuits for 10–12 minutes.

Rhymes and Finger Plays

How to Make a Happy Day

This rhyme reminds us that we can find happiness in what we do for others. As you recite the words, make up actions to match them.

Two eyes to see nice things to do;
Two lips to smile the whole day through;
Two ears to hear what others say;
Two hands to put my toys away;
A tongue to speak sweet words each day;
A loving heart for work and play;
Two feet that errands gladly run
Make happy days for everyone.

Fun and Games

Jump Rope

Jump rope

1. Jump rope with your preschooler. It may be difficult for him, but he'll have fun trying.
2. Your child may also enjoy jumping without the rope, watching you jump, or learning a few traditional jump rope rhymes.
3. If you need to brush up on your rhymes, see *Anna Banana* by Joanna Cole. Here are a few rhymes to get you started:

Postman, postman, do your duty.
Send this letter to an American beauty.
Don't you stop and don't delay.
Get it to her right away.

Not last night but the night before,
Twenty-four robbers came knocking at
  my door.
As I ran out, they ran in.
I hit them on the head with a rolling pin.

Cinderella, dressed in yellow,
Went downstairs to kiss her fellow.
How many kisses did she give?
One, two, three, four, five...

Music and Movement

Clementine

This favorite folksong goes well with *The Rag Coat* because Minna has a father who's a miner and a sister named Clemmie. If you don't know the melody, you'll find it in most children's song books and recordings.

In a cavern, in a canyon,
Excavating for a mine,
Dwelt a miner, forty-niner,
And his daughter, Clementine.

Chorus:
Oh, my darling, oh, my darling,
Oh, my darling Clementine,
You are lost and gone forever,
Dreadful sorry, Clementine.

Light she was and like a fairy,
And her shoes were number nine,
Herring boxes without topses
Sandals were for Clementine.

Drove she ducklings to the water
Ev'ry morning just at nine,
Hit her foot against a splinter,
Fell into the foaming brine.

Ruby lips above the water,
Blowing bubbles soft and fine,
But, alas, I was no swimmer,
So I lost my Clementine.

Play and Learn

Sewing Practice

This fun activity is great for developing hand-eye coordination.

Scissors
Cardboard
Glue and fabric (optional)

Large nail
Shoelace (or yarn and tape)

1. Cut a shape from the cardboard. If you like, glue fabric onto the shape.
2. With a large nail, punch holes at regular intervals around the edge of the shape.
3. Tie a knot in one end of a shoelace or piece of yarn. If you're using yarn, wrap the unknotted end with tape.
4. Show your child how to "sew" by weaving the unknotted end of the shoelace or yarn through the holes.

Enrichment Activities

- Quilts are beautiful works of art. Look at a real quilt or a picture book about quilts. We've enjoyed *Selina and the Bear Paw Quilt* by Barbara Smucker and *The Josefina Story Quilt* by Eleanor Coerr.
- The Quilting Mothers make a pattern called Joseph's Coat of Many Colors. Read the story of Joseph and his brothers in the Bible (Gen. 37) or in one of many picture books on the topic.

- Find the Appalachian Mountains on a map. Notice how they stretch from Alabama to Newfoundland.
- Find a book with pictures of Appalachia —especially of mines, miners, quilts, and schools.
- Watch the movie *Christy,* which tells of a young woman struggling to teach the children of a poor mountain community in Cutter's Gap, Tennessee, in 1912. *Christy* is based on Catherine Marshall's book by the same name, which in turn is based on her mother's life.
- Minna and her family are very poor and are forced to rely on their community for something as basic as a coat for Minna. Talk with your child about ways you can share what you have with those in need. For example, you might take good clothing to a relief agency, donate food to the local food bank, give up a pizza-and-movie night and contribute the savings to a worthy cause.

The Runaway Bunny

Written by Margaret Wise Brown
Illustrated by Clement Hurd
(Harper & Row, 1942)

Margaret Wise Brown has written many books for children; *Goodnight Moon* is probably her most well-known title. If you've read that book, you may recognize Clement Hurd's illustration style in *The Runaway Bunny.*

The Runaway Bunny tells of a little bunny who wants to run away and tells his mother so. His mother replies that if he runs away, she will run after him, for "you are my little bunny." The bunny then imagines that he will turn into a fish to get away from his mother, but she will become a fisherman and fish for him. If the bunny turns into a rock on a mountain, his mother will become a mountain climber and climb to where he is. The little bunny's imaginings continue until he finally concludes, "I might just as well stay where I am and be your little bunny."

Your child will appreciate this story's sweet illustrations and its heartwarming message that there's no escaping a mother's love.

As You Read

- Your child may enjoy pretending to be the various characters and objects imagined by the little bunny and his mother: a fish, a fisherman, a rock, a mountain climber, a flower, a gardener, and so on.

Let's Talk about It

Ask your child:

- Why does the little bunny's mother say she will run after him?
- Have you ever wanted to run away? Why or why not?

- In the end, the little bunny decides to stay where he is. Why do you think he decides this? Do you think this is the right decision? Why or why not?
- What's your favorite part of the story? Why?
- Would you like to read more books by this author? Why or why not?

Arts and Crafts

Bunny Ears

This is a quick, clean, cute craft suitable even for a toddler.

Scissors
White and pink construction paper
Glue
Stapler

1. Cut 2 bunny ears from the white paper. Cut 2 slightly smaller ears from the pink paper.
2. Glue 1 pink ear onto the center of each white ear.
3. Glue the bottoms of the ears about 6 inches apart onto a long strip of paper.
4. Wrap the paper strip around your child's head, and when you've found the proper fit, staple the ends together to form a headband.
5. If you like, make another set of ears for yourself. You can both wear your ears while you read *The Runaway Bunny* together.

Cooking and Baking

Carrot-Spice Muffins

2 eggs
⅔ cup brown sugar
½ cup oil
¼ cup milk
1 teaspoon vanilla
1½ cups finely grated carrot
1½ cups all-purpose flour
1½ teaspoons baking powder
½ teaspoon baking soda
½ teaspoon salt
½ teaspoon cinnamon
¼ teaspoon nutmeg
½ cup walnuts, chopped
½ cup raisins

1. Preheat your oven to 400°F.
2. In a large bowl, thoroughly mix the eggs, brown sugar, oil, milk, vanilla, and carrot.
3. In a smaller bowl, mix the flour, baking powder, baking soda, salt, cinnamon, nutmeg, walnuts, and raisins.
4. Combine the wet and dry mixtures and fold them together gently until they're just mixed.
5. Spoon the batter into a greased muffin pan and bake the muffins for 20–25 minutes.
6. Remove the muffins from the pan and let them cool on a wire rack.

Rhymes and Finger Plays

The Rabbits

A family of rabbits lived under a tree—
    (Hide your right hand under your left arm.)
A father, a mother, and babies three.
    (Hold up your thumb, then each finger in order.)
Sometimes the bunnies would sleep all day,
    (Make a fist.)
But when night came, they liked to play.
    (Wiggle your fingers.)
Out of the hole they'd creep, creep, creep
    (Make a creeping motion with your fingers.)
While the birds in the trees were all asleep,
    (Hold your palms together and rest your head on your hands.)
The bunnies would scamper about and run
    (Wiggle your fingers.)
Uphill! Downhill! Oh, what fun!
    (Raise and lower your hand while continuing to wiggle your fingers.)
But when the mother said, "It's time to rest,"
    (Shake your index finger as if you're scolding.)
Pop! They would hurry right back to their nest!
    (Clap your hands, then hide your right hand under your left arm.)

Fun and Games

Bunny Fishing

Your child will have as much fun fishing for bunnies as the little bunny's mother would have if she were to fish for him!

Scissors
Construction paper
Glue or tape
Metal paper clips
Stick
String
Magnet

1. Cut several bunnies from the construction paper.
2. Glue or tape a metal paper clip to the back of each bunny.
3. Make a fishing pole by tying a length of string to the end of a stick.
4. Tie a magnet to the other end of the string.
5. Place the paper bunnies on the floor and let your child dangle her line over the back of a couch or chair.
6. If you like, use this game to help your child develop basic learning skills. Draw a shape or write a letter or number on each bunny and challenge your child to identify the shape, letter, or number when it's caught.

Out and About

Visual Scavenger Hunt

Take a walk with your child and try to observe things mentioned in the story. Here's a list to get you started:

garden	rabbit
gardener	fish
bird	stream
tree	fisherman
sailboat	rock
boy	mountain
mother	crocus or other
house	small flower
carrot	wind

Snack Time

Bunny Food and More

- Snack on "rabbit food"—carrot sticks, lettuce, and water.
- The little bunny imagined joining a circus. Snack on popcorn, a traditional circus food.
- Eat Goldfish crackers.
- If the runaway bunny were a bird, he might eat worms and seeds. Snack on candy worms and sunflower seeds.

Enrichment Activities

- Read a simple nonfiction book about rabbits. Find out where they live, what they eat, and so on.
- Play hide-and-seek.
- Take a short hike and pretend to be mountain climbers.
- Plant crocus bulbs that will bloom in the spring.
- Ask your child where she'd run if she ran away, then tell her how you'd find her.
- Read *I Promise I'll Find You* by Heather Patricia Ward.
- Read other bunny stories, such as Beatrix Potter's *The Tale of Peter Rabbit* or Clare Turlay Newberry's *Marshmallow.*
- Read other books by Margaret Wise Brown, such as *Goodnight Moon* and *Home for a Bunny.*

The Snowman

Written and Illustrated
by Raymond Briggs
(Random House, 1978)

Raymond Briggs has illustrated many successful children's books. He has won the Kate Greenaway Medal twice: for *The Mother Goose Treasury* in 1966 and again in 1973 for *Father Christmas*.

The Snowman is a wordless book. It relies entirely on illustrations to tell the story of a boy's wonderful winter adventure with a snowman who has magically sprung to life. The pictures are warm despite the chilly subject, and your child will enjoy "reading" this book both with you and on his own.

Although wordless books don't actually involve reading, they do accustom children to sequential action and the left-to-right pattern of reading. More importantly, they encourage a positive attitude toward reading. Wordless books allow prereaders to "read" by themselves. Wordless books may also be the only books an illiterate or semiliterate adult can read to a child. And the story of a wordless book is easy to retell because there's no need to remember exact text.

As You Read

- As you leaf through this book, let your child do some or all of the story-telling.
- If you like, cover up some of the pictures and ask your child what will happen next. For instance, you might ask, "What do you think will happen when the snowman turns the stove on? What do you think will happen when the snowman sees the freezer?"

- Notice the expressions on the snow-man's face as he discovers the fire-place, an electric light, a skateboard, and the freezer.

Let's Talk about It

Ask your child:

- Can you tell the story of *The Snowman* in your own words?
- How do you think the little boy feels at the end of the story?
- What's your favorite part of the story? Why?
- Which picture do you like the most? What do you like about it?
- Do you think this story could really happen? Why or why not?

Act It Out

The Snowman

The snowman has fun discovering interesting things inside the boy's house. Acting out this aspect of the story is easy and fun! It's also funny and easy to improvise for friends or other family members.

Light switch, water faucet, radio, and other common household items

1. Pretend that one of you is a snowman who has never been inside a house before. The other can play the boy. If you're playing with more than one child, the additional people can play other residents of the house that the snowman visits.
2. Give the snowman a tour of your house. As the snowman puzzles over some of the household items, explain how they work.
3. Add humor to your drama. For instance, what happens when the snowman discovers shaving cream or diapers?
4. Take turns playing the different characters.

Arts and Crafts

Cotton Ball Snowman

Scissors
Clear contact paper
Stapler
Construction paper
Cotton balls

1. Cut 3 circles from clear contact paper. The circles should have 3 different diameters ranging from 1½ inches to 5 inches.
2. Staple the circles (adhesive side up) to the construction paper to form a snowman shape.
3. Peel the contact paper to expose the adhesive. Stick cotton balls to the contact paper to cover the snowman.
4. If you like, cut additional snowman features, like a hat and a carrot, from construction paper and glue them onto the cottony snowman.

Cooking and Baking

Crispy Rice Snowman

¼ cup margarine or butter
4 cups miniature marshmallows or 40
  regular marshmallows
5 cups crispy rice cereal
Shredded coconut
Toothpicks
Candy decorations

1. Melt the margarine or butter in a large saucepan.
2. Add the marshmallows and stir the mixture constantly over low heat until it's syrupy.
3. Remove the saucepan from the stove. Add the cereal and stir until it's well coated.
4. Butter your hands and use them to shape the sticky cereal into small, medium, and large balls. Roll the balls in shredded coconut to make them look snowy.
5. Join the balls with toothpicks to make miniature snowmen. Decorate your snowmen with candies.

Rhymes and Finger Plays

Snow

Snow is on the housetop.
    (Join your fingertips to make a peak.)
Snow is on the ground.
    (Spread your hands flat, palms down.)
Snow falls from the heavens.
    (Flutter your fingers downward.)
Snow is all around.
    (Make a sweeping gesture with both hands, palms up.)

Music and Movement

It Is Snowing

Sing this song to the tune of "Frère Jacques." If you don't know the tune, look for it in a children's song book or on a recording of children's music.

It is snowing, it is snowing
    (Flutter your fingers downward.)
All around, all around.
    (Make a sweeping gesture with both hands, palms up.)
Soft and silent snowflakes, soft and silent snowflakes—
    (Sing very softly while fluttering your fingers downward again.)
Not a sound, not a sound.
    (Shake your head while holding your index finger to your lips.)

Out and About

Snow Painting

You'll have the prettiest yard in the neighborhood after doing this activity!

Spray bottle
Water
Food coloring

1. Fill a spray bottle with water and add a few drops of food coloring.

2. Dress your child warmly and take him outside to paint the snow with his spray bottle.
3. Your child may also enjoy using brushes to paint the snow.

Enrichment Activities

- If you live in an area with cold winters and conditions are right, head outdoors and build a snowman with your child.
- Glue wintry magazine pictures to a sheet of construction paper to make a winter collage. Cover the collage with clear contact paper to make a place mat.

- Help your child create his own wordless book.
- Read other books about winter and snow, such as *The Snowy Day* by Ezra Jack Keats, *Owl Moon* by Jane Yolen, and *Our Snowman* by M. B. Goffstein.
- Read other wordless books, such as *Frog Goes to Dinner* by Mercer Mayer (one of a series about a boy and his frog), *Pancakes for Breakfast* by Tomie dePaola, and *Sunshine* and *Moonlight* by Jan Ormerod.
- Read other books illustrated by Raymond Briggs, such as *Jim and the Beanstalk, Father Christmas,* and *The Elephant and the Bad Baby* (written by Elfrida Vipont).

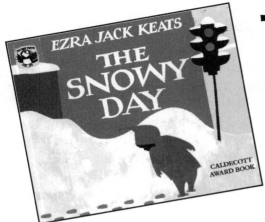

The Snowy Day

Written and Illustrated
by Ezra Jack Keats
(Viking, 1962)

The Snowy Day is the first book Ezra Jack Keats wrote and illustrated, and it won the Caldecott Medal in 1963. It tells a very simple story about a boy named Peter and the adventures he has on a snowy day. Reading the book, one can almost feel the cold as Peter walks through the snow, makes snow angels, and so on.

Like many other books by Keats, *The Snowy Day* is one that very young children will easily relate to. And adults reading it to their children will no doubt remember from their own childhoods the special joy of outdoor play on a snowy day.

Let's Talk about It

Ask your child:

- How do you think Peter feels when he wakes up and sees that it has snowed during the night? Has this ever happened to you?
- What does Peter do in the snow? What do you (or would you) like to do in the snow?
- Do you think Peter lives in the city or the country? Why?
- What happens to the snowball Peter puts in his pocket? How does that make him feel?
- What is Peter's dream? How do you think he feels when he wakes up and finds he's only been dreaming?

- At the end of the book, Peter and his friend go out into the snow together. What do you think happens then?

Arts and Crafts

Snow Paint

This recipe makes a thick paint that your child will have a ball using!

Electric mixer, eggbeater, or wire whisk
1 cup soap flakes
½ cup cold water
Popsicle stick or paintbrush
Heavy paper or cardboard

1. Beat or whisk the soap and cold water together until the mixture is stiff.
2. Let your child spread the paint on heavy paper or cardboard using a Popsicle stick, a paintbrush, or her fingers.
3. Lay your child's painting flat to dry.

Rhymes and Finger Plays

Snowflakes

Softly, softly, falling so...
This is how the snowflakes go.
Falling, falling from the sky,
Quiet as a lullaby.
Soft and silent on the ground,
Snowflakes do not make a sound.

Let's Pretend

Winter Clothing Store

Table or desk
Winter clothing and accessories
Bags from your recycling bin
Play money
Play purse or wallet (optional)
Small box (optional)

1. Set up a pretend clothing store at a large table or desk using winter clothes from your closets. Grab a few bags from your recycling bin to use as shopping bags.
2. Provide the shopper with play money. You can use store-bought play money, cut your own from paper, or use different-colored lids from plastic milk and juice jugs.
3. If you like, provide a play purse or wallet and a small "cash box" to hold the play money.
4. Take turns playing the clerk and the customer. If you want to reinforce math skills while you play, require the customer to ask for items by color and quantity: for example, "I would like two blue mittens, please." If you like, have the customer say why she wants each item. The customer should take care to pay the right amount of money, and the clerk should be sure to count the money.
5. You can also use this game to reinforce good manners by requiring (and

if necessary, modeling) courteous dialogue between the clerk and the customer.

Out and About

Walk in the Snow

If you live in an area with cold winters, bundle up in your warmest clothing and head outside for some fun in the snow!

- Take a walk in your neighborhood. Run, jump, skip, and dance as you walk along. Make tracks like Peter does. Drag a stick or a tree branch behind you and see what happens to the snow.
- Build a snow sculpture.
- Make snow angels by lying flat on your back and sweeping your arms and legs back and forth across the snow several times. Get up carefully to avoid ruining your snow angel.
- Have a snowball fight.
- Find a hill with a gentle slope and go sledding.

Play and Learn

Warm and Cold

The following activities will help your child explore the concepts of warm and cold.

- Place some play dough in your freezer to cool it. Warm another lump of play dough in a microwave oven. Let your child play with both the warm and the cold play dough to see how different they feel. Ask her, "Which play dough do you like better?"
- Place an ice cube on a tray along with several other objects. Blindfold your child or have her close her eyes and challenge her to pick out the cold object.
- Put an ice cube or two in each of three Ziploc bags. Place the bags in locations with varying temperatures. For example, you might place one bag outside, one on your kitchen counter, and one in a pan of warm water. Ask your child, "Which ice will melt first? Why?" Watch the ice to see if her predictions are correct.
- Place three bowls of water on the table. Put ice water in the first bowl, cool water in the second, and room-temperature water in the third. Have your child dip her hand in each bowl and tell which is cold, which is colder, and which is coldest. Do a similar activity with warm water.
- Put some crushed ice into a plastic dishpan or large plastic bowl. Your child will have fun using bath toys (cups, spoons, bowls, and so on) to play with the ice. If you're freezing and crushing the ice yourself (rather than buying it), add a few drops of food coloring to the water before freezing it.

Snack Time

Apple Snow

*4 tart apples, peeled, cored, and
  quartered*
Powdered sugar
3 egg whites, stiffly beaten

1. Put the apple wedges in a double
boiler and heat them over boiling
water until they're soft.
2. Mash the apple wedges and add powdered sugar to taste.
3. Fold the egg whites into the apple
mixture. Serve with custard sauce.
(See below.)

Custard Sauce

1½ cups whole milk
⅓ cup sugar
6 large egg yolks
Pinch of salt

1. In a 3-quart heavy saucepan, bring
the milk just to a boil. Remove it from
the heat.
2. Whisk together the yolks, sugar, and
salt in a bowl, then slowly add hot
milk while still whisking.
3. Pour the custard into the saucepan
and cook it over medium-low heat,
stirring constantly, until it's slightly
thickened and registers 170°F on a
candy thermometer.
4. Pour the custard through a fine sieve
into a pitcher and serve warm.

Enrichment Activities

- Glue wintry magazine pictures to a
sheet of construction paper to make
a winter collage. Cover the collage
with clear contact paper to make a
place mat.
- Help your child write and illustrate her
own book about a snowy day.
- Take a nighttime walk in the snow.
Notice how the snow muffles sounds
and makes everything seem clean and
bright.
- Make snow cones by pouring fruit
juice concentrate over crushed ice.
- Keats's illustration style resembles
those of Leo Lionni *(Frederick)* and
Eric Carle *(A House for Hermit Crab)*.
Look at books by these three illustrators and compare their illustrations.
- Read other books about snow, such
as *The Snowman* by Raymond Briggs,
Owl Moon by Jane Yolen, and *Katy and
the Big Snow* by Virginia Lee Burton.
- Read other books by Ezra Jack Keats,
such as *Goggles!* (a 1970 Caldecott
Honor Book), *Peter's Chair,* and
Whistle for Willie.

The Story about Ping

Written by Marjorie Flack
Illustrated by Kurt Wiese
(Viking, 1933)

Marjorie Flack has written many books about animals, but *The Story about Ping* is one of the best loved. Ping is a little yellow duck who lives with "his mother and his father and two sisters and three brothers and eleven aunts and seven uncles and forty-two cousins" on a boat on the Yangzte River. Ping and his family spend their days hunting for food on the river. They return to their boat quickly when their master calls, as the last duck home always gets a spank on the back. One evening Ping doesn't hear his master's call and decides to hide rather than return last to the boat. Your child is sure to enjoy what happens next as Ping learns that facing the consequence of a mistake is better than trying to avoid it.

Let's Talk about It

Ask your child:

- Where do Ping and his family live? What would it be like if you lived with not only your own family, but also all your aunts, uncles, and cousins?
- Why doesn't Ping want to be the last duck on the boat? What happens when he decides not to return to the boat?
- Why is the little boy who catches Ping tied to his boat? What's the barrel for?
- How does Ping escape? What does he do then?
- How do you think Ping feels as he gets a spank on the back for being the last duck on the boat?
- Have you ever tried to hide something you did because you were afraid of

what would happen because of it? What happened?

Arts and Crafts

Fuzzy Ping Picture

Pencil, pen, crayons, or markers
Paper
Glue
Googly eyes (optional)
Scissors
Yellow yarn
Heavy paper or cardboard (optional)
Popsicle stick (optional)

1. Trace or draw a picture of Ping on a sheet of paper.
2. Color in Ping's feet, beak, and eyes. Glue on googly eyes if you like.
3. Snip the yarn into tiny pieces to make yellow fuzz.
4. Spread glue on the parts of your Ping picture you want fuzzy.
5. Sprinkle yellow fuzz on your picture and press it lightly with your finger to make it stick.
6. If you'd like to make a Ping stick puppet, glue your picture onto heavy paper or cardboard, cut out Ping, and glue him to a Popsicle stick.

Rhymes and Finger Plays

Five Little Ducklings

Begin this rhyme by holding up one finger. Lift another finger each time another duckling is mentioned. At the end, spread your hands wide to show the ducklings growing into fine big ducks.

One little duckling, yellow and new,
Had a fuzzy brother, and that made two.
Two little ducklings now you can see;
They had a little sister, and that made three.
Three little ducklings sitting by the door—
In came a friend, and that made four.
Four little ducklings went to swim and dive;
They met a little neighbor, and that made five.
Five little ducklings—watch them grow!
They'll turn into fine big ducks, you know!

Let's Pretend

Houseboat

Sheet or blanket
Stuffed animals
Goldfish crackers

1. Spread a sheet or blanket on the floor to serve as your boat.
2. Use dolls or stuffed animals to represent the many members of your extended family.
3. Fish for Goldfish crackers, then snack on them.
4. With your child, pretend that you live on a boat on the Yangtze River. Be creative as you imagine what living on a boat might be like. Ask your child, "Would you like to live on a boat? What would be good and bad about living on a boat?"

Play and Learn

Ping's Family

Ping lives with "his mother and his father and two sisters and three brothers and eleven aunts and seven uncles and forty-two cousins." To count the total number of ducks that live on the boat, try the first two activities. To count the total number of people in your own extended family, try the last activity.

- Use objects like pennies, raisins, or LEGOs to represent Ping and his family.
- Draw a picture of Ping and his family, then count the ducks.
- Draw a picture of each member of your extended family, including your child and his parents, siblings, aunts, uncles, and cousins. You could also look at family photos. Help your child count the total number of people pictured.

Music and Movement

Five Little Ducks

If you don't know the tune of this song, look for it in a children's song book or recording. Begin singing by holding up one hand with all five fingers extended. Bend a finger down each time a duck disappears.

Five little ducks went out one day,
Over the hill and far away.
Mother duck said, "Quack, quack, quack, quack."
But only four little ducks came back.

Four little ducks went out one day,
Over the hill and far away.
Mother duck said, "Quack, quack, quack, quack."
But only three little ducks came back.

(Sing three more verses, ending the last one with the words *But none of her little ducks came back.*)

Sad mother duck went out one day,
Over the hill and far away.
Mother duck said, "Quack, quack, quack, quack."
And all her five little ducks came back.

Snack Time

Rice, Tea, and More

- Ping snacks on fish and snails. You and your child can snack on Goldfish crackers and milk.
- The little boy on the fishing boat is eating a rice cake, which Ping snatches out of his hand. Snack on rice cakes with your child.
- Have a snack of plain rice and tea, two things commonly served with Chinese meals.

Enrichment Activities

- As the sun rises in the east, Ping and his family march off the boat. Notice where the sun rises relative to your house.
- Read or watch a simple nonfiction book or videotape about ducks. Take a walk in an area where you might see a family of ducks.

- The fishing birds in the story are called cormorants. Try to find a picture and some information about cormorants.
- Locate China on a world map, then locate the Yangtze River. Read a simple nonfiction book about China. If possible, find a book with pictures of the Yangzte River or traditional Chinese houseboats. Try to identify clothing, food, or other items in your home that may have come from China. If possible, visit a Chinatown or Chinese restaurant or bakery near your home.
- Read other books set in China, such as *Tikki Tikki Tembo* by Arlene Mosel and *Shen of the Sea* by Arthur Bowie Chrisman.
- Read other books by Marjorie Flack, such as *Ask Mr. Bear, Walter the Lazy Mouse,* and the Angus series.

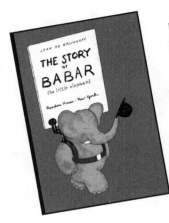

The Story of Babar

Written and Illustrated
by Jean de Brunhoff
(Random House, 1933)

Babar the elephant has been loved by generations of children around the world. Originally written in French, *The Story of Babar* is the first of many simple books about the adventures of Babar and his family. De Brunhoff's illustrations have a childlike quality not often seen in early picture books.

In this book, little Babar runs away from the forest to live in the city after hunters kill his mother. He becomes very cultured in the city, but he misses his life in the forest and decides to return there. Upon his return he is crowned King of the Elephants because "he has learned so much." He marries Celeste, and the book ends as the King and Queen set out on their honeymoon in a "gorgeous yellow balloon."

As You Read

- Challenge your child to find Babar on pages 4 and 5.
- Ask your child to guess what spats are.
- On page 28, point out the marabou, a stork that lives in Africa, to your child.
- Challenge your child to guess what a dromedary is by looking at the pictures on pages 41 and 42.

Let's Talk about It

Ask your child:

- What happens to Babar's mother? Why does Babar run away?
- What happens to Babar when he reaches the city?

- Is Babar happy living in the city? Why or why not? Why does he return to the forest?
- Why do the elephants choose Babar to be their king? Do you think this is a good idea?
- Do you think Babar and Celeste will be a good King and Queen? Why?
- What do you think happens after King Babar and Queen Celeste set out on their honeymoon?

Arts and Crafts

Babar's Photograph

Encourage your child to paint or color Babar the way the photographer might have seen him.

Pencil
White paper
Paints or markers
Yellow construction paper or poster board
Glue

1. Draw a picture of Babar. If you like, copy the illustration on page 17 or draw Babar in another pose.
2. Let your child paint or color Babar. If she's using paints, start with black, white, yellow, red, and blue. Show her how to mix black and white to make gray and how to mix yellow and blue to make green. Let her experiment with other combinations and see what colors she can create.

3. Glue Babar's "photo" onto yellow construction paper or poster board and display it prominently.

Cooking and Baking

Banana Bread

At the beginning of the book, elephants are shown eating bananas. They'd surely love this banana bread, too!

½ cup cooking oil
1 cup sugar
2 eggs, beaten
3 ripe bananas, mashed
2 cups all-purpose flour
1 teaspoon baking soda
½ teaspoon baking powder
½ teaspoon salt
3 tablespoons milk
½ teaspoon vanilla extract
½ cup chopped nuts (optional)

1. Preheat your oven to 350°F. Grease a 9-by-5-by-3-inch loaf pan.
2. Beat the oil and sugar together.
3. Beat in the eggs and bananas.
4. Sift the baking soda, baking powder, and salt into the batter, then mix in the milk and vanilla.
5. If you like, mix in the nuts.
6. Pour the batter into the greased pan and bake it for about 1 hour.
7. Let the bread cool completely before you slice it.

Let's Pretend
Department Store

Clothing, shoes, and hats
Bags from your recycling bin
Play money
Play purse or wallet (optional)
Small box (optional)

1. Set up a pretend children's, ladies', or men's department in your living room. Display clothing, shoes, and hats in separate areas. Attach a price tag to each item. Grab a few bags from your recycling bin to use as shopping bags.
2. Assemble play money in 50-cent denominations. You can use store-bought play money, cut your own from paper, or use different-colored lids from plastic milk and juice jugs.
3. If you like, provide a play purse or wallet and a small "cash box" to hold the play money.
4. Take turns playing the clerk and the customer. If you want to reinforce math skills while you play, require the customer to ask for items by color and quantity: for example, "I would like two red hats and one green jacket, please." The customer should take care to pay the right amount of money, and the clerk should be sure to count the money.
5. You can also use this game to reinforce good manners by requiring (and if necessary, modeling) courteous dialogue between the clerk and the customer.
6. Designate a corner of the room as a photo studio. Have your child dress up in the clothes she's "bought," then take her photo.

Music and Movement
Carnival of the Animals

In his symphony *Carnival of the Animals*, Camille Saint-Saëns interprets the movements of animals like the lion, elephant, tortoise, and kangaroo.

1. Buy or borrow a recording of *Carnival of the Animals*. Listen to the track called "The Elephant."
2. As you listen, walk like an elephant. Bend at the waist, clasp your hands, swing your arms like a trunk, and walk with a slow, lumbering gait.
3. Challenge your child to listen to more tracks, guess what animals the music represents, and imitate their movements.

Out and About
Pastry Shop

When Arthur and Celeste visit Babar, he takes them to a pastry shop. Do the same with your child!

- Visit a pastry shop together. Have fun looking at all the pretty baked goods. If the shop has an eating area, buy a treat and enjoy it with a cup of tea or a glass of juice.

- If visiting a pastry shop isn't possible, set up your own pastry shop at home. Bake banana bread (page 191) and cupcakes or other treats, then let your child go "shopping." Cover a table with a tablecloth and serve the "pastry" on fancy plates with tea or juice.

Play and Learn

Counting

The Story of Babar is rich with objects to count: trees, flowers, elephants, birds, monkeys, bananas, and so on. After you've read the book once, reread it and count some of the objects you see. To make the flash cards mentioned below, see "Getting Started: Play and Learn" (page 18).

Number flash cards (optional)
Object flash cards (optional)

- As you look at each page, say, "Let's count the _____ in this picture. How many _____ do you see?" Point to each object as you count it: "One, two. There are two elephants in this picture." You might then say, "What else do you see in this picture?" and go on to count other objects.
- If you like, use number flash cards as you count. When your child counts two objects, ask her to find the card with the number two on it.

- If your child is not yet able to recognize numbers, use object flash cards. When your child counts two objects, ask her, "Can you find the card that has two stickers on it?" To help her learn to associate numbers with groups of objects, show her the card with the number two on it and explain that the number two means "two things."

Enrichment Activities

- Locate Africa on a map or globe.
- Read or watch a simple nonfiction book or videotape about elephants. Find out how they live, what they eat, and why they're hunted.
- Look for information on the marabou.
- Listen to a Babar audiotape with your child.
- Watch a Babar videotape with your child. (See Appendix D for more information.)
- Read other books about Babar, such as *Babar the King, Babar and His Children,* and *Babar and Father Christmas.*
- Read other books about elephants, such as *The Elephant and the Bad Baby* by Elfrida Vipont and *Five Minutes' Peace* by Jill Murphy.

The Story of Ferdinand

Written by Munro Leaf
Illustrated by Robert Lawson
(Viking, 1936)

I loved the story of Ferdinand, the gentle bull, when I was a child. And as an adult I delighted in introducing its hero to my own children. Ferdinand is not afraid to be different. While the other bulls, hoping to be picked for the bullfights in Madrid, snort and stomp about, Ferdinand takes life easy, sits quietly under a cork tree, and smells flowers. Imagine what happens on the day of the fight, when Ferdinand is accidentally mistaken for "the biggest, fastest, roughest bull" of the bunch!

Lawson's illustrations perfectly complement Leaf's humor. Both poke gentle fun at the pomp of the bullfight. This is a book you'll be comfortable reading to your child regardless of whether you approve of bullfighting.

Let's Talk about It

Ask your child:

- How is Ferdinand different from the other bulls? Does he mind being different?
- What do you like about Ferdinand's mother?
- Why do you think the bulls want to be picked to fight in Madrid?
- What happens on the day the men come to choose a bull?
- What happens when Ferdinand enters the ring? Why are the bullfighters so mad?
- Many people think bullfighting is wrong. Why do you think this is? Would you like to see a bullfight? Why or why not?
- What's your favorite part of the story?

Arts and Crafts

Brushed Flower Picture

Scissors   Facial tissue
Heavy paper   Nontoxic hair spray
Construction paper
Colored chalk or pastels

1. Cut several blossom shapes (at least 3 inches wide) from heavy paper. If you like, copy blossom shapes from the book.
2. Place one of the blossom shapes on the construction paper. Hold the shape with 1 hand and with the other, trace the shape with a piece of chalk or a pastel.
3. Continue holding the shape and gently brush the chalk away from it with a tissue. Remove the shape.
4. Continue tracing and brushing flowers of different colors until your picture is complete.
5. Spray the picture with nontoxic hair spray to fix the chalk and give the picture a flowery scent.

Cooking and Baking

Churros

Churros are a traditional Spanish deep-fried confection. Hot oil is quite hazardous for young children, so insist on frying these churros yourself while your child is occupied elsewhere. (For safety's sake, use a sealed deep fryer if possible.) He'll enjoy helping roll the cooked churros in sugar.

1 cup water
½ cup margarine or butter
¼ teaspoon salt
1 cup flour
3 eggs, beaten
¼ cup sugar
¼ teaspoon ground cinnamon

1. Heat the water, margarine or butter, and salt to a rolling boil in a 3-quart saucepan. Stir in the flour.
2. Stir the mixture vigorously over low heat until it forms a ball (about 1 minute). Remove it from the heat.
3. Stir in the eggs.
4. Spoon the batter into a cake decorating tube with a large star tip.
5. Heat 1–1½ inches of vegetable oil to 360°F in a sealed deep fryer or deep pan.
6. Squeeze a few 4-inch strips of dough into the oil. Fry them until they're golden brown (about 2 minutes on each side).
7. Drain the churros on a paper towel.
8. Mix the sugar and cinnamon on a plate and roll the churros in them.

Rhymes and Finger Plays
Little Bull

This little bull eats grass.
    (Point to your thumb.)
This little bull eats hay.
    (Point to your index finger.)
This little bull drinks water.
    (Point to your middle finger.)
This little bull runs away.
    (Point to your ring finger.)
And this little bull does nothing at all but smell the flowers all day!
    (Point to your pinky finger.)

Fun and Games
Cork Race
Play this game in honor of Ferdinand's favorite cork tree.

1 9-by-13-inch baking pan per player
Water
1 cork per player
1 drinking straw per player

1. Fill each pan with water. Place the pans on a table or on the floor.
2. Place a cork in the water at the edge of each pan.
3. Give each player a straw to place in his mouth. Have the players place the ends of their straws near their corks.
4. At the word "Go!" each player tries to blow his cork from one side of his pan to the other.
5. The player whose cork reaches the other side of his pan first wins.

Music and Movement
Spanish Dancing

Recording of Spanish music
3- or 4-foot lengths of brightly colored ribbon
Plastic shower curtain ring or empty key chain
Chiffon scarf

1. Listen to Spanish music with your child and encourage him to physically express how it makes him feel. For example, he might run during fast music, tiptoe during soft music, hop and bounce during lively music, and so on.
2. Tie ribbons to a plastic shower curtain ring or empty key chain. Your child can wave the ribbons in the air or twirl them in time to the music as he dances.
3. Give your child a chiffon scarf to use as a dancing accessory. If the scarf is too long, tie a knot in the middle to make a handle.

Out and About
Visit the Country

- If you live in the city, try to plan a day trip to the country. As you leave the city behind, notice the changes: Big roads lead to small roads, crowded neighborhoods give way to open spaces, the air becomes fresher, and your surroundings grow quieter. If you're still in the country at night and the sky is clear, look at the sky and notice how much darker it is and how many stars you can see.

- Stop at a field where cows are grazing. Ask your child, "What's the difference between a cow and a bull?" Explain the difference if necessary. You needn't get technical; comparing cows and bulls to mommies and daddies should do. Find out if the cows you see belong to a dairy farm or a cattle ranch. Explain the difference to your child. Ask him, "Why wouldn't you see a bull on a dairy farm?"
- If you can, arrange to visit a dairy farm or cattle ranch.
- Stop at a country bakery or general store for a snack.

Enrichment Activities

- Find Spain on a map. Find its capital, Madrid, where the bullfight takes place.
- Learn to say a few words in Spanish, such as *hola* (hello), *adiós* (good-bye), *por favor* (please), *gracias* (thank you), *madre* (mother), *padre* (father), *bebé* (baby), *amigo/amiga* (friend).
- Find out a little about the custom of bullfighting: How and when did it start? In what countries was bullfighting popular? Is it still a form of entertainment today? The story mentions banderilleros, picadores, and a matador. What's the difference?
- Look at the illustration of the cork tree. Do you think this is the way cork really grows? Find a photo of a real cork tree and compare it to the illustration. Where in the world does cork grow?
- Christopher Columbus sailed from Spain to North America in 1492. Look for a simple nonfiction book that provides a balanced discussion of Columbus and his explorations.
- Read other books about characters who like to "do their own things," such as *Ira Sleeps Over* by Bernard Waber and *William's Doll* by Charlotte Zolotow.

Sylvester and the Magic Pebble

Written and Illustrated
by William Steig
(Simon and Schuster, 1969)

This picture book won the Caldecott Medal in 1970. It's a delightful tale about a donkey named Sylvester who discovers a magic pebble one day. Anything Sylvester wishes for will come true if he wishes while holding the pebble. Excited by the possibilities, Sylvester heads home, only to come face to face with a hungry lion. Flustered and panicked, Sylvester wishes he were a rock—and instantly turns into one.

While Sylvester is a rock, his parents search everywhere for him. Their sadness grows as time passes and Sylvester still doesn't return home. When the family is reunited in the end, Sylvester learns that he has had everything he wants all along.

Let's Talk about It

Ask your child:

- What does Sylvester find that makes him so excited?
- How does Sylvester end up being a rock?
- How do Sylvester's parents feel when he doesn't come home?
- How does Sylvester finally turn into a donkey again?
- What lesson do you think Sylvester learns while he's a rock?
- What are some good things about finding a magic pebble? What are some bad things? What would you wish for if you found a magic pebble?
- Could this story really happen? Why or why not?

Arts and Crafts
Seasons Book or Poster

Scissors
Gray construction paper
Glue
4 sheets of plain paper or 1 large sheet
  of poster board
Paint, crayons, or markers
Stapler

1. Cut 4 rocks from gray construction paper.
2. Glue each rock onto a sheet of plain paper. Or divide a sheet of poster board into quarters and glue each rock to 1 of the sections.
3. At the bottom of each page, write the name of a season.
4. Have your child use paint, crayons, or markers to illustrate each season. For example, in *Sylvester and the Magic Pebble,* leaves and flowers surround Sylvester in the spring. In the fall, the leaves change color and fall to the ground. In the winter, snow covers everything, and a wolf sits on Sylvester and howls.
5. Staple the pages together and add a colorful construction paper cover or follow the directions in Appendix B. Or, if you like, display your child's work on a wall or bulletin board.

Fun and Games
Pebble Hunt

Red spray paint
1 rock per child
Small treat

1. Spray-paint each rock and let it dry.
2. Choose an area of your house or yard in which to play. Have your child(ren) leave the area while you hide the rock(s).
3. Have your child(ren) search for the rock(s). Provide clues if you like.
4. As each rock is found, provide a small treat as a reward.
5. An older child may enjoy using a simple map to find her rock.

Let's Pretend
Magic Pebble

Magic pebble (rock spray-painted red)
Other props as needed

1. Take a walk with your child and pretend to find a magic pebble.
2. Together, imagine and dramatize what happens next. Use whatever props you have on hand: dress-up clothes, play money and jewelry, and so on.
3. Take turns being the one to find the magic pebble.

Out and About

Rock Fun

Take a walk with your child and collect interesting rocks. Back at home, wash the rocks in the sink or with a garden hose. If very young children are around, discard rocks small enough to pose choking hazards. Then use your rocks to do the activities listed below.

Bucket with handle
Rocks
Paint
Glue gun
Clear acrylic spray
Spray paint
Colander

- Challenge your child to sort the rocks by size or color.
- If you like, paint the rocks and glue them together to create a sculpture. If you like, finish the sculpture with clear acrylic spray.
- Spray-paint the rocks with bright colors. When the paint is dry, hide the rocks in your child's sandbox. She'll have fun sifting through the sand with a colander to find the rocks.
- Use the rocks to make a sorting game. (See "Play and Learn.")

Play and Learn

Sorting Game

48 rocks
4 empty egg cartons
Spray paint in 4 different colors

1. Spray-paint a dozen rocks each a different color and let them dry.
2. Spray-paint each egg carton a different color and let the cartons dry.
3. Give your child the rocks and egg cartons. Challenge her to sort the rocks by placing each in the egg carton of the same color.

Snack Time

Picnic

Sylvester was saved from his life as a rock when his parents decided to have a picnic one fine spring day. You and your child can brighten any day by having a picnic together!

Tablecloth or old sheet or blanket
Picnic tableware
Picnic food
Summer clothing and sunglasses

1. If the weather is fine, have a picnic lunch with your child in your yard or at a park.
2. If the weather is bad, perk up your day with an indoor picnic. Spread a tablecloth or old sheet or blanket on your living room floor. Use picnic

tableware to eat picnic food. Wear summer clothing and sunglasses.

Enrichment Activities

- Collecting pebbles is Sylvester's hobby. Ask your child, "Do you know what a hobby is? What other things do people do for hobbies? Do you have a hobby?"
- Collecting things is a popular hobby. Ask your child, "Do you have a collection? What might you like to collect?" If she doesn't have a collection already, help her start one.

- Talk about the seasonal changes Sylvester sees: leaves changing color, snow on the ground, budding trees, and so on. Ask your child, "What signs of the season can you see around you now?" Read a simple non-fiction book about the seasons.
- Read other books about being content with who we are or what we have, such as *The Whingdingdilly* by Bill Peet and *Fish Is Fish* by Leo Lionni.
- Read other books by William Steig, such as *Spinky Sulks, Doctor De Soto,* and *Brave Irene.*

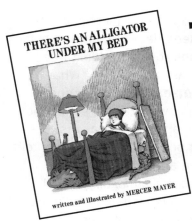

THERE'S AN ALLIGATOR UNDER MY BED

written and illustrated by MERCER MAYER

There's an Alligator under My Bed

Written and Illustrated
by Mercer Mayer
(Dial, 1987)

Mercer Mayer has written and illustrated many children's books that range from wordless books to complex fairy tales. *There's an Alligator under My Bed* is a sequel to *There's a Nightmare in My Closet*. Both books take a humorous look at common nighttime fears of young children.

There's an Alligator under My Bed tells of a boy who has an alligator living under his bed. The boy knows the alligator is there even though it does a good job of hiding whenever his parents come into his room. He devises a plan to lure the alligator out from under his bed and into the garage where it belongs. You and your child will delight in the clever words and pictures, and you're sure to find that, as the book jacket states,

"Peeking under the bed will never be the same."

Let's Talk about It

Ask your child:

- Why does the boy have to be so careful getting in and out of his bed?
- Is there really an alligator under his bed? How do you know?
- How does the boy get the alligator out from under his bed?
- Where does the alligator go? What do you think happens next?
- Do you think this story could really happen? Why or why not?
- Have you ever thought something was hiding under your bed? What did you do?

- What would you do if you found an alligator under your bed?

Arts and Crafts

Stuffed Alligator

2 large sheets of paper (each about 1 square yard)
Tape or stapler
Markers, crayons, paint, and/or paintbrushes
Scissors
Newspaper, tissue paper, or other scrap paper
Hole punch and yarn (optional)

1. Lay 1 large sheet of paper on top of the other and tape or staple the edges together.
2. Draw a big alligator outline on one side of the paper. (The illustration of the boy following the alligator down the hall is a good one to copy.)
3. Cut along the outline to make 2 alligator cutouts.
4. Tape or staple the edges of the cutouts together. Leave an opening along 1 edge.
5. Let your child color or paint both sides of the alligator, adding details like eyes, a mouth, scales, and so on.
6. Stuff the alligator with crumpled newspaper, tissue paper, or scrap paper. Staple the opening shut.

7. If you like, punch a hole in the top of the alligator and hang it from the ceiling with yarn.

Cooking and Baking

Alligator Bait Cookies

These double chocolate fudge cookies are not only delicious, they're very easy to make.

1 package chocolate fudge cake mix
1 large egg
3 tablespoons water
5 tablespoons vegetable oil
1½ cups chocolate chips
1½ cups chopped walnuts and/or walnut halves (optional)

1. Preheat your oven to 350°F.
2. Mix the cake mix, egg, water, and oil in a bowl.
3. Mix in the chocolate chips (and walnuts, if you like).
4. Drop the batter by rounded teaspoonfuls or tablespoonfuls onto a greased baking sheet. If you like, press a walnut half into the top of each cookie.
5. Bake small cookies for 10–12 minutes or large ones for 15–20 minutes.
6. Remove the cookies from the oven. They'll be soft at first, so let them cool on the baking sheet for 10–20 minutes, then use a spatula to transfer them to a wire rack.

Rhymes and Finger Plays

There Was a Little Alligator

There was a little alligator
Underneath my bed.
Sometimes I'd see his tail and
Sometimes I'd see his head.

He had a big, long body
Scaly and green,
And teeth as sharp as nails.
He was mean, mean, mean!

He snapped at a sandwich.
He snapped at some tea.
He snapped at a piece of pie.
He snapped at me.

He crunched up the sandwich.
He crunched up the tea.
He crunched up the pie, but
He didn't crunch me!

Fun and Games

Balancing Board

The boy in the book uses a board as a
ramp to get in and out of bed. Your child
will enjoy pretending there's an alligator
under his bed as you play this game.

Board about 8 inches wide by 6 feet
  long
Magazines or books

1. Place the board across two piles of
   magazines or books. Challenge your
   child to walk across the board with
   his arms extended for balance.

2. As your child grows more steady, place
   one end of the plank on his bed to
   make a ramp. Challenge him to walk
   up and down the ramp. Remember
   that the higher you place the board,
   the more supervision your child
   will need.

Let's Pretend

Dangerous Waters

Turn your living room into alligator-infested
waters. All you need are some cushions
and a vivid imagination.

Couch with removable cushions
Old sheets and towels (optional)

1. Place the cushions around your living
   room. They should be far enough
   apart so that your child must jump
   from one to another.
2. Pretend that the couch and cushions
   are islands and that the floor is
   alligator-infested water.
3. Challenge your child to jump from
   island to island without landing in the
   water. If he falls in, fight off the alligators and rescue him before he gets
   eaten!
4. If you like, play this game outside
   using old sheets and towels instead
   of cushions.

Play and Learn

Green, Green, Green

- Go on a color hunt with your child. How many green things can you spot?
- Draw a picture using crayons in various shades of green.
- Cut green pictures from magazines or catalogs. Glue the pictures onto sheets of paper, then staple the pages together. Add a green construction paper cover to make a Green Book.
- Sort DUPLO or LEGO blocks into two piles: green and not green.
- Have a Green Day in your home: Wear green clothes; play with green play dough; drink green juice (white grape juice and food coloring); eat green vegetables; snack on crackers spread with green-tinted cream cheese or honey.

Enrichment Activities

- When it's bedtime or nap time, check for alligators under your child's bed.
- Challenge your child to write and illustrate a new ending for the book. You might ask him, "What happens the next day when the boy's father goes to the garage?" or "What if the alligator hadn't followed the trail of food down the hall?"
- Pretend a dangerous animal is living in your garage. Write and illustrate a warning note to post on the garage door.
- Look for a simple nonfiction book about alligators to find out where they live, what they eat, and what the difference is between the often-confused alligator and crocodile.
- Read other books by Mercer Mayer, such as *There's a Nightmare in My Closet, A Special Trick, Terrible Troll,* and *What Do You Do with a Kangaroo?*

The Three Little Pigs

Written and Illustrated
by Paul Galdone
(Clarion, 1970)

Paul Galdone has retold and illustrated many simple folktales especially for very young children. These books are great for kids with short attention spans, and the illustrations complement the text perfectly.

In *The Three Little Pigs,* Galdone retells the well-known story of the wicked wolf on a quest for pork who is outwitted by a clever, tireless pig. This is the story I remember hearing as a child; in it the wolf eats up the first two pigs, tries to lure the third pig from his home, and is eventually boiled up and eaten for supper. If you think these aspects of the story will bother your child, read a kinder, gentler version instead.

As You Read

- Because this story is so familiar, your child will probably be able to recite the dialogue as you read it.
- Add some excitement by huffing and puffing as you read about the wolf's blowing the houses down.
- Explain what a sow, a turnip, and a butter churn are if your child asks.

Let's Talk about It

Ask your child:

- Can you tell the story of the three little pigs in your own words?
- Why do the first two pigs build their houses with straw and sticks? What happens to them?

- What does the third pig use to build a house? What happens to the house and the pig?
- How does the third pig trick the wolf?
- What happens to the wolf? How does this make you feel?
- What's your favorite part of the story?

Act It Out

The Three Little Pigs

To act out this story, you can gather straw, sticks, bricks, and other props or just use your imagination.

1. If there are only two of you, one person may play all three pigs while the other plays the wolf. In a larger group, each person may play a different character.
2. Read the book aloud as the players act their parts or dramatize the story without a narrator.
3. If time permits, act out the story again until each player who wants to has a chance to play the wolf or the third pig.

Arts and Crafts

Papier-Mâché Pig

Papier-mâché can be messy, but it's a lot of fun for children and adults. This project will take several days to complete.

Flour
Water
Small mixing bowl
Mixing spoon
Saucepan
Shallow baking dish
Newspaper, crepe paper, or tissue paper
Large, inflated round balloon
String
Scissors
Empty cardboard egg carton
Glue
Pipe cleaner
Pink and black paint (or black marker)

1. Mix ¼ cup flour with 1 cup water. Stir this mixture into about 5 cups of lightly boiling water. Gently boil and stir the paste for 2–3 minutes, then let it cool until you can touch it safely. Pour it into the baking dish.
2. Tear your paper into 2-inch squares or long strips.
3. Hang the balloon over your work area with a string.
4. Dip the paper squares or strips into the paste, then stick them on the balloon. Make sure the edges overlap. Cover the balloon with many layers of paper. Let it dry for 1–2 days, then remove it from the string.
5. Cut 6 individual sections from the egg carton. Glue 1 section to the narrower end of the balloon for the pig's nose.
6. Cut 1 section in half and glue a piece on each side of the top of the pig's head for the ears.
7. Glue 4 sections to the underside of the balloon for the pig's feet.

8. Glue a curled pipe cleaner to the rear end of the balloon for the pig's tail.
9. If necessary, prepare more paste and paper. Cover the pig's nose, ears, feet, and tail with papier-mâché and let them dry for 1–2 days.
10. Paint your pig pink. Draw a face with black paint or a black marker.

Cooking and Baking

Apple Crisp
Perhaps the third pig made this tasty dish with that basket full of apples!

¼ cup flour
¼ cup quick-cooking oats
1 cup packed brown sugar
¼ cup butter or margarine
½ cup chopped nuts (optional)
3 cups thinly sliced apples

1. Preheat your oven to 350°F.
2. Combine the flour, oats, and brown sugar in a medium bowl.
3. Cut in the butter or margarine until the mixture forms pea-size nuggets. If you like, mix in chopped nuts.
4. Arrange the apple slices in a 6-by-10-inch baking dish.
5. Sprinkle the sugar mixture evenly over the apples.
6. Bake the apple crisp for 40 minutes or until the apples are tender.
7. Serve the apple crisp hot or cold, with ice cream if you like.

Fun and Games

Pigs
This game is easy, fun, and great for three to thirteen players of all ages.

Deck of playing cards

1. Assemble four cards of a kind for each player. For three players, use four aces, four kings, and four queens. For four players, add four jacks; for five players, add four tens; and so on.
2. Shuffle the cards and deal four cards to each player.
3. Each player looks at her cards to see if she has four of a kind. If nobody has four of a kind, each player passes one unwanted card facedown to the player on her left.
4. The players look at their cards again. If nobody has four of a kind, the players pass again and continue passing until someone has four of a kind.
5. When someone has four of a kind, instead of passing a card she quietly makes a pig snout by pushing up the tip of her nose with her finger.
6. As the other players notice the player making a pig snout, they stop passing cards and do the same. The last player to make a pig snout is the wolf! The wolf deals the cards for the next round of play.

Play and Learn

Telling Time

Scissors
Colored construction paper
Paper fastener
Paper plate
Crayon, pen, or marker

1. Cut hour and minute hands from construction paper and attach them with a paper fastener to the center of a paper plate.
2. Number the plate like a clock face.
3. As you read *The Three Little Pigs*, show your child where to position the clock hands whenever a time is mentioned.

Snack Time

Homemade Butter

Heavy cream
Small jar with tight lid
Sieve or cheesecloth

1. Pour the cream in the jar and secure the lid tightly.
2. Let your child shake the jar until the cream forms soft lumps of butter.
3. Drain the lumpy cream through a sieve or cheesecloth.
4. Discard the liquid and mash the lumps in a bowl until they're smooth.
5. Spread your butter on muffins, bread, or crackers for a tasty snack.

Enrichment Activities

- Build miniature houses of straw or drinking straws, twigs or Popsicle sticks, and LEGOs or other toy building blocks. Let your child discover which house is the sturdiest.
- Recite pig rhymes like "To Market, To Market" and "This Little Piggy."
- Read a simple nonfiction book about pigs or visit a farm. Ask your child, "Are pigs always pink? Are they always cute? Are they hard-working and clever?"
- If your child has never tasted turnips, cook some for dinner one night.
- Read other folktales retold by Paul Galdone, such as *Cinderella, The Gingerbread Boy, Henny Penny, Rumpelstiltskin, The Three Bears,* and *The Three Billy Goats Gruff.*
- Read other stories about pigs, such as *Geraldine's Blanket* by Holly Keller, *Mr. and Mrs. Pig's Evening Out* by Mary Rayner, *Chester the Worldly Pig* by Bill Peet, *Olivia* by Ian Falconer, and the Oliver and Amanda Pig series by Jean Van Leeuwen.

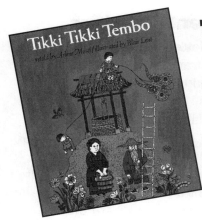

Tikki Tikki Tembo

Written by Arlene Mosel
Illustrated by Blair Lent
(Henry Holt, 1968)

According to this folktale, Chinese parents of long ago honored a first-born son with a long name but gave a younger son hardly any name at all. *Tikki Tikki Tembo* describes how the adventures of Tikki tikki tembo-no sa rembo-chari bari ruchi-pip peri pembo and his younger brother, Chang, cause the Chinese to give all their children short names.

This story makes a great read-aloud. Your child will love repeating Tikki tikki tembo's wonderfully ridiculous name, and he's sure to enjoy the funny pictures by Blair Lent, illustrator of the *The Wave,* a 1965 Caldecott Honor Book written by Margaret Hodges.

As You Read

• Encourage your child to recite Tikki tikki tembo's name with you.

Let's Talk about It

Ask your child:

• What does Tikki tikki tembo's name mean? What does Chang's name mean? Why has their mother given the boys these names?
• How do you think Chang feels about his name? How do you think Tikki tikki tembo feels about his name?
• Why does the boys' mother warn them to stay away from the well? Do they obey? What happens?
• Have you ever been warned not to do something? Why? Have you ever done

something you were warned not to do? What happened?

- Do you think this story really happened? Why or why not?

Arts and Crafts

Paper Lantern

Make some paper lanterns like the ones pictured in the dragon illustration near the end of *Tikki Tikki Tembo*.

Construction paper
Scissors
Glue, tape, or stapler
Ribbon, yarn, and/or streamers

1. Fold a sheet of construction paper in half lengthwise. Show your child how to cut from the folded edge to about 1½ inches from the opposite edge. Make cuts about 1 inch apart along the entire folded edge.
2. Unfold the paper and curl it into a cylinder by joining the short edges of the paper with glue, tape, or staples.
3. Cut a strip of paper or a length of ribbon or yarn for a handle. Glue, tape, or staple the handle to the top of the lantern.
4. Fasten ribbon, yarn, curled strips of paper, or streamers to the bottom of the lantern.

Cooking and Baking

Alphabet Cookies

This dough handles like clay and also makes delicious cookies.

4½ cups all-purpose flour
1½ cups butter
3 hard-cooked egg yolks
¾ cup sugar
3 raw egg yolks
1½ teaspoons vanilla
Colored sugar or chocolate chips
  (optional)

1. Preheat your oven to 300°F.
2. Measure the flour into a large bowl.
3. Cut the butter into small pieces and add them to the flour. Mix the flour and butter with your fingers until they form fine crumbs.
4. Mash the cooked egg yolks with the sugar and stir this mixture into the flour mixture.
5. Blend the raw egg yolks and vanilla and stir this mixture into the flour mixture with a fork.
6. Press the mixture into a firm ball. Cover and refrigerate it if you plan to shape and bake it later; otherwise, work with it at room temperature.
7. Roll out the dough. Cut 3-or-4-inch strips and roll them with your palms to make ropes.
8. Shape the ropes into the letters of your child's name. Flatten them slightly so they are about ¼ inch

thick. If you like, decorate them with colored sugar or chocolate chips.

9. Bake the letters on a baking sheet for 25–30 minutes.

Fun and Games

What's in a Name?

Tikki tikki tembo... means "the most wonderful thing in the whole wide world." Chang means "little or nothing." Does your child know what his name means?

Baby name book
Scissors
Old magazines
Paper or poster board
Glue

- Tell your child how you chose his name. Tell him about any family members or historic or biblical figures who share his name.
- Look up the meaning of your child's name(s) in a baby name book.
- Take turns making up silly names and guessing their meanings.
- Cut pictures of people from magazines and glue them onto a sheet of paper or poster board. Make up a name and a story for each person.
- Have a group of children sit in a circle facing inward. One child chooses a name (real or made up) and whispers it into the ear of the child on his left. Each child in turn whispers it into the ear of the child on his left. The last

person calls out the name he hears, then the child who chose it tells what it was at the start. It's funny to hear how the name changes as it's whispered around the circle.

Music and Movement

Chinese Dancing

Recording of Chinese music
3- or 4-foot lengths of brightly colored ribbon
Plastic shower curtain ring or empty key chain
Chiffon scarf

1. Listen to Chinese music with your child and encourage him to physically express how it makes him feel. For example, he might run during fast music, tiptoe during soft music, hop and bounce during lively music, and so on.
2. Tie ribbons to a plastic shower curtain ring or empty key chain. Your child can wave the ribbons in the air or twirl them in time to the music as he dances.
3. Give your child a chiffon scarf to use as a dancing accessory. If the scarf is too long, tie a knot in the middle to make a handle.

Out and About

Tell Me a Folktale

A folktale is a traditional story originated by the common people of a culture. It usually has little basis in fact and often tries to explain natural or cultural patterns that are hard to understand. Folktales are traditionally shared orally, so creating or telling a folktale is easy to do anytime, anywhere.

1. Take a walk with your child and brainstorm some questions about nature, such as *Why is the sky blue?*
2. Make up a folktale to answer one of your questions. If you like, write down your folktale and illustrate it.

Play and Learn

My Name

- Print each letter of your child's name on a separate index card. Lay the cards out to spell your child's name. Mix them up and have him try to put them back in the proper order.
- Pour a thin layer of sand, salt, or sugar in a 9-by-13-inch baking pan. Show your child how to write his name in the sand, salt, or sugar with his finger.
- Print your child's name in big letters on a sheet of heavy paper. Trace the letters with glue, then shake glitter, colored sand, or colored rice over the shapes. When the glue is dry, shake off the excess glitter, sand, or rice.

- Print your child's name in big letters on a sheet of paper. Cover the paper with clear contact paper. Let your child roll play dough into ropes and shape them over the letters.
- Spread peanut butter, jam, or honey on bread. Help your child spell his name on the bread with alphabet cereal.
- Print your child's name on a sheet of paper. Cover the paper with clear contact paper. Let your child trace the letters with a crayon or marker, then wipe the sheet clean with a damp cloth.

Enrichment Activities

- Locate China on a world map. Look for clothing, food, or other items from China in your home.
- Read a simple nonfiction book about China. Look for pictures of China's mountain country.
- Eat rice cakes and fortune cookies. Drink Chinese tea. Try eating a meal with chopsticks.
- Read other Chinese tales, such as *The Story about Ping* by Marjorie Flack, *The Emperor and the Kite* by Jane Yolen, or *Shen of the Sea* by Arthur Bowie Chrisman.
- Read other books by Arlene Mosel, such as *The Funny Little Woman* (also illustrated by Blair Lent).

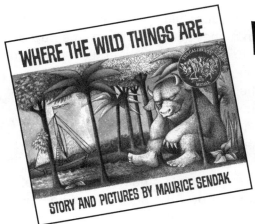

Where the Wild Things Are

Written and Illustrated
by Maurice Sendak
(Harper & Row, 1963)

Where the Wild Things Are is probably the best-known work of author and illustrator Maurice Sendak. It won the 1964 Caldecott Medal. In *Children and Books* (Addison-Wesley, 1997), Zena Sutherland lists it as a milestone in the history of children's literature. And in *The Read-Aloud Handbook* (Penguin, 1995), Jim Trelease describes it as "the picture book that changed the course of modern children's literature."

Where the Wild Things Are is a fantasy about a boy named Max who, when he's sent to his room by his mother, imagines he is the ruler of a kingdom of wild things. Adults may feel apprehensive about the illustrations of fanged and clawed creatures, but children do not find this book the least bit frightening.

Sendak's understanding of and respect for children is evident; he reassures readers when, in the end, Max returns to "where someone loved him best of all."

As You Read

- The illustrations are full of detail, so allow your child plenty of time to look at each before you turn the page.
- Notice the changes in Max's facial expressions: from defiant to angry to happy to frightened to lonely to relieved.
- After a few readings, your child will easily be able to recite Max's simple dialogue with you.

Let's Talk about It

Ask your child:

- Why does Max's mother call him a wild thing? Why is he sent to his room? What would happen to you if you made mischief like Max?
- Have you ever been sent to your room? Why? How did you feel?
- Why does Max go on a journey? Why does he return home?
- Would you like to go to a land inhabited by wild things like the ones in this book? What might happen if you did?
- Do you think this book could really happen? Which parts could happen and which parts couldn't?
- What's your favorite part of the story? Why?

Act It Out

Where the Wild Things Are

Acting out this story is easy, and it will encourage your child to relive the story and empathize with Max.

1. If you are playing with only one child, you can assume the roles of Mother and Max and simply imagine the wild things. A group of children will enjoy taking turns playing Mother, Max, and the wild things.
2. Read the book aloud as the players act out their parts.

3. If time permits, reread the book until each child has had a chance to play Max. If only one reading is possible and everyone wants to play Max, each child can mime the part of Max as you read.

Arts and Crafts

Wild Thing Picture

Markers
Paper
Glue
Googly eyes, paper or fabric scraps, yarn, toothpicks, uncooked rice, and so on
Scissors and Popsicle sticks (optional)

1. Draw or trace a wild thing on a sheet of paper.
2. Let your child color and decorate the picture however she likes. She might glue on googly eyes, paper or fabric scraps for clothes or fur, yarn for hair, toothpicks or uncooked rice for claws and teeth, and so on.
3. If you like, draw and decorate Max and several wild things. Cut out the pictures and glue them to Popsicle sticks to make stick puppets. Your child can use the stick puppets to dramatize the story on her own or as you read it.

Rhymes and Finger Plays

Five Crazy Wild Things

As you say this rhyme, do the actions it describes.

Five crazy wild things staring at me—
A scarier sight there never could be.
The first one shows its terrible claws.
The second one roars and waves its paws.
The third one rolls its terrible eyes.
The fourth one shows its fearsome size.
The fifth wild thing comes at me until
I stare at him and say, "Be still!"
Five frightened wild things tremble and fall;
They say I'm the wildest thing of all!

Fun and Games

Max Says

In this adaptation of Simon says, the leader is called Max. This is a good game for a group of children and is great fun when played quickly.

1. Have the players take turns being Max. Max performs various actions while commanding the other players to do the same.
2. The players follow Max's actions only when Max precedes a command with the phrase *Max says*. They stay still when a command isn't preceded by *Max says*.
3. If a child moves when she's not supposed to, instruct her to sit down. Award a small prize to the last child who remains standing.

Music and Movement

Wild Rumpus

When I was growing up, it seemed that every house had a rumpus room. Now that I understand the meaning of the word *rumpus* (a noisy commotion), I know why we kids were always sent to the rumpus room to play! You and your child may enjoy having a wild rumpus just like the one Max and the wild things enjoy!

Recording of loud, fast music
Snack

1. Find some appropriate "wild rumpus" music. Any loud, fast music will do. Or you might enjoy using music written especially for this purpose, such as the "Wild Rumpus" tracks from Oliver Knussen's opera *Where the Wild Things Are* (Arabesque, 1987) and/or Randall Woolf's ballet by the same title (Composers Recordings, 2000).
2. Dance, jump about, and act as silly as you can until you want to stop.
3. When your wild rumpus is over, enjoy a snack together.

Snack Time

Monster Food

Have a quick snack waiting for your wild thing when she finishes acting out the story or having a wild rumpus. Make her favorite treat or one of the following:

- **Ants on a log:** Cut washed stalks of celery into 3-or-4-inch sticks. Spread peanut butter on the celery and decorate it with raisins.
- **Apples and cheese:** Wash an apple and cut it into wedges. Serve the wedges with slices of cheddar cheese.
- **Cereal:** Give your child a bowl of her favorite cereal with or without milk.
- **Cinnamon toast:** Butter a slice of toast, then sprinkle it with brown sugar and cinnamon.
- **Instant pudding:** Follow the package directions to make a quick batch of pudding.

Enrichment Activities

- Sculpt wild things with play dough.
- This book is really a story-within-a-story. Leaving the outer story (Max's misbehaving and being sent to his room and Max's returning from his adventure) intact, ask your child to imagine another adventure Max might have. Begin with the words *That very night in Max's room....* If you like, write down your child's story and let her illustrate it.
- Listen to an audiotape of *Where the Wild Things Are* and other Sendak stories. (See page 216 and Appendix D for more information.)
- Read other books about fantasies and strange creatures, such as *There's a Nightmare in My Closet* by Mercer Mayer, *The Beast in the Bed* by Barbara Dillon, *Harry and the Terrible Whatzit* by Dick Gackenbach, or *The Amazing Voyage of Jackie Grace* by Matt Faulkner.
- Maurice Sendak won the Hans Christian Andersen Award for Illustration in 1970 and was the first American artist ever to do so. Be sure to enjoy some of his other books, including *Chicken Soup with Rice, Outside over There,* and *In the Night Kitchen.*

William's Doll

Written by Charlotte Zolotow
Illustrated by William
Pène du Bois
(HarperCollins, 1972)

Charlotte Zolotow seems especially well attuned to the emotional needs of small children and to the problems they commonly encounter. Her empathy is evident in the tender yet funny stories she writes.

William's Doll tells of a boy named William who, despite his brother's jeers and his father's efforts to give him more "suitable" toys, yearns for a doll to cuddle and care for. When Grandmother comes to visit, she understands exactly why William wants a doll and why he should have one—so that he can practice being a father.

As You Read

- Your child may enjoy acting out some of William's actions, such as hugging a doll, giving it a bottle, pushing it in a swing, and so on. He may use a real or pretend doll.

Let's Talk about It

Ask your child:

- What does William want more than anything else? How do his brother and the boy next door act when they find out William wants a doll? What does William's father do?
- What happens when William's grandmother comes to visit? Why does she buy William a doll?

- What's your favorite part of the story?
- Would you like to play with a doll? Why or why not?
- How are boys and girls the same? How are they different?
- What are some things boys can be just because they're boys? (sons, brothers, fathers, uncles, grandfathers) What are some things that boys can't be? (daughters, sisters, mothers, aunts, grandmothers)

Arts and Crafts

Daddy Collage

Old magazines
Scissors
Glue
Poster board or construction paper and clear contact paper

1. Help your child find pictures of men, children, and babies in old magazines and cut them out.
2. Glue the pictures onto a sheet of poster board or construction paper.
3. If you've made a poster board collage, display it on a wall. If you've made a construction paper collage, cover it with clear contact paper to make a place mat.

Family Album

Photos of your family
Construction paper
Glue
Clear contact paper
Hole punch
Ribbon

1. Collect photos of your family.
2. Glue the photos onto sheets of construction paper, leaving at least ½ inch of construction paper around each photo.
3. Cover the pages with clear contact paper.
4. Punch 2 holes in the left margin of each page. Be sure to punch the holes in the same position on each page.
5. Assemble the pages in whatever order you like, aligning the holes.
6. Thread ribbon through the holes and tie the ends together to form a family photo album.

Let's Pretend

House

If your child seems reluctant to play house, he may be more enthusiastic if it's just the two of you. Don't force the issue if he resists strongly.

Doll
Doll clothes
Doll bottles, diaper bag, stroller, furniture, and other accessories

1. Play house with your child. Take turns playing the roles of parent and child, or you might both play parents caring for your new baby.
2. Be sure to feed and change your doll, play with it, take it for a walk, and so on.
3. If you like, take your doll to the park and push it on a swing.

Music and Movement

Rocking Songs

- As you cuddle in a rocking chair with your child, sing him traditional rocking songs like "Rock-a-Bye-Baby," "Sleep, Baby, Sleep," or "Hush Little Baby."
- Rock dolls or imaginary babies in your arms.
- Borrow a recording of nursery songs from your local library and learn a few new songs together.

Play and Learn

Sort the Dolls

Dolls (or stuffed animals)

1. Gather all the dolls you can find.
2. Help your child count the dolls.

3. Sort the dolls by size using words like *small, smaller, smallest, big, bigger,* and *biggest.*
4. Together, think of other ways to sort your dolls. Perhaps some dolls' eyes open and shut while others don't; maybe some dolls have soft bodies and others have hard bodies; and so on.

Snack Time

Baby Food

Your child probably doesn't remember eating baby food, so he may enjoy tasting it now. If you have any special memories of his eating habits, favorite foods, or mealtime antics as a baby, describe them as you snack on any of the following:

- Arrowroot cookies
- Fruity baby food
- Mashed bananas or other fruit
- Baby cereal mixed with warm milk
- Warm milk to drink (Ask your child if he likes milk better warm or cold.)

Enrichment Activities

- Together, look at pictures of your child as a baby. Talk about when he was born, how happy he made your family, and other details about his babyhood.
- Read about a father's love for his son in Carlo Collodi's *Pinocchio*.

- Read Stan and Jan Berenstain's *He Bear She Bear,* which takes a funny look at the things girls and boys can be just because they are girls and boys, as well as the many things a child can be regardless of sex.
- Visit a friend or family member who has a small baby. Notice how the parent cares for the baby. Ask whether your child might be allowed to hold the baby.
- Read other books about "doing your own thing," such as *The Story of Ferdinand* by Munro Leaf and *Ira Sleeps Over* by Bernard Waber.
- Read other books by Charlotte Zolotow, such as *The Hating Book* and *A Father like That.*

Appendix A

Basic Craft Recipes

Children begin to develop creative skills at a very early age. Most don't care as much about what they make as about the process of working with materials of many different colors and textures. Whether it's the process or the product that interests your child, the craft materials in this appendix are essential for her artwork. On the following pages you'll find easy recipes for paint, glue, paste, modeling compounds, and more.

Paint

Each of the following recipes will produce a good-quality paint for your child's use. The ingredients and preparation vary from recipe to recipe, so choose one that best suits the supplies and time you have available.

When mixing paint, keep in mind the age of your young artist. As a general rule, younger children require thicker paint and brushes. Paint should always be stored in covered containers. Small plastic spillproof paint containers are available at art supply stores. Each comes with an airtight lid, holds brushes upright without tipping, and is well worth the purchase price of several dollars.

Flour-Based Poster Paint

¼ cup flour
Saucepan
1 cup water
Small jars or plastic containers
3 tablespoons powdered tempera paint
*   per container*
2 tablespoons water per container

½ teaspoon liquid starch or liquid
*   detergent per container (optional)*

1. Measure the flour into a saucepan. Slowly add 1 cup of water while stirring the mixture to make a smooth paste. Heat the paste, stirring constantly, until it begins to thicken. Let it cool.
2. Measure ¼ cup of the paste into each small jar or plastic container. Add 3 tablespoons powdered tempera paint and 2 tablespoons water to each container. If you like, add liquid starch for a matte finish or liquid detergent for a glossy finish.
3. Cover the containers for storage.

Cornstarch Paint

½ cup cornstarch
Medium saucepan
½ cup cold water
4 cups boiling water
Small jars or plastic containers
1 teaspoon powdered tempera paint or 1
*   tablespoon liquid tempera paint per container*

1. Measure the cornstarch into a saucepan. Add the cold water and stir the mixture to make a smooth, thick paste. Stir in the boiling water.
2. Place the saucepan over medium-low heat and stir the paste until it's boiling. Boil the paste for 1 minute, then remove it from the heat and let it cool.
3. Spoon about ½ cup of the paste into each container. Stir 1 teaspoon of dry tempera paint or 1 tablespoon of liquid tempera paint into each container, using a different container

for each color. (Use more paint for a more intense color.) If the paint is too thick, stir in 1 teaspoon of water at a time until the desired consistency is achieved.

4. Cover the containers and refrigerate them for storage.

Detergent Poster Paint

Small jars or plastic containers
1 tablespoon clear liquid detergent per container
2 teaspoons powdered tempera paint per container

1. In each container, mix 1 tablespoon of detergent and 2 teaspoons of powdered paint. Use a different container for each color.

Edible Egg Yolk Paint

Small jars or plastic containers
1 egg yolk per container
¼ teaspoon water per container
Food coloring

1. In each container, mix 1 egg yolk with ¼ teaspoon of water and many drops of food coloring.
2. Use a paintbrush to apply paint to freshly baked cookies. Return cookies to the warm oven until the paint hardens.

Cornstarch Finger Paint

3 tablespoons sugar
½ cup cornstarch
Medium saucepan
2 cups cold water
Muffin pan or small cups
Food coloring
Soap flakes or liquid detergent

1. Mix the sugar and cornstarch in a saucepan. Turn the heat on low, add the water, and stir the mixture constantly until it's thick. Remove it from the heat.

2. Spoon the mixture into 4–5 muffin pan sections or small cups. Add a few drops of food coloring and a pinch of soap flakes or a drop of liquid detergent to each cup. Stir the paint and let it cool before use.

3. Cover the paint and refrigerate it for storage.

Flour Finger Paint

1 cup flour
2 tablespoons salt
Saucepan
Wire whisk or eggbeater
1½ cups cold water
1¼ cups hot water
Food coloring or powdered tempera paint

1. Mix the flour and salt in a saucepan. Beat in the cold water until the mixture is smooth.
2. Mix in the hot water and boil the mixture until it's thick, then beat it again until it's smooth.
3. Tint the paint however you like with food coloring or powdered tempera paint.
4. Cover the paint and refrigerate it for storage.

Play Dough

The following recipes each produce a good-quality play dough. Some require cooking and some don't; some are meant to be eaten and some aren't. Choose the recipe that best suits your needs and the ingredients you have on hand. Store play dough in a covered container or Ziploc bag. If it sweats a little, just add more flour. For sensory variety, warm or chill the play dough before use.

Oatmeal Play Dough

Your child may be able to make this play dough with very little help, but it doesn't last as long as cooked play dough. This play dough isn't meant to be eaten, but it won't hurt a child who decides to taste it.

1 part flour
1 part water
2 parts oatmeal
Bowl

1. Place all the ingredients in a bowl; mix them well and knead the dough until it's smooth.
2. Cover the play dough and refrigerate it for storage.

Uncooked Play Dough

Bowl
1 cup cold water
1 cup salt
2 teaspoons vegetable oil
Tempera paint or food coloring
3 cups flour
2 tablespoons cornstarch

1. In a bowl, mix the water, salt, oil, and enough tempera paint or food coloring to make a brightly colored mixture.
2. Gradually blend in the flour and cornstarch until the mixture has the consistency of bread dough.
3. Cover the play dough for storage.

Peanut Butter Play Dough

2 cups peanut butter
6 tablespoons honey
Nonfat dry milk or milk plus flour
Bowl
Cocoa or carob powder (optional)
Edible decorations like chocolate chips, raisins, candy sprinkles, and colored sugar

1. Mix the first 3 ingredients in a bowl, using enough dry milk or milk plus flour to give the mixture the consistency of bread dough. Flavor the dough with cocoa or carob powder if you like.
2. Shape the dough, decorate it with edible treats, and eat your artwork!

Salt Play Dough

1 cup salt
1 cup water
½ cup flour plus additional flour
Saucepan

1. Mix the salt, water, and ½ cup of flour in a saucepan. Stir and cook the mixture over medium heat. Remove it from the heat when it's thick and rubbery.
2. As the mixture cools, knead in enough additional flour to make the dough workable.

Colored Play Dough

Cream of tartar makes this play dough last 6 months or longer, so resist the temptation to omit this ingredient if you don't have it on hand.

1 cup water
1 tablespoon vegetable oil
½ cup salt
1 tablespoon cream of tartar
Food coloring
Saucepan
1 cup flour

1. Mix the water, oil, salt, cream of tartar, and a few drops of food coloring in a saucepan and heat the mixture until it's warm.
2. Remove the mixture from the heat and stir in the flour. Knead the dough until it's smooth.

Kool-Aid Play Dough

This dough will last 2 months or longer.

½ cup salt
2 cups water
Saucepan
Food coloring, powdered tempera paint, or Kool-Aid powder
2 tablespoons vegetable oil
2 cups sifted flour
2 tablespoons alum

1. Mix the salt and water in a saucepan and boil the mixture until the salt dissolves.
2. Remove the mixture from the heat and tint it with food coloring, powdered tempera paint, or Kool-Aid powder. Add the oil, flour, and alum. Knead the dough until it's smooth.

Clay

Use the following recipes to make clay that can be rolled or shaped into sculptures. Some clays should be dried overnight, while others are best baked in an oven. When hard, sculptures can be decorated with paint, markers, and/or glitter and preserved with shellac, acrylic spray, or clear nail polish. Store leftover clay in a covered container or Ziploc bag. Please note that none of these clays is edible.

Modeling Clay

2 cups salt
⅔ cup water
Saucepan
1 cup cornstarch
½ cup cold water

1. Stir the salt and ⅔ cup of water in a saucepan over heat for 4–5 minutes. Remove the mixture from the heat.
2. Blend in the cornstarch and cold water until the mixture is smooth. Return it to the heat and cook it until it's thick.
3. Let the clay cool, then shape it however you like. Let your sculpture dry overnight before decorating and finishing it.

Baker's Clay

4 cups flour
1 cup salt
1 teaspoon alum
1½ cups water
Large bowl

Food coloring (optional)
Rolling pin, cookie cutters, drinking straw, and fine wire (optional)
Baking sheet
Fine sandpaper

1. Preheat your oven to 250°F.
2. Mix the flour, salt, alum, and water in a bowl. If the clay is too dry, knead in another tablespoon of water.
3. If you like, tint the clay by dividing it and kneading a few drops of food coloring into each portion.
4. Shape the clay however you like. To make hanging ornaments, roll or mold the clay as follows, then attach a loop of fine wire to each ornament.
   - **To roll:** Roll the clay ⅛ inch thick on a lightly floured surface. Cut it with cookie cutters dipped in flour. Make a hole for hanging the ornament by dipping the end of a drinking straw in flour and using the straw to cut a tiny hole ¼ inch from the ornament's edge. You can also use the straw to cut more clay dots for press-on decorations.
   - **To mold:** Shape the clay into flowers, fruits, animals, and so on. The figures should be no more than ½ inch thick.
5. Bake your sculpture(s) on an ungreased baking sheet for about 30 minutes. Turn and bake them for another 90 minutes until they're hard and dry. Remove them from the oven and let them cool, then smooth them with fine sandpaper before decorating and finishing them.

No-Bake Craft Clay

Food coloring (optional)
1¼ cups cold water
1 cup cornstarch
2 cups baking soda
Saucepan

Plate
Damp cloth

1. If you want tinted clay, mix a few drops of food coloring into the water. Then mix the water, cornstarch, and baking soda in a saucepan over medium heat for about 4 minutes until the mixture has the consistency of moist mashed potatoes.
2. Remove the mixture from the heat, turn it onto a plate, and cover it with a damp cloth until it's cool.
3. Knead the clay until it's smooth, then shape it however you like. Let your sculpture dry overnight before decorating and finishing it.

No-Bake Cookie Clay

2 cups salt
⅔ cup water
Medium saucepan
1 cup cornstarch
½ cup cold water
Rolling pin, cookie cutter, drinking straw, and fine wire (optional)

1. Mix the salt and ⅔ cup of water in a medium saucepan and boil the mixture until the salt dissolves. Remove it from the heat.
2. Stir in the cornstarch and cold water. If the mixture doesn't thicken right away, heat and stir it until it does, then let it cool.
3. Shape the clay however you like. To make hanging ornaments, follow the instructions on page 225.
4. Let your sculpture dry overnight before decorating and finishing it.

Glue and Paste

The following recipes use a variety of ingredients, and the resulting glues and pastes have a variety of uses. Choose the one that best suits your project. For fun, add food coloring to glue or paste

before using it. Cover and refrigerate all glues and pastes for storage.

Glue

¾ cup water
2 tablespoons corn syrup
1 teaspoon white vinegar
Small saucepan
Small bowl
2 tablespoons cornstarch
¾ cup cold water

1. Mix ¾ cup of water, corn syrup, and vinegar in a saucepan. Bring the mixture to a full rolling boil.
2. In a small bowl, mix the cornstarch and cold water. Stir this mixture slowly into the hot mixture until it begins to boil again. Boil the mixture for 1 minute, then remove it from the heat. When it's cooled slightly, pour it into another container and let it stand overnight before you use it.

Homemade Paste

This wet, messy paste takes a while to dry.

½ cup flour
Saucepan
Cold water

1. Measure the flour into a saucepan. Stir in water until the mixture is as thick as cream.
2. Simmer the mixture, stirring constantly, for 5 minutes. Remove it from the heat and let it cool before you use it.

Papier-Mâché Paste

6 cups water
Saucepan
¼ cup flour
Small bowl

1. Lightly boil 5 cups of water in a saucepan.
2. Measure the flour into a small bowl. Stir in 1 cup of water to make a runny mixture. Stir this mixture into the boiling water.
3. Stir and gently boil the paste for 2–3 minutes. Let it cool before you use it.

No-Cook Paste

Bowl
½ cup flour
Water
Salt

1. In a bowl, mix the flour and water until the mixture is gooey.
2. Stir in a pinch of salt.

Other Craft Recipes

Use the following recipes to make interesting supplies for use in various arts-and-crafts projects.

Colorful Creative Salt

Use this salt as you would use glitter.

Small bowl
5–6 drops food coloring
½ cup salt
Microwave or wax paper

1. In a small bowl, stir the food coloring into the salt.
2. Microwave the mixture for 1–2 minutes or spread it on wax paper and let it air-dry.
3. Store the salt in an airtight container.

Dyed Pasta

½ cup rubbing alcohol
Food coloring
Small bowl
Dry pasta
Newspaper and wax paper

1. Mix the alcohol and food coloring in a small bowl.
2. Add small amounts of dry pasta to the liquid and mix it gently. The larger the pasta, the longer it will take to absorb the color.
3. Dry the dyed pasta on newspaper covered with wax paper.

Dyed Eggs

Small bowls
¼ teaspoon food coloring per bowl
¾ cup hot water per bowl
1 tablespoon white vinegar per bowl
Hard-boiled eggs

1. In each bowl, mix ¼ teaspoon food coloring, ¾ cup hot water, and 1 tablespoon white vinegar. Use a different bowl for each color.
2. Soak hard-boiled eggs in the dyes. The longer you soak an egg, the more intense its color will be.

Ornamental Frosting

This frosting is an edible glue; use it for gingerbread houses or other food art. It can be made several hours or the day before you use it.

Electric mixer or eggbeater
3 egg whites
1 teaspoon cream of tartar
Bowl
4 cups powdered sugar

1. Beat the egg whites and cream of tartar in a bowl until stiff peaks form.
2. Add the powdered sugar and continue beating the frosting until it's thick and holds its shape.
3. Cover the frosting with a damp cloth when you're not using it. Store it in an airtight container in the refrigerator.

Appendix B

Making Books with Children

Creating books with your child is fun to do and can be as simple or complex as you wish. Some home-schoolers spend weeks creating professional-looking bound books, but the process needn't be time consuming. If you like, you can simply staple sheets of paper inside a construction paper cover or use a small notebook, scrapbook, photo album, or three-ring binder with plastic sleeves. Print the story your child dictates at the bottom of each page, then let your child illustrate the pages with his own artwork, photos, or pictures cut from magazines.

Making a bound book with your child takes a little more time, but the quality of the finished book makes it well worth the effort. The following instructions were adapted from the book *Parents Are Teachers, Too* by Claudia Jones (Williamson, 1988).

Scissors
1 sheet of construction paper
Up to 8 sheets of plain white paper (8½ by 11 inches)
Sewing machine or needle and thread
Utility knife (optional)
Cardboard or matte board
Nonstretch fabric
Paintbrush
White glue thinned with water
Wax paper
Several heavy books

1. Cut the construction paper to 8½ by 11 inches. Stack up to 8 sheets of plain paper on top of the construction paper. Fold the whole stack in half, with the construction paper on the outside. Stitch along the fold with a sewing machine or needle and thread.

2. Use a utility knife or scissors to cut 2 pieces of cardboard or matte board, each measuring 5½ by 6¾ inches. Lay the 2 pieces side by side about ¼ inch apart on the wrong side of a piece of nonstretch fabric. Trim the fabric, leaving a 1-inch border on all sides of the cardboard or matte board.

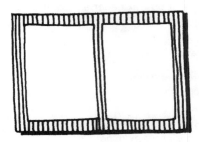

3. Paint a layer of watery white glue on 1 side of each piece of cardboard or matte board. Place the pieces of cardboard or matte board back in position (glue side down) on the fabric and press on them to glue them to the fabric.

4. Brush glue on the 1-inch fabric border, then fold the fabric over onto the cardboard. Smooth out the edges of the fabric as best you can, but don't worry about them too much, as they will be covered up in the next step.

5. Open the paper booklet you made in step 1. Paint the entire outside surface of the construction paper cover with glue. Press the gluey construction paper onto the inside of the fabric-covered cardboard cover.

6. Place wax paper inside the front and back covers. Close the book and place more wax paper around the outside of the book. Then place it under a stack of heavy books so it will dry flat.

Appendix C

Children's Book Awards

Numerous awards are presented each year to authors and illustrators of books for children. The first such award was presented in 1922. Since then, well over a hundred awards have been created to recognize excellence in children's books.

It can be difficult to keep all these awards straight, so I've included descriptions of the most prominent children's book awards on the following pages. These descriptions are reprinted by permission of Addison-Wesley Educational Publishers, Inc. from *Children and Books, 9th edition* by Zena Sutherland, © 1997 by Addison-Wesley Education Publishers, Inc.

For fuller descriptions of these awards, as well as lists of the award winners and runners-up, please refer to *Children and Books*.

The Newbery Medal

Frederic G. Melcher, editor of *Publishers Weekly,* donated and named this award as a tribute to John Newbery (1713–1767), the first English publisher of books for children. Beginning in 1922 and every year since, the Newbery Medal has been given by an award committee of the Association for Library Service to Children, a division of the American Library Association, to the author of the most distinguished contribution to literature for children published in the United States during the preceding year. The author must be a citizen or resident of the United States.

The Caldecott Medal

This award is named in honor of Randolph Caldecott (1846–1886), the English illustrator whose pictures still delight children. In 1937,

Frederic G. Melcher, the American editor and publisher who had conceived the idea of the Newbery Medal some years earlier, proposed the establishment of a similar award for picture books. Since 1938, the Caldecott Medal has been awarded annually by an award committee of the Association for Library Service to Children, a division of the American Library Association, to the illustrator of the most distinguished picture book for children published in the United States during the preceding year. The award is limited to residents or citizens of the United States.

The Laura Ingalls Wilder Award

This prize, administered by the Association for Library Service to Children, was first awarded in 1954. Since 1960, it has been given every five years to an author or illustrator whose books, published in the United States, have made a substantial and lasting contribution to children's literature. It is now given every three years.

International Reading Association Children's Book Awards

Given for the first time in 1975, this award is presented annually for a book, published in the preceding year, written by an author "who shows unusual promise in the children's book field." Sponsored by the Institute for Reading Research, the award is administered by the International Reading Association. As of the 1987 awards, separate prizes were established for older and younger readers, and in 1995, a prize for a book of information was added.

National Council of Teachers of English Orbis Pictus Award for Outstanding Nonfiction for Children

First presented in 1990, this award for outstanding nonfiction for children is named in honor of Johannes Amos Commenius, whose book *Orbis Pictus,* published in 1657, is considered to be the first work created exclusively for children.

National Council of Teachers of English Award for Excellence in Poetry for Children

First presented in the fall of 1977 by the National Council of Teachers of English, the award is given to a living American poet in recognition of his or her aggregate work. After the 1982 award, it was decided to present the award every three years instead of yearly.

The Scott O'Dell Award for Historical Fiction

The award was established in 1981 by Mr. O'Dell. The book must be historical fiction, have unusual literary merit, be written by a citizen of the United States, and be set in the New World. It must have been published in the previous year by a United States publisher and must be written for children or young adults. In some years, no award may be given.

Coretta Scott King Awards

First presented in 1970, this award was "designed to commemorate and foster the life, works and dreams of the late Dr. Martin Luther King Jr. and to honor Mrs. Coretta Scott King for her courage and determination to work for peace and world brotherhood." The award is given annually to an author for an outstanding inspirational and educational contribution, designed to promote better understanding and appreciation of the cultures and contributions of all peoples to the American dream. In 1979 another category was added to this award to honor illustrators. The awards are sponsored by the American Library Association Social Responsibilities Roundtable under the Coretta Scott King Task Force.

The Regina Medal

The Regina Medal is given annually by the Catholic Library Association to an author for his or her aggregate work.

The Carnegie Medal

The Carnegie Medal, established in 1937, is awarded annually by the British Library Association to an outstanding children's book written in English and first published during the previous year in the United Kingdom.

The Kate Greenaway Medal

This medal is awarded each year by the British Library Association for the most distinguished work in illustration of a children's book first published in the United Kingdom during the preceding year.

The Canadian Library Awards

This award, first presented in 1947, was established by the Canadian Library Association. It is given annually to a children's book of outstanding literary merit, written by a Canadian citizen. Since 1954 a similar medal has also been awarded yearly to an outstanding children's book published in French.

The Hans Christian Andersen Awards

The Hans Christian Andersen Award was established in 1956 by the International Board on Books for Young People and is given every two years to one living author who, by his or her complete work, has made an important international contribution to children's literature. Since 1966 an artist's medal has also been given. Each national section of the International Board proposes one author and one illustrator as nominees and the final choice is made by a committee of five, each member of which is from a different country.

The Mildred L. Batchelder Award

This award was established in 1966 by the American Library Association in honor of a woman who promoted internationalism and encouraged translations of books from other countries. The award is given annually to a distinguished book first published in a foreign language, translated, and then published in the United States.

Appendix D

Picture Book Resources

Because all the picture books featured in *Picture Book Activities* have enjoyed long lives and great popularity, many are available from multiple publishers in multiple formats. You should be able to borrow all fifty titles from any library system in the United States or Canada. If you wish to buy any of the titles, the chart below will help you obtain them through your local bookseller or the World Wide Web. The chart lists each title and its author followed by its publisher(s) in each major format at press time for *Picture Book Activities.*

	Hardcover	Softcover	Audiotape	Videotape
Alexander and the Terrible, Horrible, No Good, Very Bad Day (**Judith Viorst**)	Atheneum (Simon & Schuster) Econo-Clad (Sagebrush)	Aladdin (Simon & Schuster)	HarperAudio (HarperCollins)	Golden Books
And to Think That I Saw It on Mulberry Street (**Dr. Seuss**)	Random House	Random House		
Blueberries for Sal (**Robert McCloskey**)	Viking Penguin (Penguin Putnam) Econo-Clad (Sagebrush)	Viking Penguin (Penguin Putnam)	Puffin (Penguin Putnam)	Children's Circle (Look for *Corduroy; Panama; Blueberries for Sal.*)
Bread and Jam for Frances (**Russell Hoban**)	HarperCollins	HarperTrophy (HarperCollins)		
Caps for Sale (**Esphyr Slobodkina**)	HarperCollins Econo-Clad (Sagebrush)	HarperTrophy (HarperCollins) Scholastic	HarperAudio	Weston Woods
A Chair for My Mother (**Vera B. Williams**)	Greenwillow (HarperCollins) Econo-Clad (Sagebrush)	Greenwillow (HarperCollins)		
Chicka Chicka Boom Boom (**Bill Martin Jr. and John Archambault**)	Simon & Schuster	Aladdin (Simon & Schuster)	Simon & Schuster	Canadian Learning Company
Corduroy (**Don Freeman**)	Viking Penguin (Penguin Putnam) Econo-Clad (Sagebrush)	Viking Penguin (Penguin Putnam) Puffin (Penguin Putnam)	Puffin (Penguin Putnam)	Paramount Home Video. (Look for *The Adventures of Corduroy: Home.*) Children's Circle (Look for *Corduroy; Panama; Blueberries for Sal.*)

	Hardcover	Softcover	Audiotape	Videotape
"Could Be Worse!" (James Stevenson)	Greenwillow (HarperCollins) Econo-Clad (Sagebrush)	William Morrow (HarperCollins)	Spoken Arts	
Curious George (H. A. Rey)	Houghton Mifflin Econo-Clad (Sagebrush)	Houghton Mifflin	Houghton Mifflin Audio	Churchill Films (Look for *The Adventures of Curious George.*)
Fortunately (Remy Charlip)		Aladdin (Simon & Schuster)		
Frederick (Leo Lionni)	Knopf (Random House) Random House	Dragonfly (Random House)		
Frog and Toad Together (Arnold Lobel)	HarperFestival (HarperCollins) HarperCollins Econo-Clad (Sagebrush)	HarperTrophy (HarperCollins)	HarperAudio (HarperCollins)	
George and Martha (James Marshall)	Houghton Mifflin Econo-Clad (Sagebrush)	Houghton Mifflin	Houghton Mifflin Audio	
Geraldine's Blanket (Holly Keller)	Econo-Clad (Sagebrush) Demco Media	William Morrow (HarperCollins)		
Gilberto and the Wind (Marie Hall Ets)	Viking (Penguin Putnam) Econo-Clad (Sagebrush)	Viking (Penguin Putnam)	Live Oak Media	
The Happy Lion (Louise Fatio)	*The Happy Lion* is out of print. However, used editions are widely available. Consult your local used book store or any major on-line bookseller.			
Harold and the Purple Crayon (Crockett Johnson)	HarperCollins Econo-Clad (Sagebrush)	HarperTrophy (HarperCollins)		
Harquin (John Burningham)	*Harquin* is out of print in North America. It remains in print in the United Kingdom and may be purchased from its publisher, Red Fox (Random House U.K.). Used North American editions are also available. Look for *Harquin, the Fox Who Went Down to the Valley* at your local used book store or any major on-line bookseller.			
Harry the Dirty Dog (Gene Zion)	HarperCollins Econo-Clad (Sagebrush)	HarperTrophy (HarperCollins)		
A House for Hermit Crab (Eric Carle)	Simon & Schuster			
If You Give a Mouse a Cookie (Laura Joffe Numeroff)	HarperCollins	HarperCollins	HarperCollins	
Imogene's Antlers (David Small)	Crown (Random House) Econo-Clad (Sagebrush)	Crown (Random House)		
Ira Sleeps Over (Bernard Waber)	Houghton Mifflin Econo-Clad (Sagebrush)	Houghton Mifflin	Houghton Mifflin Audio	
Just Plain Fancy (Patricia Polacco)	Econo-Clad (Sagebrush) Demco Media	Yearling (Random House)		

	Hardcover	Softcover	Audiotape	Videotape
Little Bear (Else Holmelund Minarik)	Harpercollins Econo-Clad (Sagebrush)	HarperTrophy (HarperCollins)	HarperAudio (HarperCollins)	Nick Jr. (Nickelodeon) Look for *Little Bear: Meet Little Bear.*
The Little Engine That Could (Watty Piper)	Grosset & Dunlap (Penguin Putnam) Dutton (Penguin Putnam) Price Stern Sloan (Penguin Putnam)	Puffin (Penguin Putnam)	Price Stern Sloan (Penguin Putnam)	MCA Universal
The Little House (Virginia Lee Burton)	Houghton Mifflin	Houghton Mifflin	Houghton Mifflin Audio	
Little Toot (Hardie Gramatky)	Putnam Juvenile (Penguin Putnam) Grosset & Dunlap (Penguin Putnam) Econo-Clad (Sagebrush) Demco Media	PaperStar (Penguin Putnam)		Disney MCA Universal (Look for *Shelley Duvall's Bedtime Stories.*)
Madeline (Ludwig Bemelmans)	Viking (Penguin Putnam) Econo-Clad (Sagebrush)	Puffin (Penguin Putnam)	Puffin (Penguin Putnam)	Heron Communications Tri-Star Pictures
Millions of Cats (Wanda Gág)	Putnam Juvenile (Penguin Putnam) Econo-Clad (Sagebrush)	PaperStar (Penguin Putnam)		
Mirette on the High Wire (Emily Arnold McCully)	Putnam Juvenile (Penguin Putnam) Econo-Clad (Sagebrush)	PaperStar (Penguin Putnam)		
Mittens (Clare Turlay Newberry)	Smithmark (U.S. Media Holdings)			
Noisy Nora (Rosemary Wells)	Dial (Penguin Putnam)	Puffin (Penguin Putnam)	Weston Woods	
One Monday Morning (Uri Shulevitz)		Aladdin (Simon & Schuster)		
Owl Moon (Jane Yolen)	Philomel (Penguin Putnam)		Weston Woods	
Purple, Green and Yellow (Robert Munsch)	Annick Econo-Clad (Sagebrush)	Annick		
The Rag Coat (Lauren Mills)	Little, Brown (Time Warner)			
The Runaway Bunny (Margaret Wise Brown)	HarperCollins Econo-Clad (Sagebrush)	HarperTrophy	HarperAudio (HarperCollins)	
The Snowman (Raymond Briggs)	Random House	Random House	Columbia TriStar	
The Snowy Day (Ezra Jack Keats)	Viking (Penguin Putnam) Econo-Clad (Sagebrush)	Viking (Penguin Putnam) Puffin (Penguin Putnam)	Live Oak Media Kimbo Educational Audio	

	Hardcover	Softcover	Audiotape	Videotape
The Story about Ping (Marjorie Flack)	Viking (Penguin Putnam) Econo-Clad (Sagebrush)	Puffin (Penguin Putnam)	Puffin (Penguin Putnam)	
The Story of Babar (Jean de Brunhoff)	Random House	Random House	Harper Children's Audio (HarperCollins) Look for *The Babar Audio Collection.*	Children's Video Library (Look for *The Story of Babar the Little Elephant.*) Vestron Video (*Look for Babar the Little Elephant.*)
The Story of Ferdinand (Munro Leaf)	Viking (Penguin Putnam) Econo-Clad (Sagebrush)	Puffin (Penguin Putnam)	Puffin (Penguin Putnam)	
Sylvester and the Magic Pebble (William Steig)	Simon & Schuster Econo-Clad (Sagebrush) Demco Media	Aladdin (Simon & Schuster)	Weston Woods	
There's an Alligator under My Bed (Mercer Mayer)	Dial (Penguin Putnam)			
The Three Little Pigs (Paul Galdone)	Houghton Mifflin Econo-Clad (Sagebrush)	Houghton Mifflin		
Tikki Tikki Tembo (Arlene Mosel)	Henry Holt Econo-Clad (Sagebrush)	Henry Holt	Weston Woods	
Where the Wild Things Are (Maurice Sendak)	HarperCollins Econo-Clad (Sagebrush)	HarperTrophy (HarperCollins)	HarperAudio (HarperCollins)	
William's Doll (Charlotte Zolotow)	HarperCollins Econo-Clad (Sagebrush)	HarperTrophy (HarperCollins)		

Appendix E

Resources for Ideas and Activities

While many of the ideas and activities in this book are original, many have appeared in print elsewhere, and many you have probably read about, heard about, or done yourself. In writing this book I gleaned ideas and information from personal experience, friends and family, and the following books:

Bartlett, Nancy Lewis. *Children's Art and Crafts (The Australian Women's Weekly Home Library).* Sydney: Australian Consolidated Press, 1991.

Cianciolo, Patricia J. *Picture Books for Children, 4th Edition.* Chicago: American Library Association, 1997.

Donavin, Denise Perry. *American Library Association Best of the Best for Children.* New York: Random House, 1992.

Ellison, Sheila and Judith Gray. *365 Foods Kids Love to Eat.* Naperville, Ill.: Sourcebooks, 1995.

Gilbert, Labritta. *Do Touch: Instant, Easy Hands-On Learning Experiences for Young Chidren.* Beltsville, Md.: Gryphon House, 1989.

Gillespie, John T. *Best Books for Children, 7th Edition.* New York: R.R. Bowker, 2001.

Hearne, Betsy with Deborah Stevenson. *Choosing Books for Children: A Commonsense Guide, 3rd Edition.* Champaign, Ill.: University of Illinois Press, 2000.

Hunt, Gladys. *Honey for a Child's Heart, 3rd Edition.* Grand Rapids, Mich.: Zondervan Books, 1989.

Jones, Claudia. *Parents Are Teachers, Too.* Charlotte, Vt.: Williamson Publishing, 1988.

Kohl, MaryAnn. *Preschool Art.* Beltsville, Md.: Gryphon House, 1994.

Kuffner, Trish. *The Preschooler's Busy Book.* Minnetonka, Minn.: Meadowbrook Press, 1998. (Published in Canada as *Surviving Your Preschooler* by Lighthouse Books, 1998.)

Kuffner, Trish, *The Toddler's Busy Book.* Minnetonka, Minn.: Meadowbrook Press, 1999. (Published in Canada as *Surviving Your Toddler* by Lighthouse Books, 1999.)

Lambert, Jane Claire. *Five in a Row.* Grandview, Mo.: Five in a Row, 1996.

Landsberg, Michele. *Reading for the Love of It.* New York: Prentice Hall Press, 1987.

Lansky, Vicky. *Feed Me I'm Yours.* Minnetonka, Minn.: Meadowbrook Press, 1994.

Lappé, Frances Moore. *What to Do after You Turn Off the TV.* New York: Random House, 1985.

MacDonald, Margaret Read. *Bookplay: 101 Creative Themes to Share with Young Children.* North Haven, Conn.: Library Professional Publications, 1995.

MacDonald, Margaret Read. *Booksharing: 101 Programs to Use with Preschoolers.* North Haven, Conn.: Library Professional Publications, 1988.

Martin, Elaine. *Baby Games.* Philadelphia: Running Press, 1988.

Mayesky, Mary. *Creative Activities for Young Children, 6th Edition.* Albany, N.Y.: Delmar Publishers Inc., 1997.

Meilach, Dona Z. *Papier-Mâché Artistry.* New York: Crown Publishing, 1971.

Miller, Karen. *Things to Do with Toddlers and Twos.* Chelsea, Mass.: Telshare Publishing, 2000.

Mohrmann, Gary, ill. *1001 Rhymes & Fingerplays.* Everett, Wash.: Warren Publishing House, 1994.

Paré, Jean. *Kids Cooking.* Edmonton, Alta.: Company's Coming Publishing, 1998.

Peek, Don. *Finger Plays for Early Childhood.* Minneapolis: T.S. Denison, 1975.

Rossi, Mary Jane Mangini. *Read to Me! Teach Me!* Wauwatosa, Wis: American Baby Books, 1982.

Rothlein, Liz. *Read It Again!* Glenview, IL: Scott, Foresman and Company, 1989.

Sanford, Anne R. *A Planning Guide to the Preschool Curriculum.* Winston-Salem, N.C.: Kaplan Press, 1983.

Simons, William L., ed. *The Reader's Digest Children's Songbook.* Pleasantville, N.Y.: The Reader's Digest Association, 1985.

Stenmark, Jean Kerr, Virginia Thompson, and Ruth Cossey. *Family Math.* Berkeley, Calif.: University of California, 1986. (For information, contact Lawrence Hall of Science, University of California, Berkeley, CA 94720, Attn: FAMILY MATH.)

Sunset-Lane Editors. *Sunset Children's Crafts.* Menlo Park, Calif: Lane Publishing, 1976.

Sutherland, Zena. *Children and Books, 9th Edition.* New York: Addison-Wesley Educational Publishers, 1997.

Trelease, Jim. *The Read-Aloud Handbook, 4th Edition.* New York: Penguin Books, 1995.

Wicks, Ben. *Born to Read.* Toronto, Ont.: Ben Wicks, 1995.

The United States General Services Administration makes available many free and low-cost Federal publications of consumer interest, including many on learning activities and parenting. If you would like a free copy of the *Consumer Information Catalog,* write to Catalog, Pueblo, Colorado 81009, call 888-8PUEBLO (888-878-3256), or order a catalog on-line at www.pueblo.gsa.gov.

Activity Index

Author/Illustrator Index